P9-CMP-606

Making Sense of Place

THE DEVELOPING BODY AND MIND

Series Editor: Professor George Butterworth, *Department of Psychology, University of Sussex.*
Designed for a broad readership in the English-speaking world, this major series represents the best of contemporary research and theory in the cognitive, social, abnormal and biological areas of development.

Infancy and Epistemology: An evaluation of Piaget's theory
  George Butterworth (ed.)
Social Cognition: Studies on the development of understanding
  George Butterworth and Paul Light (eds)
The Mental and Social Life of Babies: How parents create persons
  Kenneth Kaye
Evolution and Development Psychology
  George Butterworth, Julie Rutkowska and Michael Scaife (eds)
Developmental Psychology in the Soviet Union Jaan Valsiner
Language and Representation: A socio-naturalistic approach to conceptual development
  Chris Sinha
Causes of Development: Interdisciplinary perspectives
  George Butterworth and Peter Bryant (eds)
An Introduction to the Psychology of Children's Drawings
  Glyn V. Thomas and Angèle M. J. Silk
Child Prodigies and Exceptional Early Achievers John Radford
The Child's Point of View, second edition Maureen Cox
Making Sense of Place M. H. Matthews

Making Sense of Place

Children's understanding of
large-scale environments

M.H. Matthews

HARVESTER WHEATSHEAF

BARNES & NOBLE BOOKS

First published 1992 by
Harvester Wheatsheaf
Campus 400, Maylands Avenue
Hemel Hempstead
Hertfordshire HP2 7EZ
A division of
Simon & Schuster International Group

First published in the United States of America in 1992 by
Barnes & Noble Books
8705 Bollman Place
Savage, Maryland 20763

Typeset in 10/12 Ehrhardt
by VAP Publishing Services, Kidlington, Oxford

Printed and bound in Great Britain by
BPCC Wheatons Ltd, Exeter

Library of Congress Cataloging-in-Publication Data is available from
the publisher.

ISBN 0-389-20987-2

British Library Cataloguing in Publication Data
Matthews, M.H.
  Making sense of place: children's understanding of large-
  scale environments. — (The developing body and mind)
  I. Title   II. Series
  153.7083

  ISBN 0-7450-0930-1
  ISBN 0-7450-0931-X (pbk)

1 2   3   4   5   96 95 94 93 92

For David and Gilly, with love

Contents

Figures

Tables

Acknowledgements

I would like to thank Shirley Addleton for her excellent artwork. Also, I am most grateful to Professor George Butterworth who provided the opportunity for me to write this book.

1

Introduction

For most of us, our childhood appreciation of the environment expands from the floor, walls and furniture of the room we grew up in, to links with other rooms, steps, corridors and stairs, on to the outside world beyond the front door of yards, gardens, streets, shops and parks. What becomes forgotten on the way is how we managed to piece these disparate elements together into some form of comprehension of places and large-scale space. Colin Ward (1977), in his influential book *The child in the city*, muses on whether we are ever able to recapture these visions of childhood. Like Yi Fu Tuan (1974), he believes the world of young children is so full of miracles, the word miracle can have no precise meaning for them. As we move on to adult life we may gain subtlety, but we lose a wondrous sense of richness.

The world viewed from the eye-level of a young child is bound to be different to that of a fully developed adult. So, too, must the environmental experiences of childhood, simply because of differences in scale. When Lukashok and Lynch (1956) asked adults what they remembered about their upbringing in the city it was the tactile rather than the visual quality of place that was recalled. According to Moore (1986), who reviews a number of *environmental autobiographies*, a step or ledge to sit upon, a shady corner by a rough wooden fence on which to lean on a hot summer's day, a soft grassy glade, are persistent recollections of childhood. For Edith Cobb (1977) it is significant that adult memories of this kind are frequently accompanied by a deep desire to renew the ability to see the world as a child and to 'participate with the whole bodily self in the forms, colors, and motions, the sights and sounds of the external world of nature' (p 130). There is, however, a great deal of difference between the adult who is able to recall rich and memorable images of childhood and the young child encountering a place or an environmental experience for the first time. How can we ever step back to the sense of wonder experienced on that first unaccompanied walk outdoors? Are adults inevitably to be cast as outsiders able to gain only the most meagre glimpses of the magical world of the very young?

This book attempts to unravel some of mysteries of childhood. Its focus is on how children make sense of place. Place in this context refers to the macroenvironment or large-scale environment. Macroenvironments are gener-

1

ally defined as being larger than people, whereas microenvironments are smaller. The prototype of a microenvironment is an object, whilst the prototype of a macroenvironment is a place (Blaut, 1991). In the context of this book, place is particularly defined as those macroenvironments encountered out-doors.

How, why and at what age or stage children acquire an understanding of place is proving a difficult issue to uncover. Researchers from a broad range of backgrounds, notably psychology (and its sub-disciplines of cognitive, develop-mental, ecological, environmental, social and educational psychology), artificial intelligence, geography, anthropology, and planning, have all contributed to the subject. Although considerable debate surrounds the most satisfactory way of explaining children's grasp of macroscale locational and spatial relationships, there is a growing school of thought which argues that the environmental capability of children needs to be reassessed. A burgeoning body of empirical evidence has shown that the environmental skills and competence of children have been underestimated. This has occurred partly because of an uncritical acceptance of Piagetian, age-dependent state theory of human development, and partly because of an over-reliance on novel, small-scale, laboratory tests, divorced from the child's world of experience, to assess macroenvironmental expertise. This book offers a contemporary review of many of these disparate studies with the aims of providing an insight into how children make sense of the world about them, as well as suggesting how it is up to adults to make provisions which take into account children's environmental needs and capabilities.

The reader will have already detected that *making sense of place* is interpreted as a multifaceted process. On the one hand, it includes transactional behaviour or *place behaviour*. Children's various experiences of near and distant environ-ments are likely to shape their impressions of place. On the other hand, *place learning* involves abilities to handle and process environmental information of different kinds. In this regard, Liben's (1981) typology of spatial information processing offers a useful distinction between *spatial products, spatial storage,* and *spatial thought.* Spatial products refer to any external products that represent space in some way, whether graphic or verbal. Spatial storage refers to the cognitive representation of environmental information and how it might be acquired, coded, and stored in the memory. Spatial thought refers to the mental manipulation of spatial data, such as the planning of a route or the selection of wayfinding strategies.

The organization of the book reflects these various issues and strands. Four Parts are presented. Part One focuses upon children's place behaviour; a distinction is made between children's direct and indirect transactions with place. For example, some places are encountered directly through children's movement through space, whereas other places are only heard about or seen, as a result of information flow. In many respects, this distinction corresponds to how children encounter near and more distant places. In highlighting children's varying contact with the geographical environment, the book draws attention to the importance of ecological studies and suggests that place learning cannot be fully understood without reference to children's world of experience. Reality for a child is a constantly evolving entity, which depends in part upon socio-personal circumstance, geographical setting, and social and cultural milieux. These factors are discussed, as well as how mass communication and interpersonal communication contribute to environmental imagery.

Part Two follows on from this experiential frame by examining differing theoretical expectations on the environmental capabilities of young children. The origin and development of children's place-learning ability are not clearly understood. Whereas *nativists* contend that children are naturally predisposed towards spatial information processing and *empiricists* argue that spatial skills are the outcome of experience alone, *constructivists* espouse a viewpoint which suggests that an understanding of large-scale space awaits the unfolding of different kinds of thought processes through successive stages and the active construction of space by individuals. Related to this debate is the methodological issue of how best to explore children's understanding of the environment. The process of uncovering children's grasp of large-scale space is a difficult task. Recent work suggests that children's abilities can be moved *upwards* or *downwards* dependent on the nature of the exercise and its locational setting. In Chapter 5 the results provided by different environmental stimulus techniques (spatial products) are compared and their implications examined. A widely used procedure for gaining an insight into children's environmental imagery is free-recall mapping. The different ways of coding, classifying and analyzing children's cartography are discussed.

Part Three reviews studies which have examined children's environmental competencies in different geographical settings. An attempt is made to distinguish between *spatial storage* and *spatial thought*, noted above. Initial attention is upon a broad body of empirical work which has revealed sets of factors likely to affect children's environmental cognition and hence their storage of environmental information. The importance of activity-in-space to environmental awareness is given prominence in Chapter 6, as well as ecological factors likely to impinge upon spatial information processing. The net result of the process of environmental cognition is commonly referred to as a *cognitive map* or *mental map*. However, the concept of a map should be seen as no more than a convenient metaphor, used to summarize the extent of a person's environmental knowledge. The remaining chapters examine the abilities of children to comprehend and solve locational problems of different kinds (spatial thought) and those factors likely impinge upon performance. For example, Chapter 7 discusses children's strategies for early spatial learning, place learning, route learning and distance estimation; Chapter 8 looks at children's ability to read and use maps; Chapter 9 considers the debate on whether gender variations in environmental experience induce sex contrasts in spatial abilities between girls and boys; and Chapter 10 evaluates how recent studies on children's age-related abilities have contributed to the debate between nativists, empiricists and constructivists. Cognitive mapping is not just about how children structure and organize space. Children's *maps* include a wealth of information about how children feel and think about places. Chapter 11 looks at the kind of environments that children consider enriching or boring and highlights their affective images of place.

Part Four considers the implications and outcomes of these studies of children's environmental capability to their environmental needs. Two issues are discussed. Chapter 12 looks at how recent work on young children's environmental competencies challenges many of the educational assumptions of established classroom practices. There is now sufficient evidence to suggest that mapping and other graphical skills can be introduced at the time of school entry and that graphicacy deserves to be placed alongside numeracy, articulacy and literacy in the primary school curriculum. By bringing together research in child development, education and geography, more satisfying syllabuses can be designed which build upon children's protomapping capabilities. Chapter 13 discusses how, through the study of children's place images and space preferences, adults are offered peepholes into the private geographies of childhood. A common finding is that children rarely play in those spaces currently set aside by adults for their use. Instead, children often prefer streets and vacant plots to play in, areas which link them to the larger community and which work against practices of child *ghettoization*. This sort of information can be used by planners to provide outdoor environments which reflect the real environmental needs of children.

The aims of this book are ambitious. Undoubtedly, there are topics and issues which have not been covered which others would argue are essential. What is striking, however, is that children's ability to acquire and handle environmental information as they encounter geographical space is a process not convincingly understood. Despite a plethora of research many questions remain unanswered, and no theoretical viewpoint offers an exclusive explanation. In this light, my preferences for explanations which are based upon real-world studies, and my suspicions of laboratory-based performance tasks which lack ecological rigour, together with a view of children that sees them as early environmental mappers or *protogeographers*, are presented in the hope that less adultocentric views of childhood will predominate in future.

Part I

Children's experience of place and space

Environments of childhood vary in their scope, complexity and significance. They consist not only of *spatial and design attributes,* like objects, length, size, shape, distance and scale, but also of *meanings,* provided by prevailing social, cultural and organizational systems. In a sense these spatial and design features represent the *geographical environment,* those aspects of the setting that exist as objective characteristics of places. Meanings, on the other hand, define a behavioural context within which a child makes sense of or gives significance to a particular environmental transaction. Both these qualities exert a particular power and affect of their own. Not only does the geographical environment condition and shape experience, but also how a child reacts, responds and feels within a particular environmental setting will be a product of surrounding social, cultural and organizational systems. There is a third dimension, too, which impinges upon this close interrelationship between space and meanings and this is the capability of the child as a processor of environmental information. Every child brings to a situation an arrangement of personal resources and a varying level of environmental skill. Hence, different individuals will react differently to the same environment. This Part is organized into two chapters. First, in Chapter 2 we shall explore how children of different ages and from different social backgrounds encounter different types of environment through their own direct experiences. Secondly, in Chapter 3 attention will be on how children develop an understanding of place and space by indirect means, such as through various communication and media sources. Issues relating to children's environmental capability are reserved for later discussion.

2

Children's direct experience of place and space

An ecological framework

Ecological studies provide a useful starting point for examining how children come into contact with different types of environment. Environmental experience is seen as a product of a complex transaction between children and the world about them. Initially, the ecological approach drew attention to how the larger social context affects what goes on in the child's immediate settings (Barker and Schoggen, 1973; Barker 1979). More recent work recognizes how the geographical context also impinges upon the quality of the child's life (Bronfenbrenner, 1979; Garbarino and Gilliam, 1980; Garbarino and Plantz 1980).

According to Garbarino (1985), children's environments are multi-layered and multi-faceted. Each level is defined by a complex set of physical (geographical) and social forces, which *press* upon the child. Bronfenbrenner (1979) describes these combined forces as *environmental systems*. He goes on to define four general environmental systems (see Figure 2.1), categorized by their proximity and effects upon children. These systems, which are like a set of nested structures, each inside the next, can either support or inhibit a child's environmental experience.

Microsystems. These are the places where children live, the people who are with them and how they interact together in the course of day-to-day events. At first, most children experience one microsystem, the home, involving interaction between close family members within a restricted spatial context. As the child grows complexity normally increases, with the child doing more, with more people, in more places. Play, work and love are the main environmental opportunities provided to the child by the microsystem. However, the extent to which these activities take place and their level of sophistication are variable. Negative effects result from a microsystem characterized by a narrowly defined set of activities, impoverished environmental experiences and a lack of social interaction. In contrast, wide-ranging, enduring and reciprocal social relationships in diverse geographical settings provide enriching environmental circumstances for the child.

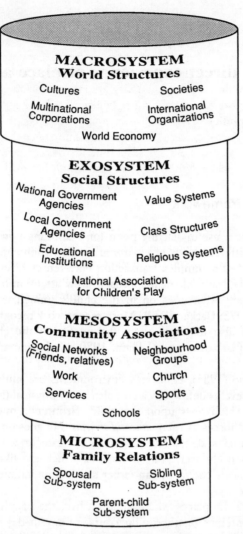

Figure 2.1   The environmental systems of childhood: an ecological framework
(Based on: Bronfenbrenner, 1979)

Mesosystems are the social and geographical contexts in which a growing child comes into contact with the world beyond the home. Important mesosystems for children include the relationships between the home (microsystem) and school and other local community organization. In essence, the stronger, the more diverse and the more positive the links between settings, the more beneficial and influential will the resulting mesosystem be upon a child's environmental opportunity. A dense ecology of links is seen as a positive influence, whereas a poor set of mesosystems produces impaired opportunities.

Of particular significance to the way in which children encounter geographical environments, especially in an urban context, is the relationship between the family and the neighbourhood. Warren (1980) sees neighbourhoods as important *ecological niches*, serving to bolster parents or conspiring to compound family difficulties. In general, the most wealthy are freer to inhabit a neighbourhood of their own choosing and children of these families are more likely to come into contact with ecologically more rewarding and richer geographical settings. On the other hand, poorer families may well live in neighbourhoods of multiple social and physical deprivation and decay. The ecological perspective highlights not only the emotional risk to these children but also their geographical impoverishment. Often, in poor neighbourhoods families and individuals exist in social isolation and their lack of involvement in local affairs compounds their sparse environmental background.

Exosystems are broad social and organizational structures which affect the quality of children's lives, but in which the child does not play a direct role. Children's exosystems are those contexts which shape and influence environmental opportunities, yet in which children do not participate. These include the wider value-systems of societies and their related institutional mechanisms. These settings surround children's mesosystems and result in decisions that frequently affect everyday life. According to Michelson and Roberts (1979), an example of a very important exosystem for children is a local planning authority. This agency can play a decisive role in determining land uses at a local level and how well the interests of children are represented. Given that the needs and expectations of children about the geographical environment are likely to be very different to those of adults it is important that their ideas be recognized. An illustration of this view comes from Barker (1979), who points out that children may thrive on vacant urban plots, which they fill with games, but these are the very spaces that many adults regard as economically wasteful and physically unattractive. Typically, the behaviour of independently-acting institutions of this kind has a significant bearing on how children come into contact with the world around them.

Macrosystems. Both mesosystems and exosystems are themselves set within the broad ideological and institutional structures of a particular culture or sub-culture. Macrosystems reflect a society's or a sub-culture's shared assumption of how things should be done, including cultural ideas about child rearing and home range behaviour. As a result of a macrosystem effect, it is likely that children from different ethnic backgrounds living within similar environments will engage in different transactions with their surrounding geographical settings. In consequence, particular cultural or ideological alignments induce various environmental opportunities. Risk occurs when any social pattern or societal event impoverishes the ability or willingness of adults to care for children and for children to learn from adults.

In summary, what Bronfenbrenner's model suggests is that children enter into a complex relationship with the environment and it is axiomatic that their development and understanding of the world is advanced or held back by different social and physical settings, which operate at different levels within society: the daily circumstance of family life, the quality of community associations, the effectiveness of social structures and the general state of pervading ideological and cultural arrangements. Such observation is particularly useful in the context of our discussion on children's experience of place in that it recognizes the broad local–global connections of most environmental transactions. However, the emphasis of Bronfenbrenner's work is upon the social ecology of childhood and whilst those mechanisms by which children acquire a grasp of large-scale space are implied, there is no explicit treatment of this subject.

In contrast, Moore and Young (1978) provide an alternative conceptualization of how children encounter everyday environments, which they set up as a 'behaviour–environment ecological framework' (p. 83). In this case the effect of the geographical environment is clearly acknowledged. The model suggests that every child lives simultaneously in three interdependent realms of experience: the physiological–psychological environment of body–mind; the sociological environment of interpersonal relations and cultural values; and the physiographic landscape of spaces, objects, persons, and natural and built elements (see Figure 2.2). Interaction between these three realms controls children's use of the geographical environment and, in turn, leads to the acquisition of both an image and a sense of place.

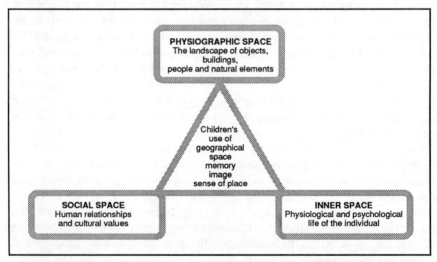

Figure 2.2   Realms of environmental experience (Based on: Moore and Young, 1978)

When they were developing this framework, Moore and Young were strongly influenced by the writings of Edith Cobb (1977). In *The ecology of imagination in childhood* she discusses what she calls 'the natural genius of childhood and the spirit of place'. Cobb identifies an 'evolutionary biocultural process' which is rooted in 'a *genius loci*: a living, ecological relationship between an observer and an environment, a person and a place' (p. 44). She suggests that through experiences like play, the child is able to 'finger over the environment in sensory terms' (p. 46) and gain a spatio-temporal understanding of place. However, the environment is more than just an objective phenomenon, it is interpreted and reconstructed through personal, social and cultural lenses, and the outcome is never a copy. Later, Bjorklid (1982), takes up these *interactional and ecological* notions of child–environment relationships in her book, *Children's outdoor environment*. Here, she recognizes the importance of a reciprocal and adaptive process whereby the individual is not only influenced by but also influences the environment, 'and has an inner need to do so' (p. 67).

What emerges from these ecological studies is a compendium of factors and situations likely to control, shape and mould how children encounter large-scale environments. In this chapter the effect of some of the more important of these influences will be examined and considered. Three major organizational headings are used. These relate to, first, the physiological and socio-personal characteristics of the child and include factors like age, sex, social class and ethnicity; secondly, the nature of the geographical environment, such as the opportunities provided for play, whether it is natural or built and its effects upon children's outdoor activities; and thirdly, the societal and cultural context of these child–environment transactions.

The importance of physiological and socio-personal characteristics to environmental experience

Age-related factors

Young children, like adults, gain information about their surroundings through increasingly sophisticated environmental transactions, which themselves are conditioned by important age-related influences such as, levels of locomotor capability, the emotional import and purpose of the events (often provided by the mother–child relationship) and developing *range* behaviour. We will use these influences as convenient headings for our discussion.

Levels of locomotor capability
Locomotor development is of undoubted importance in any consideration of how children come into contact with the world around them. Comprehensive research on the locomotor-related behaviour of infants and young children has been undertaken by Gesell and his associates at the Yale Clinic of Child Development (Gesell, 1940; Gesell *et al.*, 1946). Gesell's work was carried out with children from birth to 10 years of age. The average age of significant locomotor developments include:

16 weeks	moves from crib to cot.
28 weeks	sits; moves to chair; much time spent in active manipulation.
44 weeks	crawls on hands and knees.
12 months	stands momentarily alone; walks with one hand held.
18 months	runs stiffly; walks alone, seldom falls.
2 years	rides toy car; runs without falling.
3 years	rides tricycle.
5 years	climbs with sureness.
5–6 years	first bicycle (two-wheeler) ride.
7 years	rides bicycle some distance.

The sequence of these abilities is very important in any conceptualization of how children experience place. Although Gesell's studies were with American children, other research (Dennis, 1938; 1940) suggests that within the first 12 months there does appear to be a certain universality of performance skills. It is worth highlighting the environmental significance of particular locomotor skills within this first year of life.

The first environment which neonates explore are their mother. Exploration of this new world begins with the mouth which adjusts to the contours of the mother's breast, providing a sense of buccal space (Spitz, 1965). Sucking is a highly rewarding activity which brings into motion the other senses of touch, smell and taste. Whilst infants suckle, their hands are busily used to examine the tactile and morphological qualities of this environment. Long before an infant's eyes can focus on an object, its shape and form will have been recognized by touch (McKenzie and Day, 1972).

By the end of their first month infants are able to fixate on objects in their direct line of vision and by the third month binocular control and convergence appear (Scaife and Bruner, 1975). However, even in the fourth month infants show little interest in visually exploring their surroundings beyond a range of 3 ft (McKenzie and Day, 1972). For some time the visual world of the very young remains different to that of older children. Visual space lacks organization and permanence; objects are impressions which exist only as long as they remain within the visual field. With age, children become capable of focusing more sharply on objects, their outline and characteristics are clearly seen and become understood.

According to McComas and Field (1984) we should not underestimate the developing spatial competence of pre-locomotory children. Even before crawling, infants have already acquired relational experiences through the coordination of head, hand and body movements. With the ability to sit up and to control head movements, which comes before trunk rotation and develops at about 6 months, children may well be able to distinguish 'position relative to the body, position relative to the head and position relative in the external world' (Bremner and Bryant, 1985). Although much of the young child's earliest environmental experiences is a product of the passive reception of sensory data, by about 10 months onwards there is considerable evidence to suggest that children are actively seeking to explore their surroundings. For example, Smith and Smith (1962) have shown that children at about one year of age will attempt to change the position of their playpen in order to bring into view objects which are visually obscured. Kessen *et al.* (1970) have demonstrated the importance of *surprise* and *complexity* as significant rewards to novel environmental events. As Ittelson *et al.* (1974) argue, such pursuits are seemingly unrelated to the alleviation of primary drives of hunger and thirst, nor are they conditioned by the action of others, such as parents when playing with children. 'As active explorers of their environment children are pleased simply by their accomplishments' (Ittelson *et al.*, 1974, p. 174).

However, for a heightened sense of large-scale space and for an understanding of concepts like forwards, backwards and sideways, both Acredolo (1978) and Bremner and Bryant (1985) claim that moving the body along a more or less straight line is essential. Unlike most mammals, who gain some feel of orientation after birth, the slow maturing child acquires these skills more gradually (Tuan, 1979). Most children do not crawl confidently on their hands and knees until about 10 months. It is a further two months before many are able to stand alone. Locomotor independence of this kind widens the opportunities for confronting increasingly varied spatial properties and for the first time children can take a more active role in exploring their everyday environments. Yet at first, as Bremner (1978) reminds us, the very act of taking part in such novel, mobile experiences may be so demanding of concentration that the child's attention is actually diverted away from the surrounding environment for a while.

At this age the physical environment provides few signals of danger. Anything which can be grasped by the child adventurer is grasped and often put into the mouth for closer examination; fear has to be learnt through experience. To the crawling child the horizontal world appears to be safe. Children seem to be only aware of one kind of physical danger, the cliff. Gibson (1969) has shown that infants will not crawl onto a glass plate which lies over a vertically sided pit, despite encouragement from the mother. The young child's visual acumen is already sufficient to distinguish sharp changes of gradient.

An important aspect of children's early environmental experience is the *stability* of their surroundings. Children have to be able to trust their everyday world (Erikson, 1950). With locomotor independence the scope and range of places to be discovered are enormously expanded. More and more, the moving child will want to seek out and create his/her own novel environmental experiences. Important in this context is the mother–child relationship.

Emotional setting: The mother–child relationship
As soon as children learn to walk they will want to follow their mother and explore the environment. As with young animals, the instinctive nature of the mother–child attachment has an important effect upon the territorial behaviour

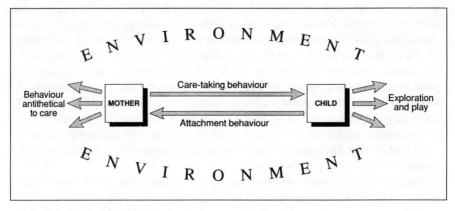

Figure 2.3   Spatial dynamics of mother–child interaction (Based on: Bowlby, 1969)

of children. Bowlby (1969) suggests that this relationship generates four classes of behaviour, each with its own territorial consequences (see Figure 2.3).

Care-taking behaviour is 'any behaviour of a parent . . . by which . . . the young are brought either into the nest, or close to the mother, or both' (Bowlby, 1969, p. 291). Most acts of maternal care-taking are a response to organismic conditions, but Bowlby recognizes two environmental situations which are of interest. The first is when a child wanders beyond a certain distance; the second is when a child cries due to some external influence. In both cases a mother is likely to respond by retrieving the child so closing the distance between her and what is perceived to be the external threat. An exception would be if the child was playing among other infants in her vicinity, when she may simply let things be, whilst keeping a watchful eye. Bowlby notes that recovery behaviour appears to be a consistent and universal maternal reaction to environmental threat and replicates what has been observed within the animal world.

Attachment behaviour describes the distance children are prepared to move away from their mother with confidence. At first, children will cry when their mother leaves the room or will attempt to follow their parent as much as possible. From about 6 to 9 months children will gradually make excursions from their mother and occasionally go out of sight. In a study of the outdoor behaviour of English children aged 18–24 months, Anderson (1972) noted that they seldom strayed more than 200 ft from their mothers. At this age children move only short distances at a time from their mother, frequently stopping to look around, fixating sources of sounds and visual objects and constantly endeavouring to attract their mother's attention. The more hostile the environment the closer the child's proximity to the protective adult. This can be shown in two contexts. First, children appear to explore less freely in the presence of a stranger and when visiting an unfamiliar place (Rheingold, 1969; Ainsworth *et al.*, 1969; Rheingold and Eckerman, 1973). Secondly, Konner (1972) has shown that Bushmen children of Namibia are less ready to stray from their mother when playing and are more likely to run to her than Western children. Bowlby suggests that a maturational threshold occurs from about 4 years of age. At this age children show an abrupt change in behaviour, becoming capable of accepting their mother's temporary absence and able to accept alternative attachment figures, such as play-group leaders and nursery teachers. In this way, environmental exploration begins to take on a new and even more active dimension as children reduce their degree of attachment to their mothers.

Behaviour antithetical to care by the mother includes both *competing behaviour* and *withdrawing behaviour*. Some household chores or the demands of other family members inevitably compete with the needs of infant care. Bowlby distinguishes these from behaviour incompatible with care, such as a dislike of young children or an annoyance of crying. In both cases an infant's proximity-maintaining behaviour with his/her mother is disrupted, often producing emotional states which interfere with environmental opportunities. A number of studies confirm that an environment characterized by social attentiveness and stimulation is vital for the healthy development of the child. Goldfarb (1945), Spitz (1945) and Bowlby (1953) all document how a lack of mothering or a lack of environmental stimuli, or both, has important and negative consequences upon the early intellectual capabilities of children. What these works imply is that rich social and geographical environments in early childhood prepare the child for the perceptual complexities of later life.

Lastly, *exploration and play* provide a class of behaviour which increasingly draws a young child away from the mother. Schoggen and Schoggen (1985) define exploration as behaviour which is designed to reduce uncertainty about an unfamiliar object or environment. Exploration is seen as preceding play; once the object or environment becomes familiar play may occur (Hughes, 1978). Both are mechanisms by which the growing child becomes acquainted with large-scale environments.

Exploration and play are essential experiences in childhood and since they take place within a spatial context they are means by which children become familiar with place. Schoggen and Schoggen (1985) suggest that there is a great deal of similarity about how children explore and play with objects and how they use the environment. In ontogenetic terms object exploration and exploration of space display similar sequences. Object exploration begins with *attention*, especially visual fixation, followed by increasing involvement with the object by reaching, grasping, inspection and manipulation (Hutt and Hutt, 1970; Sherrod *et al.*, 1978). Enhanced exploration of large-scale space awaits *locomotor mobility*, but very young children, of their own volition, stay within aural and visual contact with their mother when they enter and explore new situations or encounter new objects (Goldberg and Lewis, 1969; Hartup and Lempers, 1973). Increased locomotion serves both to increase the number of objects encountered and to entice the child more and more from the parent figure, until full and independent interaction is achieved with the environment. Older children not only encounter more objects but also traverse more space and take responsibility in increasingly varied geographical settings (Scott, 1968).

Exploration and play are frequently regarded as significant developmental mechanisms (Bruner and Connolly, 1974; Mead, 1974; Bruner et al., 1976; Vandenberg, 1978). Both are seen as *energizers* which encourage mastery of and adaptation to the surrounding environment (Scott, 1968; Arnaud, 1974; Groos, 1978). Other effects include control of the environment through fantasy, control of danger and the learning of new skills (Csikszentmihalyi, 1975; and Dolhinow and Bishop, 1970). In these ways a close relationship develops between exploration–play–curiosity and environmental transactions. This relationship is important at a variety of levels, not only with respect to the discovery and familiarization of objects in small-scale space, but also to the location of objects in large-scale space and to a growing appreciation of space itself.

In *Children's experience of place*, Hart (1979) asserts that children's environmental interaction assumes developmental significance as it is much easier for a child to affect the physical environment through their encounters than the social environment, simply because the physical world is less complex, more stable and more accessible. Play is the child's way of coping with the geographical environment and offers a means for differentiating it. For children objects derive significance from their use: a tree which can be climbed or bushes which provide a screen for a hidden camp. By experiencing the world in some evocative way children achieve a sense of fulfilment, which in turn encourages further interaction (Bjorklid, 1982). The physical environment is nothing more than a rich reservoir of experience waiting to be tapped by children's play.

As direct dependence on adults declines so children assert their urge to negotiate with their surroundings. The growing significance of *outdoors* to children as they become older has been shown in a number of surveys. The Newsons (1977), in their study of Nottingham, note that by the age of 7 years children had made the transition from being relatively homebound to being outdoor explorers, spending much of their day in environments away from the home. This period coincides with what Cobb (1977) describes as 'the middle age of childhood', a special age 'between the strivings of animal infancy and the storms of adolescence' when children have the greatest chance to strike out alone or with peers 'to explore an ever-expanding repertoire of reachable places, in search of new experiences' (Cobb, 1969, p. 124). In Nottingham, the Newsons found that their 7-year-olds enjoyed many interests which often tempted them to the next street and beyond. 'The fact that they go to and from school each day familiarises them with short journeys, and widens the circle of children that they know by sight, who in turn act as lures away from their home territory' (Newson and Newson, 1976, p. 32). On asking 700 mothers 'Would you call your child an indoor child or an outdoor child?', the answers revealed both a class and a sex difference. Overall, 60 per cent of children were described as outdoor children, but this rose to 71 per cent for those whose parents were scaled as Social Class V, compared to 44 per cent from Social Class I and II backgrounds. Also, more boys than girls were said to be outdoor children: 67 per cent against 52 per cent. The Newsons explained these differences with reference to living conditions and parental attitudes. They found that with lower social class, accommodation dwindles and family size increases, so that mothers were less prepared to tolerate their children playing indoors. In this way the street becomes *overspill space*, where children can play with others within calling distance. The higher the social background of the family the more likely that children would have some place in the house of their own; this means that indoor play is both more positively encouraged and more inherently attractive. These influences are further conditioned by parental sanctions on the play behaviour of young girls. In many cases girls were encouraged to play indoors and to help with family chores, whereas boys were given greater freedom to explore the outdoor world. We will return to the importance of these socio-personal factors on territorial opportunities later on.

The Department of the Environment (1973) in their study of children's play on a public housing estate noted that for all resident children aged 5–6 years 22 per cent were seen regularly outdoors, and this figure rose to 30 per cent for children aged 8–10 years. When 237 children aged 5–10 years, living both on and off the public housing estate, were asked what they liked about where they lived, 75 per cent of estate children and nearly half of non-estate children answered in terms of 'places to play outdoors' (p. 76). Moore (1978), in his 'Childhood use of the urban landscape' project looked at the environmental relationships of 8–12-year-olds in both Britain (n=96, from London, Stevenage and Tunstall, Nottinghamshire) and the United States (n=265, from six San Francisco Bay area communities). Children were asked about their favourite places to play after school and at weekends. Replies were divided into three groups: homesites; community and commercial facilities, such as libraries, churches, shops, etc.; open spaces/outdoor elements both formal, such as parks and playgrounds, and informal, such as streets, vacant plots and open ground. In all cases, taking combined average mention rates of favourite play spaces, the majority of children preferred open spaces/outdoor elements. Some cross-cultural variation was found: in the United States 50 per cent of children mentioned open spaces compared to 70 per cent of British children, whereas preferences for community facilities ranged from 23 per cent in the former case to only 7 per cent in Britain.

An interesting source of temporal data is Himmelweit *et al.*'s, (1958) study, cited by Hole (1966), which looked at the average hours spent outdoors by a group of 10–11-year-olds in five English towns. They found that the majority, 58 per cent, spent at least one to two hours outside, whilst a further 14 per cent spent in excess of this. Although temporal averages are misleading in that they obscure the importance of particular time periods, such as the weekend, what emerges from this and other studies (Poag *et al.*, 1985; Cohen and Cohen, 1985) is the special emotional importance of the outdoors for children. Clearly, from an early age children are increasingly drawn into a close and intimate relationship with territories beyond their home.

Environmental range

Closely related to children's play and exploration is range behaviour. Many studies have examined human territorial behaviour. To some it represents an expression of biological function (Ardrey, 1966; van den Berghe, 1974), to others it is an outcome of socio-cultural patterns, which vary through time and across space (Hall, 1966; Sommer, 1969; Altman, 1975). There is, however, broad agreement that with increasing age children show the capacity and motivation to cover larger and larger territories when they are not required to be at home or attend school (Pollowy, 1977; Hart, 1979; Michelson and Roberts, 1979; van Vliet, 1983).

Territorial range has been variously defined. Among the first to refer to the concept were Barker and Wright (1955). To them, territorial range was 'the number of community settings inhabited'. However, in their discussions they make little attempt to account for the diversity of spatial contexts likely to be experienced in childhood. More useful with regard to children's varying transactions with large-scale space are the ideas of Moore and Young (1978). They see territorial range as being the collective spatial realm of experience, encompassing children's leisure and play spaces, and the pathways connecting them. In this way, territorial range embraces 'the totality of a child's space–time domain' (p. 91). Moore and Young (1978) propose that territorial range is a dynamic concept composed of two parts: *growth* and *development*. Range growth describes the child's constant search for new places and environmental experiences. This can be crudely represented by what van Vliet (1983) terms the 'cradle–room–house–doorstep–neighbourhood sequence'. Children's natural inquisitiveness, coupled with developing locomotor ability, is seen to result in the incessant search of new destinations. Each extension introduces a new place, which then becomes the 'temporary landscape marker of the child's range boundary' (Moore and Young, 1978, p. 93).

Range growth is not a continuous process. Instead it occurs in spurts as new landscapes are discovered and added to children's environmental repertoire. Important to range extension are both *primary social events* and *range conditions*. In the first instance, range growth is likely to develop most rapidly when children start attending school. Thereafter, gradual extension occurs via trips to friends' houses, visits to parks and shops and membership of various clubs and societies. In addition, the foundations of environmental experience are conditioned by parental care-taking practices, children's levels of mobility and the nature of the surrounding environment.

Range development, on the other hand, is a more ongoing process. Partly, it relates to the capability of children to handle, explore, manipulate and transform their newly acquired environmental experiences. Also, range development provides a source of new material for the continuing drama of a child's discovery of the world, without which the acquisition of environmental competence and understanding would be impossible (Pearce, 1977). The environmental potential of different places varies greatly: some places are visited and soon forgotten, whereas other places provide an endless fascination. Discovery need not be confined to the first visit, as with each successive trip new environmental opportunities may open up.

Home range – most studies on the territorial behaviour of children refer to this concept, which is the distance children travel away from their home in the course of their outdoor play and leisure pursuits. Donaldson (1970) sees the growth and development of home range following a well-defined pattern. In his model Donaldson distinguishes the *home base*, a secure and well–known node for the child, from the *region* (territorial range), an area undergoing active exploration through usage. With age and increasing ability, the region at one level of experience assumes the role of home base for a succeeding stage of territorial exploration and activity. Donaldson proposes that home range expands from a relatively small and continuous area known by young children to an increasingly diffuse and discontinuous set of activity nodes covering large areas for adults.

Empirical support for this model was provided by Coates and Bussard (1974). They looked at the home range development of a group of thirty children living in a moderate density, planned, suburban housing estate in Calgary. For the youngest children, aged 4/5 years, their range was 'bounded in a compact home base bubble extending about 50 feet from the front doors . . . and between 90 feet and 140 feet laterally'. Territorial range extensions occurred along short paths to playgrounds. For children aged 6 years to 9 years, their home base was significantly larger, often up to ten times greater in size. At this age children travelled five to eight times further afield than their younger counterparts and many explored territories beyond their home base. For the oldest children, aged 10 years to 12 years, the home base remained about the same, but territorial range and the number of destinations had greatly increased.

Not surprisingly, a number of studies have confirmed that the distance children travel away from their homes increases with age. For most children, the limits of their home range are negotiated with their parents. In his examination of child–parent relationships in a New England township, Hart (1979) identified three range conditions sanctioned by parents: *free range*, places children are allowed to go alone without asking permission; *range with permission*, places where children are allowed to go alone, but where they must ask permission first; *range with permission with other children*, places where children are allowed to go, but only when accompanied by another child. Hart interviewed a sample of sixty-four children to find out the limits of these range boundaries (see Table 2.1). Each range condition showed an increase with age. For the youngest children *free range* was very small and amounted to little more than 100 yards. Hart found that this distance related to the mother's desire to

Table 2.1 The range limits of children in a New England township, in yards

	Grades 1–3 (age 6–8 years)	Grades 4–6 (age 9–11 years)
Free range	213	514
Range with permission	518	792
Range when accompanied	1013	1610

Source: Hart (1979)

see or hear her children at all times. Even mothers of older children used these vocal and visual criteria as *markers* of range boundaries. For example, a 9-year-old girl reported that she could 'only play in the driveway and around the hen houses' but not 'in the field, cause once Joseph and I went to the brook, and we couldn't hear her [mother] shouting, and she was ever so worried' (Hart, 1979, p. 54).

The first significant increase in average free range came at grade 3 (8 years). This was the earliest age that children were allowed to ride bicycles on pavements and roads and some were permitted to cross over nearby streets. In grade 5 (10 years) a dramatic increase in range occurred, especially for boys. For the first time children were seen crossing over major roads in the town and wandering well beyond their immediate home base. At this age, fear of traffic was no longer given as the major reason by parents for limiting the travel of their children, although major highways were still feared by fifth- and sixth-grade cycling children. Instead, social factors were mentioned as barriers to movement. Parents were fearful of the 'bad influences' of other children, of 'hanging around and doing nothing' and the worries of drugs and petty theft. Some sixth-grade boys even boasted that they could go well beyond the town without having to tell their parents, although Hart found that none had actually done so.

The pattern for *range with permission* is similar to that of free range, but with some important differences. Like free range, there is an age-related progression, but while there is a marked jump in the size of range from grade 2 to grade 3, there is no corresponding increase between grade 4 and grade 5. It appears that children in the fourth grade were content to play within their free range and although parents were prepared to sanction further movements children of this age showed little desire to explore further afield. Nevertheless, failure to inform parents about trips beyond their free range frequently resulted in children being reprimanded by 'grounding'.

Range when accompanied by other children also grows with age. By the sixth grade some of the boys' ranges had grown so free that Hart observed two of them daring to join their seventh-grade colleagues in hitching a 2-mile ride to a local beach. Younger children, who attempted to tag along with older brothers and sisters, were frequently seen looking on despairingly when more interesting playmates took their revered siblings into places they were not allowed to venture.

Table 2.2 The range limits of children in a Coventry suburb, in metres

	Age group					
	6	7	8	9	10	11
Free range	100	190	252	533	784	866
Range with permission	219	333	338	638	749	899
Range when accompanied	288	383	426	813	856	939

Source: Matthews (1987a)

Using the same range categories as Hart (Matthews 1987a), I looked at the home range behaviour of children in suburban Coventry and was able to confirm a strong relationship between age and territoriality (see Table 2.2). In this case, by far the greatest jump in children's range came between the ages of 8 and 9 years, when parental constraints became sufficiently relaxed to enable children to wander freely within the confines of their suburban estate. However, only the oldest children were allowed to cross a major road which separated their estate from surrounding housing areas.

Moore (1978), in his 'Childhood use of the urban landscape' project, identifies a number of common environmental and social fears important to parents when controlling the range behaviour of their children (see Table 2.3). Although these fears are out of proportion to their statistical probability, none the less, they play an important part in determining the limits of range boundaries.

In summary, as children grow older so their opportunities to encounter and explore large-scale environments increase. We have seen that, in part, environmental experience is a product of both biological development and parent–child relationships, which, themselves, condition range behaviour. For each child there exists 'a repertoire of necessary range behaviours, extending from the routine to exploratory involvements in a shifting spectrum of places' (Moore and Young, 1978, p. 93): from the familiar to unfamiliar, from the known to the yet-to-be-discovered. Moore suggests that both ends of this 'involvement cycle' are important. On the one hand, routine trips to well-known destinations consolidate the child's growing appreciation of place; on the other hand, trips to unfamiliar parts lead to the discovery of new properties of the world and so contribute to the child's environmental awareness.

Sex-related factors

Although sex is distinguished as a separate influence on environmental opportunity, most sex-related differences are strongly conditioned by age considerations. In play, games and tasks around the home, young boys and girls are often given very different opportunities to experience and learn, manifesta-

Table 2.3 Environmental and social fears of parents

Fear	%
Traffic danger	27
Social fear (fear of attack)	25
Lack of competence (too far, get lost, not old enough)	17
Environmental dangers (dogs, snakes, open water, high places)	17

Source: Moore and Young (1978)

tions of how gender influences socialization and upbringing. Harper and Sanders (1975) suggest that incipient sex-stereotyping of this kind becomes established at an early age and is recognizable even among pre-schoolers. In a study of children's early socialization, Landy (1965) noted that 4-year-old girls were restricted more in their physical mobility by parental sanctions than similarly aged boys. Landy devised a scale of restrictedness, where 4.0 is an index of extreme restriction. Unfortunately, Landy gives no indication as to what this index represents in terms of distance, area or control. Nevertheless, the median value for boys was 2.5, whereas for girls it was 3.0. Landy also identified another difference between boys and girls, the frequency with which the mother checked them when they played alone. With 4.0 set as the highest value, girls had a median index of 3.5, compared to 3.0 for boys.

The Newsons (1977), whilst recognizing the importance of early socialization, argue that the degree of parental involvement in sex-differentiation and sex-role play increases with the age of children. They found more pronounced parental behaviour and attitudes based on sex-role expectations towards 7-year-old children than was the case for 4-year-olds. Similarly, Mary Lynch (1975) found that children between the ages of 9 and 11 years already showed many sex-role differences, with girls taking on 8 minutes of housework for every 5 minutes the boys contributed. However, these differences increased with age: girls aged between 12 and 18 years spent twice as much time on household chores than boys. In her survey four girls in five, among 16-year-olds, helped to clear up after meals compared to less than one boy in five. A consequence of such gender variation is that boys and girls often lead very different outdoor life styles.

Both Coates and Bussard (1974) and Payne and Jones (1977), working in Calgary, found the territorial movements of girls to be more strictly controlled than for boys, with their range boundaries, such as roads, fences and streams, clearly defined. The environmental fear of many parents was seen to give rise to emphatic sex-differentiation towards the spatial control of young children, with more protective attitudes shown towards girls. These observations were confirmed by a further study by Bussard (Coates and Bussard, 1974). On this occasion she looked at the factors affecting the spatial behaviour of a group of thirty-five children aged 4–12 years from a medium-density, moderate income

Table 2.4 Sex differences in home range behaviour

	4–5-year-olds	6–9-year-olds	10–12-year-olds
Home base	Compact bubbles: 50ft out of front door, by 90ft to 140ft lateral extension, within a 120° cone of vision. Out of back door: 30ft. No sex differences	Expands by a factor of 10 in area and 5 to 8 in path length. Often includes homes of friends. Typically, girls' friends are within same or adjacent street; boys' friends in same neighbourhood. Boys' home base larger	Similar to 6–9-year-olds. Boys' range more a product of choice; girls' range more a result of parental sanction
Activities	No sex differences: triking, biking, play with dolls, toys, in dirt, ball games, hide and seek	Girls: quiet, e.g. jacks, dolls, role-play. Boys: active, e.g. ball games, tag	Girls *define* play as playground activity and dominate this setting. Boys *define* play as activities that occur in wild areas with friends
Zones	Mainly family public and family private. Group public only if within sight. Includes playgrounds and near friends' house	Girls: mostly family public and family private, friends' houses and formal play settings. Boys: informal play settings, and unowned areas	Girls now regularly use public settings. Boys regularly use unowned areas.
Territorial range	Existed for only 50 per cent of children. Usually short path to playground	Girls: 50 per cent had none or only one node on-site, remainder went to nearby shop or, rarely, to nearby scrubby area. Boys: all had off-site range, to shops and wild areas	All children had off-site ranges. Girls: all went to nearby shops only 50 per cent went to wild areas. Only one went to water area. Boys: go to wild areas more than shops. Visit distant wild areas and water areas
Parental attitudes	All wanted children within view. Children only allowed out of sight to go to playgrounds or to known friend's house. Firm boundaries	Much stricter for girls. Girls: often kept within view of home; not allowed off-site alone; required to ask permission to leave house. Boys: not kept within view of house; all allowed off-site: permission needed only for movement off-site. Firm boundaries set for girls	Girls: directly supervised: allowed to go shorter distances with friends: required to inform parents when leaving home base. Boys: had no boundaries, except main highway: no distinction between going with friends and alone

Source: Coates and Bussard (1974)

housing development in a small industrial city in New York State. Some of the principal findings are summarized in Table 2.4.

In a study of 166 children aged between 6 and 11 years in Coventry (Matthews, 1987a), I found a growing differential between the activity spaces of boys and girls within their home area during early childhood (see Figure 2.4).

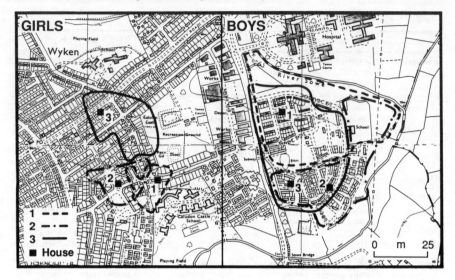

Figure 2.4   Free range of 9-year-old girls and boys in suburban Coventry

Table 2.5 The home ranges of girls and boys in a Coventry suburb, in metres

	Age group					
	6	7	8	9	10	11
Boys						
Free range	100	189	305	795	967	1083
Range with permission	210	345	389	915	900	1136
Range when accompanied	290	391	461	963	1021	1132
	$H = 10.4, df = 2, p = 0.01$					
Girls						
Free range	100	190	199	283	600	649
Range with permission	228	320	257	360	597	662
Range when accompanied	285	364	391	664	691	745
	$H = 10.4, df = 2, p = 0.01$					
Range distance sex ratio (boys/girls)						
Free range	1.0	1.0	1.5	2.8	1.6	1.7
Range with permission	0.9	1.1	1.5	2.5	1.5	1.7
Range when accompanied	1.0	1.1	1.2	1.5	1.5	1.5
	$H = 11.9, df = 2, p = 0.01$					

Source: Matthews (1987a)

Table 2.6 Range distance sex ratios of children, by age in different environments

	Younger[1]	Older[2]	Difference
Urban	1.46	1.65	0.19
Suburban	1.0	1.7	0.7
Rural	1.32	2.56	1.24

Source:	younger[1]	older[2]	
urban	2nd grade	4th grade	(Anderson and Tindall, 1972)
suburban	6 years	11 years	(Matthews, 1987a)
rural	3rd grade	6th grade	(Hart, 1979)

These gender-based differences in activity patterns seemed to develop in a staged progression, confirmed by Kruskal-Wallis H tests (see Table 2.5). Three phases were identified, each associated with a widening differential between the sexes. Among the youngest chidren there was little difference in their home ranges. Nearly all of the children played in sight of, or near to, their house, rarely venturing beyond calling distance. Even with permission or when accompanied territorial movements were clearly defined and tightly sanctioned. At the age of 8 years gender differences in spatial range became evident, with boys enjoying considerably more freedom than girls. Some boys of this age often roamed more than twice as far as girls of their own volition and most continued to enjoy the advantages of broader place experience for the remainder of their middle childhood. The third stage extended from the age of 9 years and was associated with pronounced variations in range behaviour. By the time they were 11 years boys were seen to have had much more opportunity to contact and learn about nearby places, whereas girls' territorial activities had seldom exceeded their immediate locality. In my sample, I noted that 11-year-old girls played within and explored environments located at distances which 8- or 9-year-old boys would have treated as commonplace. Conversely, the eldest boys frequently began to wander beyond the limits of their housing estate, many crossing a major road nearby in their play. Parental concern and fear were thought to be instrumental to these patterns of behaviour: when escorted by older children girls were allowed greater freedom than otherwise. Most children, however, were keen to point out their dislike of this type of accompaniment and stressed its infrequent nature. My findings are in accordance with other studies which have looked at children's range behaviour in a suburban context (see Table 2.6). For example, Anderson and Tindall (1972) examining the maximum daily distance travelled to play, generated range distance–sex ratios of 1.38 for children in the second grade and 1.58 for those in the fourth grade. The implication is that younger children's range appears a great deal more sex-equitable than older children's.

The combined importance of both temporal and environmental factors on the outdoor behaviour of boys and girls has been examined by van Staden (1984). He looked at the range behaviour of 11–13-year-olds from two different urban areas: Clinton Hill (Brooklyn) and Murray Hill (Manhattan).

Table 2.7 Mean free time (hours) spent within neighbourhood

	Murray Hill		Clinton Hill	
Winter				
	Weekday	Weekend	Weekday	Weekend
Boys	2–3	4–5	1–2	1–2
Girls	1–2	1–2	<1	1–2
Summer				
Boys	5–6	>6	3–4	5–6
Girls	3–4	3–4	3–4	4–5

Source: van Staden (1984)

Both areas were predominantly middle-class neighbourhoods of mixed high-, middle-, or low-rise apartment blocks, although the Murray Hill area contained somewhat greater diversity with regard to children's recreational opportunities. The results showed that in both areas boys tended to spend more free time within their neighbourhoods than girls, whilst all groups spent more time in their neighbourhoods during the summer and on weekends than during winter and on weekdays (see Table 2.7). Murray Hill boys spent consistently more time in their neighbourhoods than did Clinton Hill boys. This pattern was not repeated for the girls. Van Staden concluded that girls experience less freedom and more social restrictions in exploring and actively interacting with their extended surroundings. While this state of affairs can in part be *socio-culturally* determined, its expression also appears to be *socio-physically* supported by high density urban situations which give rise to parental perceptions of anxiety, challenge and threat, and girls' feelings of insecurity. These findings appear to be supported by a number of studies (Booth and Johnson, 1975; Loo, 1972; Murray, 1974; Loo and Smetland, 1977), which all relate more active environmentally-oriented styles of interaction to boys and more passive styles to girls.

Other studies have highlighted the importance of the environmental context, and commensurate changes in parental attitudes, upon children's potential spatial behaviour. Comparison of the differences between range distance–sex ratios reveals increasing disparity between age groups as we move from urban (0.19) to suburban (0.7) to rural (1.24) environments. In the city, van Vliet (1983) and Sager (1977) suggest, although sex-related differences in home range are initially well pronounced, as children grow older sex–range variation diminishes because parents commonly relax their control of older children's movements in order to allow their offspring an opportunity to cope with surrounding environmental contingencies. In contrast, studies of rural places have repeatedly shown that girls' ranges are especially restricted by parental fears and domestic chores. Hart (1979) in his investigations at 'Inavale' found that with increasing age boys progressively enjoyed greater freedom, travelling further afield to a wider variety of places. On the other hand, girls were encouraged to stay in the safe confines of the home and encouraged to participate in the routines of family life. Moore and Young (1978) propose that another reason for the very large differences in the rural ratios, especially when compared to suburban values, is that rural landscapes offer many more attractive opportunities for range extensions compared to the more mundane, homogeneous and compact environments of suburbia.

Ward (1977) cites much anecdotal evidence of what he terms, 'the invisibility of girls' in city life:

> Whenever we discuss the part the environment plays in the lives of children, we are really talking about boys. As a stereotype the child in the city is a boy. Girls are far less visible . . . . The reader can verify this by standing in a city street at any time of day . . . and counting the children seen . . . the majority . . . will be boys. (p. 152)

Gwenda Blair (1976) takes up this point. To her the street in the city belongs to men, women are allowed to use the street but only with permission; being a man gives you a 'pass key'.

In summary, considerable evidence suggests that the outdoor behaviour and commensurate environmental experiences of boys and girls are very different. Girls are given less chance to seize the environmental opportunities provided by the world outside their front doors. Although the importance of sex is itself imbedded in other considerations, like age and parental attitudes, none the less, it appears to be instrumental in shaping contact with large-scale space.

Class-related factors

Few studies have looked at the effects of a child's social class background upon environmental experience. Those which have been undertaken provide contradictory findings. In a survey of American research on class differences in child-rearing practices, Bronfenbrenner (1967) notes findings of national surveys carried out in 1932 which showed a tendency by middle-class parents to restrict their children's spatial freedom outside the home much more than working-class parents. However, later work, conducted in Detroit during the 1940s and 1950s, suggested that middle-class parents were more lenient in sanctioning their children's range behaviour. This included less restrictions on how far children were allowed to play away from home; less supervision of play activities outside the home; less 'keeping tracks of their whereabouts'; and earlier age permission for downtown journeys. Landy (1965) corroborates some of these findings in his study of the attitudes of mothers to the outdoor behaviour of their kindergarten children in Massachusetts. He interviewed 372 mothers and he categorized these into two groups, upper middle class and lower middle class. The study found that middle-class mothers checked less on their children's play than the more protective lower middle-class mothers.

In another early investigation, Bernard (1939) studied the 'neighbourhood emancipation' of 420 middle- and upper-class American children. Bernard found the emancipatory effect of social class to be greater than that of age with respect to neighbourhood attitudes, such as feelings of attachment, but smaller regarding children's activities. These findings suggested to Bernard that social class acts as a catalyst in the process of spatial emancipation, accelerating or impeding attitudinal and behavioural range extension. Bernard's study does not consider whether these effects of social class were attributable to differences in family resources that enable mobility. This point was taken up by Farley (1977) who examined the effects of socio-economic status on the activities of children aged from 6 to 16 years in Toronto. In this case no relationship was found, simply because all children had access to an efficient, low-cost, city-wide, mass transportation system.

Van Vliet (1983) carried out another study in Toronto. He investigated the effect of social class upon the home range of children aged between 14 and 16 years. Mean home range was found to differ significantly in both city and suburb: children of higher social classes travelled further than did those from lower social classes. Apparently, both higher social class and suburban location were associated with the largest home range, such that suburban children from higher social classes had the largest home range, and city children from lower class backgrounds had the smallest.

In Britain, the Newson study (1971) of Nottingham families provides a wealth of data on how children, aged from infancy to adolescence and from different social backgrounds, experience their city home. The families involved in the study were divided into five social classes based on parental occupation. Charles Mercer (1976), looking at the evidence collected by the Newsons from the point of view of an environmental psychologist, extracted a series of seven propositions from the data on working-class 4-year-olds, none of which applied to their middle-class counterparts:

1. Working-class children live in more crowded environments, with more siblings and less space.
2. The play of working-class children must take place in the street or other communal areas and not on the 'home territory'.
3. Working-class children are more likely to come into contact with all sorts and a greater number of children.
4. Working-class children's choice of friends is not generally guided by parents, as all children play on communal areas.
5. For the same reason, the play of working-class children is not generally supervised by adults.
6. Parents of working-class children are reluctant to interfere in children's play, because this may lead to conflict with other parents who are also neighbours.
7. Conflict with neighbours is less easily tolerated in working-class environments because of the greater propinquity of families.

In a similar vein, Ward (1977), in his seminal work *The child in the city*, highlights the environmental plight of many inner city children. He quotes an infant schoolteacher working in Islington, inner London.

> The experience of many of these children during the first 5 years of their lives has been so limited that they come to school like so many blank pages. Near the school is a park and a busy underground station, but many of the children have never been inside a park and some of them don't know what a tube train looks like. (Ward, 1977, p. 42).

Ward draws attention to the fact that many children from low social class backgrounds are simply 'not hooked onto those educational networks of fantastic riches and variety that the city through its very existence provides' (p. 42). According to Deutsch (1973), the home environment for a large proportion of low-class families offers children a minimal range of stimuli. The sparsity of objects and lack of diversity of home artifacts together with a lack of parental involvement, a lack of knowledge of how to get about and high public transport costs, combine to restrict children's environmental opportunities and thus 'perceptually to organise and discriminate the nuances of that environment' (p. 103). 'The child from the better-off, or simply a more sophisticated family is far better able to exploit the wonderful potential that any city offers' (Ward, p. 106).

In summary, present evidence generally suggests that children's environmental opportunities are likely to increase with a rise in socio-economic status. However, van Vliet (1983) argues that the *independent* significance of different social class measures has not been clearly established and much more work is needed on this subject.

Ethnic-related factors

There is a paucity of work upon the influence of ethnicity to environmental experience. This reflects not only the difficulty of disentangling discrete ethnic effects from other social considerations, for example class, but also a recognition that generalization is compounded by differences in attitudes, behaviour and opportunities among different ethnic groups. In essence, there is no single ethnic effect. Nevertheless, the limited amount of work which has been carried out suggests that ethnicity is an important determinant of children's outdoor behaviour.

The term ethnic group is used to mean any minority population distinguished by colour, religion, nationality or culture from the surrounding charter population. Ethnic groups in this sense include blacks, Italians, Jews, Puerto Ricans, Mexicans, Vietnamese and Indians (Asian) in American society; West Indians, Asians and Irish in British society; Greeks, Yugoslavs and Turks in West German society, and so on (Knox, 1987). Whilst the host society may not be homogeneous it always contains a charter group which represents a

Table 2.8 Dissimilarity indices at varying spatial scales

Author	Place	Scale	Ethnic group	Index
Jones & McEvoy (1978)	Huddersfield	Kilometre square	Asian	66.6
Woods (1976)	Birmingham	Polling district	Asian	69.0
Jones & McEvoy (1978)	Huddersfield	Half kilometre grid	Asian	70.4
Robinson (1981)	Blackburn	Enumeration district	Asian	73.3
Cater & Jones (1979)	Bradford	Quarter kilometre grid	Asian	78.3
Robinson (1981)	Blackburn	Street level	Asian	75.3
Cater & Jones (1979)	Bradford	Street level	Asian	81.0
Jones & McEvoy (1978)	Huddersfield	Street level	Asian	81.6

dominant ideology into which these ethnic groups are inserted.

The extent to which ethnic groups are spatially segregated and isolated within a society varies from place to place and city to city. Segregation is taken here to refer to situations where members of ethnic groups are not distributed uniformly in relation to the rest of the population. A widely used method for quantifying the degree to which an ethnic group is residentially segregated is the index of dissimilarity, which produces a range of values from 0 (no segregation) to 100 (total segregation). Index values calculated for census tract data in the United States show that blacks are the most segregated of ethnic groups. Taeuber and Taeuber (1965) found a median index value of 88, whilst van Valey *et al.* (1977), in a study of 237 cities, had index values of 70 or more, with some cities like Chicago, Dallas, Fort Lauderdale and Los Angeles with values over 90. Rose (1969; 1970; 1972) points out that the characteristic black settlement form in the northern cities of the United States is the ghetto, a territory rigidly segregated from white neighbourhoods and a permanent base rather than a springboard for dispersal. So large and populous are these black ghettoes that they have been labelled 'a-city-within-a-city' (Cater and Jones, 1989).

In comparison, ethnic residential segregation in European cities is relatively low. For example, in Britain index values calculated for New Commonwealth and Pakistani populations at enumeration district level range between 40 and 70 (Baboolal, 1981; Jones, 1979; Robinson, 1980). In West Germany even less evidence of segregation is found with index values for Turks, Greeks and Yugoslavs rarely exceeding 45. However, a number of authors have shown that levels of segregation are strongly related to issues of scale (see Table 2.8). Increasing indices have been found with finer spatial frames.

Lieberson (1981) points out that dissimilarity indices of this kind are insensitive to the ethnic composition of the total population. This is best understood in the following example. If we assume a city has a mixed black and white population and a dissimilarity index of 0, the residential distribution of blacks and whites is the same at any given scale. Where the city has a 10 per cent black population this corresponds to each district having a representative 10 per cent who are black. In such a situation the average black person will find that 90 per cent of the neighbours are white. Let us now suppose that the population of blacks rises to 50 per cent and the index stays at 0, the neighbouring characteristics of both blacks and whites dramatically change. Now the average black person has become markedly more isolated from contact with whites. Lieberson describes this measure of neighbouring contact as P, the probability of an ethnic minority mixing with someone from the same background. To date, there has been little testing of this P index, but Robinson (1984) working in Blackburn has shown that, at the enumeration district level, the statistical probability of Asian contact with Asian increased from 28 per cent to 51 per cent between 1971 and 1977. He suggests that, over time, many other ethnic groups are clustering in this manner.

What emerges from such evidence is that many ethnic groups are highly segregated from the charter group. Moreover, because many of these ethnic groups are concentrated at the lower end of the occupational structure, most segregation is associated with poor housing, in areas unattractive to the charter group, such as the inner city. Whilst charter group attitudes, structural effects and occupational status are frequently cited as instrumental factors in explaining residential segregation of this kind, Boal (1976) suggests that these factors do not satisfactorily explain the clustering of ethnic groups into increasingly discrete and ethnically homogeneous territories. According to Boal, in situations of intense segregation such clusters are basically conservative and serve four principal functions: defence, support, preservation and resistance. Together these functions combine to produce enduring group cohesion and growing social and physical isolation.

Despite a great deal of work on the social consequences of ethnic clustering, few studies have examined the effect of living in an ethnic enclave upon the environmental experiences of children. Two studies provide some insight into the likely outcomes, although, in both cases, examination of environmental range is implicitly rather than explicitly discussed. Maurer and Baxter (1972) examined children's images of their home area in Houston, Texas. They found that age had little effect on children's imagery, a rather surprising result since their study focused on a group of ninety-six children aged between 7 and 14 years. In contrast, the effect of ethnicity was very strong. White children's images were more extensive than those of black or Mexican American children: black children in particular emphasized their home site.

These variations were considered to be products of different environmental experience. Anglo children, in particular, had greater mobility through access to more varied transport, their mothers were more likely to be at home during the day giving more parental stimulation, and their friends were scattered more widely, giving motives for travel. On the other hand, black children's environmental range was strongly linked to those limited parts of the city associated with black residency.

Table 2.9 Measures of locality interaction

Place	Friends adjacent to own neighbourhood %	Involvement in local voluntary organizations %
Hollywood (white, middle class)	47	39
Watts (black, working class)	87	80

Source: Orleans (1973)

In another study, Orleans (1973) compared the views of residents, drawn from different ethnic and class backgrounds, of Los Angeles. Although his sample comprised an adult population, he was able to demonstrate such startling differences in urban imagery that it is unlikely children's views would have significantly differed from those of their parents. Three principal groups took part in the survey: a white, middle-class population from Westwood; members of a black ghetto neighbourhood near Watts; and, residents of a Spanish-speaking quarter in Boyle Heights. The results revealed that the high-status Westwood population had a well-formed, detailed and generalized image of the entire Los Angeles basin. This compares to the rather vague image of the city held by blacks. Whereas white images were structured around the major east–west boulevards and freeways, the black group's view was dominated by the gridiron layout of the streets between Watts and the city centre. Orleans suggested that reasons for these differences are not hard to find. The greater wealth and broader activity space enjoyed by residents of Westwood meant that their *orbit* (spatial movements) led them to encounter large sections of the city. In contrast, the less mobile blacks resided within a physically and socially bounded ghetto and in consequence, their horizons were locally defined and set. Where language barriers further buttress this introversion the likely outcome is an extremely narrow *orbit*, as reflected in the very restricted image of the city provided by the Spanish speakers of Boyle Heights.

In a follow-up study, which further compared the spatial behaviour of white and black groups, Orleans sought information on the location of the respondents' three best friends and their involvement, if any, in voluntary associations (see Table 2.9). His findings reinforce the notion that the varying territorial behaviour of different ethnic groups often leads to contrasting range experiences.

One of the most striking examples of activity segregation linked to residential segregation has been described by Boal (1969; 1970; 1971) working in the city of Belfast. His studies provide a penetrative insight into the anatomy of a province divided by religious segregation for over 300 years. Looking at the situation before the present 'troubles' in Ulster, Boal describes a society polarized into separate residential areas on the basis of Protestant and Roman Catholic allegiance. His survey highlighted the socio-spatial cleavage that separated the mutually antagonistic Shankhill and Clonard districts of west Belfast. Residential segregation was matched by equally pronounced activity segregation, to the extent that the main criterion in any movement was the desire to avoid crossing the territory of the other group rather than to minimize the distance of the trip.

Lynch and Bannerjee (1976) maintain that in the absence of any major change of external circumstance, social neighbourhoods of this kind are perpetuated by an on-going process of socialization. Children are taught to fear adjacent territorial groups and to avoid contact with such areas. Working with small samples of 13–15-year-olds in Argentina, Australia, Mexico and Poland they showed that the existence of socially defined territorial boundaries was important in explaining the spatial behaviour of these schoolchildren. Whilst there were some distance-related factors that acted as barriers to children's range movements, important controls were personal fear, social barriers, parental sanction and lack of spatial knowledge. The fact children learn that many parts of the city are dangerous and inaccessible places perpetuates the existence of the 'defended neighbourhood' (Suttles, 1972). At the same time these children will become socialized into the ways of the area, they will come to understand its social milieux and this will colour their views of place and space.

However, defended neighbourhoods need not intensify over time. Tilly (1974) has shown that in Boston the old Italian district of the West End lost its attraction for second-generation Bostonians. Without their support those who were left behind found it impossible to continue with their customs and practice of social isolation. He suggests that the overarching process of acculturization is, for many ethnic groups, an inevitable road to incorporation into large-scale society.

In summary, there is sufficient evidence to suggest that membership of particular ethnic groups considerably influences children's environmental opportunities. Those children who reside in strong territorial enclaves, frequently located within the inner city, experience a relatively impoverished activity space compared to their charter group counterparts.

The importance of the geographical environment to environmental experience

Play settings

We have seen already how, as children grow older, the world beyond the front door becomes of increasing environmental significance. In this section we will review those studies which have examined where children play within their habitual outdoor territories.

Opportunities for play are an important aspect of children's ecological relationship with the environment. However, Bishop and Peterson (1971) point

Table 2.10 Children's favourite places to go after school and at weekends

Places	After school %	Weekends %	Mean-rate %
Home and home site (e.g. own room/home/garden/ yard, friend's home, relative's home)	21	19	20
Streets and associated space (e.g. streets, alleys, front grass areas, garage courts, around flats)	19	4	11.5
Formal/official open space (e.g. parks, playgrounds, sports field)	37	32	34.5
Informal/unofficial space (e.g. fields, vacant plots, building sites)	15	11	13
Commercial areas (e.g. shops, town centre)	4	10	7
Institutions/community facilities (e.g. church, cinemas, swimming club, youth club)	3	20	11.5
Nonspecific/other (e.g. anywhere outside, non-local recreation)	1	4	2.5

Source: Moore (1986)

out a major paradox. At an age when children would benefit the most from increasing independence and expansion of home range they are faced with constraints in terms of range of travel, times for outdoor activity and facilities for play. Bishop and Peterson have demonstrated that many adults (designers and park officials included) are quite insensitive to the play preferences of school-age children. Therefore, the play spaces planned by adults have a questionable relationship to the opportunities desired by children (see Chapter 13).

Moore (1986) interviewed ninety-six children, aged between 9 and 12 years, drawn from three urban neighbourhoods in England, to find out their favourite places to go after school and at weekends. He categorized the results into seven classes (see Table 2.10). The first three items, formal/official open space (34.5 per cent), home sites (20 per cent) and streets and associated open spaces (11.5 per cent), account for two-thirds of all mentions. The results confirm for him 'the experiential investment that children make, by necessity, in their homesite and their immediate surroundings' (Moore, 1986, p. 44). Some interesting temporal variations are also evident. Streets, for example, are used much more after school than at weekends, most likely because there was no time after school to go anywhere else. The greater amount of time available at weekends leads to greater involvement in community facilities and trips and outings to local swimming pools, football clubs and cinemas.

These results closely accord with an earlier study carried out by Moore (1978), based on a sample of children aged between 8 and 12 years from San Francisco Bay region neighbourhoods. In this case children were asked to make a map or draw 'all your favourite places, where you go after school or at weekends, around your neighbourhood, including the summer'. Features were ranked in order of their mention-rate from 1 to 72. Primary emphasis was on the subject's own person (3) and closest friends (4), together with their own homes (1), the surrounding streets (2) and immediately accessible play areas, such as schools (5), parks (8), playgrounds (12) and community facilities (14).

Two other characteristics are worth highlighting from Moore's (1978) survey. First, four categories of pathway are repeatedly mentioned: through streets (2); trails, short-cuts, paths, alleys (20); sidewalks (21); deadends and driveways (26). Moore proposes that pathway systems, such as these, are important elements in childhood, as they frequently serve as ways of escape from adult domination. He observes that in many cases, children mentioned pathways which acted as short-cuts through small openings, inpenetrable to adults, and which gave access to stimulating private landscapes. Sometimes, child-only routes are an end in themselves 'as places to dilly-dally on the way, not so much as movement channels as endless sequences of exploration-for-its-own-sake in *ad hoc* sidetrips' (Moore and Young, 1978, p. 121). Secondly, and according to Moore, the most impressive finding is that the collective rank of natural systems accounts for just over 25 per cent of the aggregate mention-rates. Nature, too, has a powerful presence in the world of children.

From the results of both surveys we can also see what elements are not frequently mentioned by children. In either case features such as traffic, asphalt and commercial facilities (including local shops and shopping centres) all received such low scores that we can presume they represent items of such 'ubiquity and mundaneness' that presumably children saw no point in mentioning them.

What these surveys show is that the outdoor recreation of children takes place in both planned and unplanned settings. Hayward *et al.* (1974) recognize the importance of planned playgrounds to the environmental experience of children. Three types of playground are commonly encountered: traditional; contemporary, and adventure. Each varies according to the sort of equipment available, the form of activity and play engaged in by children and the age of the users. The traditional playground contains swings, slides and climbing frames; the contemporary playground features mounds, tunnels and sandpits; the adventure playground features materials, like wood, tyres, ropes, that can be used in a variety of ways. From an environmental view there are at least two important attributes of such play settings and their equipment: availability and responsiveness (Ittelson *et al.*, 1974). Many such settings, like traditional playgrounds, may be available and near to home, considered safe by parents and popular with children, but their responsiveness may be questioned. Responsiveness in this case is the 'ability to engage the child in a personal and reactive manner, the capability of giving the child a sense of discovery' (Ittelson *et al.*, 1974, p. 182).

In their study Hayward *et al.* observed that pre-school children and their parents were the main users of traditional and contemporary playgrounds, whereas most of those attending adventure playgrounds were school-aged children and young teenagers. Mason *et al.* (1975) noted similar age-related usage in their study of parks in Berkeley. At one adventure playground adolescents had built a self-styled clubhouse in which they would meet, talk and play music. Poag *et al.* (1985) suggest that organized play spaces, like these, contribute to the evolving outdoor experiences of children and because children's play behaviour changes, different types of playground gain in significance at different times. In a similar vein, Coates and Sanoff (1972) make the point that formal play settings are not only important to children's social development but also to their environmental development as they enable close interaction with both the social and physical landscape. For Ittelson *et al.* (1974) the adventure playground provides the most environmentally responsive setting for children's play in that it encourages the child to deal with 'the degree of environmental complexity he is ready for' (p. 182).

Whilst playgrounds may be a source of environmental invention, and offer children privacy and freedom, they also remove the child from play opportunities available in the natural environment. Studies of playgrounds of all types indicate that they are frequently underused (Gold, 1972). Given the choice, children from the age of 6 and 7 years often prefer the complexity of the real world, even though parental sanctions and physical danger make this a less convenient setting.

Not all outdoor recreation takes place in areas designated for play. To van Vliet (1983) these areas beyond the home, school and playground constitute *the fourth environment*. Informal play settings like yards, streets, vacant plots and open ground and other *found* areas are frequently preferred by children (Sanoff and Dickerson, 1971; Coates and Sanoff, 1972; Dresnel, 1972; Hart, 1979; Moore, 1986). For example, car parks offer opportunities to ride bikes or practise skateboarding and child-made paths provide more convenient and exciting routes than formal pathways. Furthermore, as Coates and Sanoff (1972) suggest, a greater variety of play may occur in ambiguous play settings than in those designated for play and this, in itself, may prove to be environmentally more stimulating.

In summary, the study of the play settings of children reveals the importance of both formal and informal space to children's environmental activities. Through play children are given an opportunity to learn, not only about themselves, but also about their everyday worlds. Furthermore, the opportunities to play enhance a child's ability to initiate independent activity, which is crucial to environmental interaction. However, play environments are themselves enmeshed into broader environmental settings, to which our attention now turns.

Residential settings

Where children live has a profound effect on their opportunities for play, exploration and environmental interaction beyond the home. For example, Wright (1971) reported that children in a large town (33,000) were presented with more behaviour settings and of more varied kinds, than children from a smaller town (786). However, the number and kinds of setting and the opportunities for involvement did not increase in proportion to the total population. Although the large town had a population about forty times greater than that of the small town, there were only ten times as many behaviour settings and three times as many different kinds of setting. Furthermore, the children of the smaller place knew more about the settings of the town and its people than those from the larger settlement. For these children exploration was more than just physical distance, it was entrance to town life and a forerunner to adult participation. Gump and Adelberg (1978) arrive at similar conclusions. They point out that although the absolute number of things to do is greater in cities than small towns, the presence of many people lessens the urban child's chance to participate. For the small town's children, repeated exposure to fewer behaviour settings allows them to learn more about the people, places and activities of their community than city children.

Michelson and Roberts (1979) recognize the diversity of places relevant to children's activities and how different residential settings can affect children's environmental opportunities. They suggest that at any age some of the places where children spend their time will be intended for children's use whereas others are *hidden spaces*. But as children get older a greater percentage of the environment they effectively use will almost certainly be of the hidden kind. What is important is that children draw upon both types of spatial setting for their environmental experiences, although it is likely that the significance of hidden space goes beyond its unintended nature. For example, the vivid memories of childhood are often to do with these 'invisible environments' and 'hidden structures' (Grabow and Salkind, 1976) which although insignificant to adults are very attractive to children. Jane Jacobs (1976) recounts how her young son brags that 'I know Greenwich village like the back of my hand', and how he takes her to see a 'secret passage' he has discovered under a street and a secret hiding place some 9 inches wide between two buildings where he hides treasures found on his way to school. Jacobs writes, 'I had such a hiding place, for the same purpose, at his age, but mine was a crack in a cliff on my way to school instead of a crack between two buildings and he finds stranger and richer treasures' (p. 548).

Michelson and Roberts propose a fourfold classification into which residential areas can be fitted according to the presence and absence of hidden and intended play spaces (see Figure 2.5). Cell 1 represents the kind of area where there is a broad range of amenities for any given age group, whether man-made or from nature. An example of such a setting would be a well-planned urban

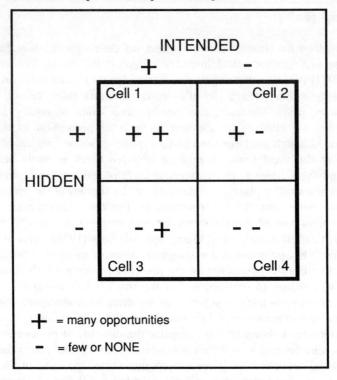

Figure 2.5   Configuration of environmental opportunities (Based on: Michelson
and Roberts, 1979)

area, where facilities have grown organically over the years and where children
can still create their own environmental opportunities.

In contrast, Cell 2 is the kind of area where formal amenities for children are
lacking, but where young people, none the less, can keep occupied in activities
which they find satisfying. Michelson and Roberts believe that such settings are
often found in established, inner city locations, where intense use is made of
back alleys, building plots, vacant sites and other informal spaces.

Cell 3 represents the situation found in many new residential areas. In this
case many natural amenities have been destroyed in the haste for development,
and at the same time the new environment appears too sterile and uniform to
attract the interest of children. In the course of time playgrounds and swimming
pools may be built, but in the absence of any other hospitable places for
children, the overall outcome is still relatively unstimulating.

Cell 4 represents those places with the least environmental opportunities.
Such areas not only lack informal spaces, but also, because of insufficient
investment, formal amenities geared towards children. In Britain, many public

sector housing estates fall into this category. In this context Figure 2.5 helps explain why many new housing developments turn out to be no more attractive to children than the slums they were meant to replace.

Porteous (1977) argues that although urban, suburban and rural settings are becoming increasingly similar, their distinction remains relevant to the environmental opportunities presented to children. Anderson and Tindall (1972) compared the home range of black second-grade and fourth-grade schoolchildren drawn from two contrasting locations: an urban ghetto in Baltimore and a suburban area, some 25 miles from the city. They found that the home range of black elementary schoolchildren was much less restricted than that of their urban counterparts: the mean home range for suburban children was 4,810 ft compared to 4,074 ft for urban children. A number of possible explanations was suggested. For example, suburban areas offer fewer threats and hazards, their lower density of facilities means that suburban children have to travel further to reach potential destinations such as schools, shops, play areas, and friends' homes, and a higher percentage of suburban children have bicycles, an outcome of higher family income. Anderson and Tindall also investigated children's 'activity nodes', the focal points or areas where certain activities are carried out. They classified these nodes into four groups: recreational, commercial, educational and social. The results confirmed a higher density of attractions in the urban environment. Differences were most emphatic between the recreational nodes of Fourth Graders. In the urban case, children regularly visited 4.4 nodes, on average, compared to 2.9 nodes in the suburbs; a possible reason being that 'suburban backyards are simply more sufficient play areas than the sidewalks and vacant lots of the central city' (p. 5).

Moore and Young (1978), draw together the findings from five studies, four American and one German, which report on children's outdoor activities in contrasting suburban and urban contexts (see Table 2.11). A number of observations can be made from these results: first, each environment generates its own opportunities for play and exploration, such that children inevitably grow up in different worlds of experience; secondly, it is difficult to disentangle the separate effects of social and physical factors upon environmental behaviour. For example, both Aiello et al. (1974) and Sanoff and Dickerson (1971) studied similar density, suburban developments and yet in the former case there is a much greater emphasis on home site activities, compared to the strong orientation towards the street found in the latter. Moore and Young speculate that this difference may simply be explained by cultural preferences among the two populations; thirdly, housing density and estate design appear to be important influences on play opportunities. All three studies carried out in high-density settings show limited or no use of the home site and its amenities. In the suburban case this can be explained by the provision of smaller house plots, whereas both urban studies were carried out around low-rise, super-block developments where the absence of private gardens and yards inevitably forced children into the public domain.

Table 2.11 Where children play: a comparison of five studies

Location	Suburb[1] low-density white American 4–14 years %	Suburb[2] low-density black American 3–13 years %	Suburb[3] high-density white American 3–13 years %	Urban[4] high-density white German na %	Urban[5] high-density white American 1–11 years %
Home/home site	77	44	8	–	–
Streets/associated spaces	18	46	14	29	56
Formal/official open space	–	2	25	42	15
Informal/unofficial space	5	3	20	12	29
Institutions/ community facilities	–	5	33	17	–

Notes:
1. Aiello et al. (1974)
2. Sanoff and Dickerson (1971)
3. Coates and Sanoff (1972)
4. Dresnel (1972)
5. Cooper Marcus (1974)

Source: Moore and Young (1978)

Table 2.12 The location of children's outdoor activities on British public housing estates

Location	Low-rise[1] (4 estates) 1–15 years %	Medium-rise[1] (6 estates) 1–15 years %	Mixed-rise[1] (5 estates) 1–15 years %	Old housing[1] (1 area) 1–15 years %	High-density[2] (9 estates) na %	Low-density[2] (6 areas) na %
Home/ home site	18	2	1	9	2	–
Streets/ associated spaces (access areas)	63 (–)	75 (23)	72 (40)	68 (7)	48 (15)	76 (7)
Formal/offical open space	4	11	13	3	23	9
Informal/ unofficial open space	20	17	28	20	12	13

Sources: 1. Department of Environment (1973)
2. Hole and Miller (1969)

Table 2.12 compares the findings of two British studies of children's outdoor activities on an assortment of public housing estates. The results further attest to the importance of estate design and density on the opportunities for children's play. In all cases, there is a tendency to play on hard surfaces near to the home. In areas of low-rise, of old housing, and of low-density development, considerable use is made of streets and paved areas. However, in medium-rise and mixed-rise developments, and to a lesser extent in residential areas of high density, there is a shift towards access areas like balconies and stairways, spaces that are immediately available and which offer some enclosure and security. Play in formal playgrounds was low, with the exception of the high-density estate where, as with many similar situations, there was virtually nowhere else for children to play in any safety.

The way in which the built environment affects play and play patterns has been further demonstrated by Berg and Medrich (1980). They observed 11- and 12-year-olds in four different neighbourhoods: a low-density suburb of large houses in spacious plots; a higher density suburb of small houses with small yards; a densely populated urban site located near industry; and, an inner city setting. What they found was that although the children of the higher density neighbourhoods mostly lacked areas to play near to their homes, they often displayed a more active relationship with the environment, in that they created their own play spaces in vacant plots and open ground. Conversely, children from the low-density neighbourhood played within or close to their home site, were less mobile and often felt isolated. In general, although the parents favoured the low-density neighbourhood as a place of residence, the children preferred the independence from adults which the high-density environments conferred.

Hart (1979), too, expresses doubt about the benefits of suburban living. According to him, suburban landscapes may provide better auditory and visual contact between parent and child, which encourages greater spatial freedom at an early age, but the spaciousness of the suburban setting presents children with fewer opportunities to develop their environmental competence. Further- more, the highly prescriptive toys and play equipment given to suburban children compared to the 'loose' environment of many rural and urban children, convinced Hart that, on balance, suburban living is detrimental to the development of post-kindergarten children. Wohlwill (1981) lends support to these ideas, by suggesting that whilst a suburban home may be more advantageous to a young child than a high-rise flat, as the child's territorial range expands and opportunities to explore beyond the home site increase, the complex urban setting may be more favourable, especially for adolescents.

Not all agree on the benefits of urban childhood. Coates and Bussard (1974), for example, point to the problems of traffic danger and the limited nature of formal open space: both, they feel, conspire to limit the child's free exploration of the neighbourhood environment. When social conditions are also taken into account, like overcrowded homes, intolerance by neighbours of the presence of children and the noise that they make, working parents, and single parent households, it becomes clear that the urban child's freedom is severely restricted.

One urban setting which has generated considerable interest is that of high- rise living. Children living in high-rise blocks face the following common problems which considerably affect their opportunities to explore neighbouring macrospace environments. First, access to and from the home is usually by lift. Young children, in particular, cannot use lifts and many adults feel that older children frequently misuse them. In consequence, several studies have shown (Fanning, 1967; Stewart, 1970) that there is considerable reluctance by parents to let their children play beyond the 'block', and, furthermore, this reluctance increases with the number of floors one has to climb.

Secondly, most high-rise blocks contain few interior, public spaces suitable for children's play. Some may contain wide passageways, accessed by broad entrance bays, but the attractiveness of these potential play spaces are tempered by such factors as the climate, neighbours' attitude to noise and parental concern about safety. In general, any formal play spaces on high-rise estates are separated from the dwelling units. This kind of separation is seen by many to hinder the opportunities for young children's outdoor play (Homenuck, 1973; Kaminoff and Proshansky, 1982). Parents have been shown to restrict the comings and goings of younger children in high-rise blocks when they cannot visually supervise the scene of their outdoor activities. For example, Morville (1969) found, from a study of 434 flats in a 15-storey block in Copenhagen, that pre-school children in high-rise environments are less likely to play outside alone, come out less frequently and have less contact with playmates, than children in low-rise settings. Pollowy (1977) has shown that many children prefer to stay close to their home block when they do play outside, congregating around entrances. This not only gives rise to a restricted environmental range, but also leads to problems with adults who dislike congestion, noise and bother.

Thirdly, children living in high-rise buildings are more likely to engage in passive recreational activities, for example, sitting, watching and talking, whilst children residing in low-rise apartments are more inclined to play actively outdoors, riding bicycles and sliding on hills (Becker, 1976). According to Parke (1978) the restrictive play schedule of children who live in high-rise blocks may have several negative effects: insufficient exercise may lead to poor health; the forced and continued contact with parents may contribute to family tension; and the inability of parents to supervise their children's outdoor play activities may impair their social and cognitive development.

Finally, the scale of high-rise buildings presents opportunities for children to have contact with many more children than on low-rise estates. Wallace (1972) points out that parents frequently worry about the lack of control they have over their children' potential playmates, an outcome of which is to inhibit further their children's opportunities for play.

However, not all studies are critical of high-rise buildings as hostile and difficult environments for children. Both Farley (1977) and Hagarty (1975) found no differences between children living in high-rise buildings and on low-rise developments with respect to children's contact with each other, number of friends, and outdoor play activities. Also, the classic, home-based, passive recreation of watching television was no more pronounced among those living in high-rise blocks than those from suburban houses. Michelson and Roberts (1979), in their review of children in the urban physical environment, conclude that at present there does not appear to be 'a solid empirical basis for ... blanket condemnation of high-rise buildings for children as has come from some quarters' (p. 450).

When high-rise living is combined with high-density development more conclusive negative effects have been identified. Kaminoff and Proshansky (1982) review a number of studies that support the notion that such a combination of settings is likely to severely restrict children's normal play activities. It appears that children from such residential backgrounds are more likely to portray behavioural problems, for example, hyper-activity and antisocial behaviours, than their low-density counterparts (Cohen et al., 1978; Booth and Johnson, 1975). Van Staden (1984), in a study of a middle-income, high-rise, high-density neighbourhood of Manhattan, noted that his sample of 11–13-year-olds emphasized the spatially restrictive effects of crowding. For them, movement in and around the local area was constrained by feelings of insecurity and an awareness of possible threat and harm. Dislike of city noise, litter and dirt intensified their negative perceptions. In addition, van Staden identifies information overload as another aversive characteristic of crowding, in that physical and social diversity were seen to create residential settings of high stress.

In summary, the residential settings of childhood are important in providing opportunities for children to explore macrospace environments. Hart (1979) attempts to draw together some of the common forces influencing children's spatial behaviour (see Figure 2.6). Although Hart's observations are based on a small town/rural environment his observations are relevant to a broad range of residential settings. For all children, the home is the secure base from which they explore. From this base children gradually extend their familiarity with the environment. In their transactions children will develop different relationships with the environment. For example, some environments will be avoided because they are perceived to be dangerous (a dark wood or a place beyond the child's habitual range), some environments will act as physical barriers simply because of the child's inability to overcome them (for example, a busy road or a deep river), whilst some environments will be *out of bounds*, simply because of parental sanctions. However, it is important to remember that different individuals are not exposed to the same physical contexts, even though they may share the same environment. Also, different individuals will respond in different ways to the same environments. Whether the physical context actually has effects on children's environmental capabilities remains a matter of conjecture.

The societal and cultural context of child–environment transactions

Culture can be defined as 'a group of people who have a set of values and beliefs which embody ideals and are transmitted to members of the group through enculturation' (Rapoport, 1980). This leads not only to a world view and a characteristic way of looking at the world, but also to common patterns of

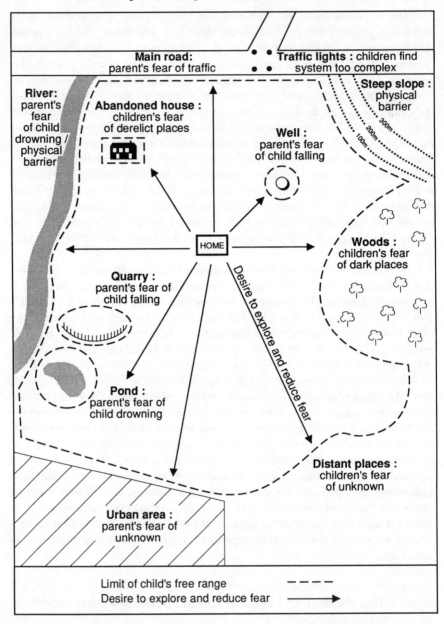

Figure 2.6   Common factors influencing children's spatial behaviour (Based on: Hart, 1979)

life-style which affect how people make choices about how to behave and condition environmental experience. Accordingly, different cultures give rise to different child–environment relationships. Rapoport (1977) believes that any activity can be analyzed into four components:

1. The activity proper.
2. The specific way of doing it and where it is done.
3. Additional, adjacent or associated activities which become part of the activity system.
4. Symbolic aspects and meaning of the activity.

Consider children's developing environmental range. The activity is rooted in pleasure and exploration and play. The nature of environmental range, at any given age, depends on parental expectation combined with children's locomotor capability, ritual and tradition. Location and distance depend on such factors as parental care-taking practices, residential settings and the societal provision of formal and informal activity nodes. Associated activities may include socialization, exchanging information and environmental learning. The symbolic meaning, for the child, may be a means of acquiring peer group status or a way of asserting some special social identity or group membership, and for the parent, it may offer a means for enculturation.

The variability of points 2 to 4 leads to different environmental outcomes. Rapoport suggests that the relationship between environmental activities and the rules and meanings which accompany them is strongly conditioned by culture. This includes such decisions as what is acceptable or unacceptable, who is allowed or not allowed, when permission should be granted or not granted, who is admitted or not admitted. It also includes the form and type of the 'setting system', the most significant of which is the house-settlement system (Rapoport, 1978). There is great cultural variability in the elements, their design and the relationships among them, of such a system, which leads to different childhood domains, habitats and environmental opportunities.

For Moore and Young (1978), in their review of children's outdoor activities, 'a conclusion which stands out is the evident cultural dependency of children's outdoor relationship' (p 121). By this they are suggesting that children's activity space is set within a culturally defined context, which inevitably impinges upon and shapes likely environmental opportunity and interaction. This impression is shared by Bruner (Bruner and Sherwood, 1981). Although Bruner is more concerned with the development of language and the social cognition of young children, his ideas on the importance of culture to children's early life experiences are relevant, by implication, to how children come into contact with large-scale environments. For Bruner, society consists of communities of people who are linked together by the bond of shared culture. Culture, in itself, is not an arbitrary creation. The historical changes of a society and that society's present form have necessarily proceeded alongside changes in culture. Culture supplies the skills, attitudes and beliefs which link people in societies together. It follows that children's experiences are constructed out of culturally supplied material. This is not to deny a place for individual experiences, but such a view does stress the idea of a common basis out of which individual variations are based.

From Bruner's perspective, the world of childhood is far from a process of accumulating experience through chance encounters with the environment. Rather, it is a highly structured activity, in which the child's opportunities are largely affected by decisions beyond their own control. Children are surrounded by cultural artefacts of different kinds. These include not only the physical or material trappings of a society but also patterns of behaviour. To be adept in participating in society children have to constitute their minds in a form which can assimilate and reflect the patterning of meaning within their culture. Children have to shape their thoughts, communications and actions to those people with whom they share their everyday world. For example, many of children's playground games involve chanting, role playing and elaborate rules, and children spend a great deal of time practising their form, gaining great satisfaction from such cultural mastery. By the same token, the way in which children encounter the environment is strongly ritualized by both parental sanction and children's age- and sex-related expectations. The process of being drawn into a culture begins, says Bruner, from the earliest days. Thus, the more children develop, the more closely their thoughts and actions become structured along the lines provided by the culture through which they interact. However, culture is not seen as a deterministic and controlling force. For Bruner, culture *enables* us to become what we are capable of; although society expects and requires certain things of us, also, by the same process, it draws out our potential and supplies cultural tools.

A wealth of studies, many anthropological in nature, draws attention to how culture can affect children's experiences of place and space. Tuan (1978) describes how children living in contrasting societies, such as those dominated by natural and man-made settings, are given very different opportunities to encounter large-scale environments. Whereas the Bushman infant plays in a natural world with twigs, leaves and pebbles, the New Guinean child roams in an intricate world of sea and sand, the Western child is restricted to the play spaces, the buildings and paths of a largely man-made world. Tuan muses whether the Western child's imagination suffers, in any sense, because of this lack of contact with nature.

Tuan (1979) points out that human groups vary widely in their spatial skills and environmental experiences. For example, Nance (1975) has shown that small, primitive groups, such as the Tasaday of Mindanao (Philippines) occupy a small, ecological niche in the tropical rain forest and hesitate to move beyond their home base. Compare their behaviour to that of the mobile, Western child, who is brought up in a society where geographical knowledge and an ability to circumnavigate space are seen as signs of mastery over the physical environment. However, as Tuan argues, it is not a rule that children from large integrated societies will have greater environmental knowledge than small, loosely organized groups. The environmental skills and experiences of primitive hunters can far exceed those of sedentary agriculturalists bound to locality.

> The hunter's skill is not simply one of identifying trails, water holes, and feeding grounds in a broad tract of land. . .spatial knowledge extends beyond details of the terrain to reference points in heaven, and may be expressed in the abstract notation of maps. (Tuan, 1979, p. 76).

Hutorowicz (1911) has shown that children of several hunting groups in Siberia, such as the Yakuts and Buriats, take a keen interest in the spatial–geometry of the night sky and are able to distinguish with the naked eye stars in the Pleiades not usually discernible without a telescope. Nearby, children of the Chucki, are introduced to elaborate maps etched on bark, leather and wood, showing more information than is needed for any particular reason and which have come to act as stores of these people's material culture.

The physical setting of a society can have a profound effect on environmental experience. Berry (1968) has compared the environmental behaviour of the Temne of Sierra Leone and the Eskimo of Arctic Canada. The environmental skills of the Eskimo are far superior to those of the Temne. Eskimos possess a large vocabulary of spatial-geometric terms with which to articulate their environment compared to the meagre terminology of the Temne. Berry explains these differences by looking at how these groups respond to nature. The land of the Temne is covered with bush and other vegetation. There are many visual stimuli and nature is fairly benign. Temne children are seldom alone and they have no need to make conscious efforts to structure space. Occasions seldom arise when the Temne child has the task to orient himself in an unfamiliar and inhospitable place. Eskimo society is very different. Arctic Canada is a bleak environment, almost uniformly grey-brown, broken only by the colours of moss and lichen in summer and ice and snow in winter. The environmental challenges which come from such a harsh landscape are legion. Eskimos are hunters. They are not supported by the workings of an organized society. Instead their behaviour is individualistic and venturesome, traits which they encourage in their children. Eskimo children need self-reliance to survive. They are encouraged to develop a sense of curiosity and their success often depends upon such early environmental mastery.

Tuan (1979) draws a likeness between the environmental skills of Eskimo children and the navigational capabilities of the Puluwatans (Pacific Islanders) as described by Gladwin (1970). Puluwatans, like Eskimos, place considerable importance upon their relationship with nature. Instead of the undifferentiated landscapes of Arctic snow and ice, the survival and success of Puluwatans are set in a watery world of sea and islands. Puluwatan children are given considerable freedom. Boys of 6 or 7 years are deliberately taken on long boat journeys in order to introduce them to navigational skills and to condition them to the changing moods of the sea and weather.

Not all island societies share the same regard for nature. Mead (1930) describes the play behaviour of the Manus children of the Admiralty Isles, north of New Guinea. The Manus children were free to play all day. Their physical environment was safe and secure and the children had plenty to play with, including many natural artefacts like palm leaves, raffia, rattan and coconut shells. Yet she found that these children had a dull, uninteresting child life, making little use of their natural environment for lack of adult guidance. Their culture was simply not predisposed towards encouraging a sense of environmental awareness.

Sometimes the nature of the physical environment gives rise to local orientation and language systems for expressing spatial relationships. Haugen (1957) describes how children in Iceland are introduced to two complementary spatial reference systems, which are still in everyday use. The first is based on *proximate orientation*, and relies on the visual judgement of relationships: for example, the farm is south of the town. The second depends on *ultimate orientation*, a system which has evolved to help land travel. At the time that this system was established, travel was by horseback along winding coastal trails. Movement across the uninhabited and environmentally harsh interior was impossible. As a result of common agreement, Iceland was divided into quarters: north, east, south and west. The trail that led around the island linked each quarter. Anyone travelling along the trail would say where they were going in the direction of the next quarter: so, 'going west' meant that they were travelling to the western quarter even though the compass direction may have been north-east. Haugen points out that the spatial logic of these systems depends entirely on local environmental conditions.

An ambitious attempt to evaluate children's relationship with the urban environment, in a range of cultural settings, was undertaken by Kevin Lynch (1979) for UNESCO. This project looked at the environmental experiences of children aged 11–14 years in Cracow, Melbourne, Mexico City, Salta (Argentina), Toluca (Mexico) and Warsaw. Some interesting contrasts were found between the groups. Lynch describes 'the hunger' for activity and stimulus expressed by the children brought up in the austere housing blocks of the Polish cities. Their play and activity was largely confined to the grey, asphalted spaces between 'the blank ranges of apartments' and their maps showed islands of activity linked by 'bridges' of public transport. In Ecatepec, too, a largely self-built settlement on the northern fringe of Mexico City, the children bemoaned the highly repetitive nature of their utilitarian environment. In particular, the maps drawn by boys revealed a narrow environmental range, confined to their housing district, and there was very little evidence of sensuous detail or stimulation. These children were the poorest of the survey and their environment was bleak, harsh and monotonous. Their only 'beacon' was their neighbourhood school, which the children consistently named as their favourite place and they gave it 'a loving emphasis on their maps'. In all these cases, Lynch found that children rarely travelled more than half a kilometre in any direction from their homes.

Yet, urban poverty need not give rise to a childhood of environmental impoverishment. The Las Rosas district of Salta consisted of 'standard houses, put down to a rather haphazard plan on an old garbage dump next to the penitentiary', but in the view of the children it had 'blossomed into a coherent society and place'. The children roamed freely and confidently throughout their slum. To them the place was 'nice' and 'friendly', 'protected' and 'fun'. They talked of their neighbourhod, and their feeling of belonging. The children drew attention to the plaza as an important meeting point. They were aware of environmental detail, emphasizing the beauty of the local trees, although, in reality, there were not too many. The children claimed that they preferred their own area to any other in Salta and most believed that things would change for the better.

Equally, affluence and material well-being need not guarantee a childhood filled with rich environmental experience. The children of Melbourne were certainly the most affluent of the international sample. Yet, very few were able to identify with their locality. There was a feeling that there were better areas elsewhere. The children mimicked their parents' resentment that they had not quite made it to the top and this stigmatized the area. In consequence there was very little environmental pride. Lynch describes the suburb as a place 'where football clubs and schools have a two-metre-high mesh fence around the periphery topped with barbed wire' and 'the parks are flat featureless tracts of haphazardly grassed unused land'. Children were uncertain about the area and so roamed widely, frequently travelling more than 5 km to visit friends and to take part in activities. However, whether these differences in environmental range and environmental attitudes are a product of culturally-defined child-rearing practices or whether they are outcomes of the social and/or physical environment is difficult to establish with any certainty. Lynch does summarize what the most important factors to movement are from these studies: personal fear, dangerous traffic, cost of public transport, parental controls (especially for girls) and lack of spatial knowledge. But what comes first in order of importance and whether these are, in any way, culturally induced must remain a matter of some conjecture.

How parental attitudes towards children's outdoor behaviour vary in different cultural settings has engaged the attention of a number of studies. Landy (1965) provides a useful cross-cultural comparison of parental care-taking practices. We have already noted how Landy interviewed eighteen Puerto Rican mothers and observed 113 island families in order to develop an index of spatial restrictedness for children (see page 22). Landy went on to examine the extent to which Puerto Rican mothers checked on the whereabouts of their children when out of doors. He replicated this methodology in a study of 372 mothers of kindergarten children drawn from two housing areas in Massachusetts. The results were scaled from 10 (rarely checks) to 90 (often checks). Puerto Rican mothers were found to have an index of 89 compared to 47 for mothers from Massachusetts. Landy observed that Puerto Rican mothers were clearly more protective towards their children, checking regularly on their whereabouts, and, indeed, failure to do so was regarded as a transgression of maternal responsibilities.

We have noted that in Western societies the outdoor behaviour of boys and girls is likely to be very different. Sex-differences of this kind were seen to increase with age and to be strongly related to parental sanction. Whether these differences are consistently found in other cultures was examined by Maccoby and Jacklin (1974). Drawing upon a large body of ethnographic literature they concluded 'the bulk of the evidence is that there is little or no differences in the socialisation of boys and girls when it comes to independence-granting' (p. 374). However, Hart (1979) calls this finding 'surprising' (p. 370) and explains their conclusion by the fact that most of the studies they reviewed were of 4- to 5-year-old children. Hart goes on to refer to two other studies on the spatial range of children (Munroe and Munroe, 1971; Nerlove et al., 1971), both of them with Bantu-speaking populations in Kenya, which challenge Maccoby and Jacklin's assertion.

In the first study, fifteen boys and fifteen girls were sorted into age-matched pairs. Each of these children were then observed on twenty separate occasions in their natural setting in and around the village. Analysis of children's distances away from their homes revealed a non-significant tendency for boys to be further away from their homes than their girl counterparts. However, these scores included observations on which children had been instructed by an older person to carry out some assigned task. In the process of carrying out a chore, a child would often follow a route which involved leaving the immediate home site. For example, obtaining water, typically a girl's job, required a trip of several hundred feet from most houses. In such cases the child would indeed be experiencing a different part of the environment than the child who stayed at home, but the nature of the task meant that a mechanical, unvarying route was being followed. This suggested to the Munroes that directed activities should be excluded from consideration. More pertinent, they felt, was a measure of a child's distance from home in 'free time'. When average distances were calculated for instances in which children were undirected, it was found that in thirteen of the fifteen pairings boys were rated as more distant from home on average than girls. In addition, the Munroes observed that boys were free for a greater proportion of their time, as girls were commonly involved in parentally directed tasks.

The second study, by Nerlove, Monroe and Monroe (1971), followed the same procedure as the initial investigation, with another Bantu-speaking group. Unlike the first study, the 'free range' of boys and girls proved to be non-significant. However, because this society was very different in its activities it was decided to modify the analysis. Nerlove et al. recognized that much of the older boys' time was taken up with herding. They concluded that although herding was a directed activity, it left the child relatively free to wander around and to explore different places, using varying routes and hence was effectively the same as 'free range'. What these studies show is that sex-related differences in spatial behaviour can be recognized beyond Western societies, but the cultural context of environmental behaviour needs to be recognized in order to comprehend its full significance.

Another, more recent, study undertaken in Kenya was carried out by Matthews and Airey (1990). We were concerned with the environmental experiences of a sample of Kimeru-speaking children drawn from an urban (Meru) and a rural (Kanyakine) area. Altogether eighty children (forty from each place), aged 7, 9, 11 and 13 years (twenty from each age group), matched by sex, were interviewed, together with a sample of their parents. Questions were asked about their environmental range, play activities and attitudes towards their everyday environments.

Matthews and Airey found that the environmental range of these children was much more strictly sanctioned than for comparable age groups in Britain. Up until the age of 9 years, children were seldom allowed to play beyond the safety of their home compounds, unless visiting a neighbouring friend or a close relative. After this age, children in Meru were given some further freedom, although in rural Kanyakine children's free range remained limited until they were at least 11-years-old. Even then, children were expected to play in parentally designated 'safe environments', such as the playing fields of the local school, or on 'visible' open ground. Children were very aware of the environmental and social reasons which their parents used to justify their sanctions. Some differences were apparent between the two locations. For example, in Meru, fear of traffic, of drowning in a nearby river and of the 'bad' influence of older children, were typically quoted, compared to the fear of open bush-country, wild animals and witchcraft in Kanyakine.

Although significant differences between the range behaviour of boys and girls were not evident in either place until the age of 11– when boys began to move further afield – without exception, parents readily admitted to strong sex-stereotyping. From an early age, girls were expected to take a full and active part in all housework in preparation for becoming 'responsible mothers'. To quote a typical response by a parent of Kanyakine children,

> I have taught my girls that they are different to the boys . . . my girls are still very young (3 years and 5 years), but when they grow up I will treat them differently . . . They will do all the jobs I do, kitchen work mostly . . . They will become good wives . . .

Throughout the course of their interviews with children it was clear to Matthews and Airey that these Kenyan children 'knew their place' within society and were responsive to the strong discipline of the home. Play activities were subsumed by domestic responsibilites and when asked to distinguish between where they played (and for how long) after school and at weekends many reported that they did not have any time to play during the week. Whether such societally generated differences in environmental range affect children's capacity to handle and understand spatial knowledge formed a further part of

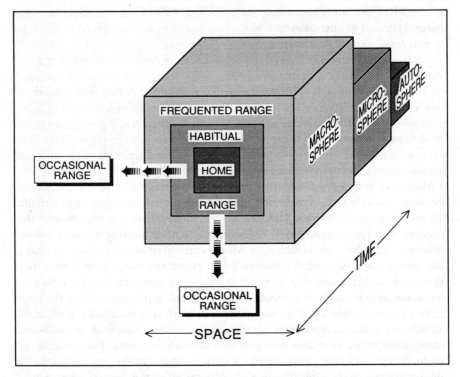

Figure 2.7   A model of children's territorial range development: a space–time framework

this study.

In summary, what these studies suggest is that children's environmental transactions are set within a societal context defined and shaped by varying cultural systems. Accordingly, the opportunities that children have to make sense of place and space are often beyond their control. Not only is their outdoor behaviour constrained by cultural expectation, but also many of the artefacts of place are products of these same cultural mores. Clearly, societal structures of this kind have a significant effect upon environmental knowing.

Summary

In this chapter we have seen that children's relationship with the environment is complex and multi-layered. Figure 2.7 attempts to summarize some of the major factors considered to be important in shaping children's developing contact with the environment. A space–time framework is postulated, as the model recognizes that children's experience of place and space depends upon an on-going transaction with the world about them. The model, itself, incorporates the developmental ideas of Erikson (1977) and the ecological perspectives of Moore (1986).

Erikson theorizes that environmental *mastery* comes about through a continuing relationship between the child and three successive scales of environmental contact: the *autosphere*, the *microsphere*, and the *macrosphere*.

The autosphere is the child's first environment. It begins and centres on one's own body (autocosmic). Initial play is simple, repetitious and sensual. The exploration which follows, Erikson describes as the child's 'first geography'. With time, so the child's map of the world extends to incorporate familiar objects and persons, his or her competence depending on the comfort and refuge these provide. The microsphere is the small world of manageable toys. Children's performance in this environment of small objects can have a direct bearing on subsequent development. On the one hand, if frightened or disappointed the child may regress to the autosphere. On the other hand, success and proper guidance will encourage further mastery and exploration. The macrosphere is the world shared with others. At this level children begin to encounter spaces beyond the immediate settings of the home. Exploration leads the child further afield, but, like the other two realms, children have to learn what sort of transaction can be safely carried out within it.

At this point Figure 2.7 recognizes the broadening spatial range of children. In *Childhood's domain*, Moore (1986) proposes a socio-spatial model which attempts to summarize the development of children's territorial range. Every child has a number of overlapping ranges that reflect various personal, environmental and cultural constraints. He suggests a threefold typology of range which evolves 'with age, from the coaction of children's personalities, parents, cultural circumstances, and the play opportunities and access barriers of the physical environment' (p. 17).

Habitual range is more or less contiguous space which extends around the child's home. This area is highly accessible for daily use and is bounded by temporal rather than distance and age constraints. For example, the use of surrounding streets as play spaces is often 'wedged between homework and suppertime'.

Frequented range comprises less accessible extensions of habitual range and is bounded by physical constraints, particularly busy roads, and parental prohibitions. This expands with age, use of bicycles, availability of traffic-free routes and the presence of older children to travel with. These places are more likely to be used at weekends and holidays, especially during the summer.

Occasional range consists of highly variable extensions of frequented range, made on foot, by bicycle or public transport. These places are visited once in a while, perhaps as part of a special outing. Such range is dependent on the child's personality, the degree of freedom and training offered by parents, the availability of travelling companions and the presence of attractive destinations. Occasional range defines the child's ultimate territorial frontier. As the child grows older, and moves around more easily, former occasional places become *frequented* and some become absorbed into everyday *habitual* range.

What Figure 2.7 is suggesting is that children's understanding of macrospace environments depends a great deal upon environmental experience. In subsequent chapters we shall examine other considerations which impinge upon children's views of their everyday worlds.

3

Children's indirect experience of place and space

In the preceding chapter we have considered how children from different socio-personal, environmental and cultural backgrounds develop varying relationships with the world about them. Not all knowledge about large-scale environments will be the result of direct and active exploration; some will be generated by indirect and more passive means, such as flows of information. In this chapter we will review those studies which have considered how children construct their knowledge of the environment, especially of distant places, from various communication sources. Communication (information flow) takes two forms: the transmission of information by means of technological devices of the mass media (newspapers, magazines, radio, television, cinema), known as *mass communication*, and the transfer of information through face-to-face contact, termed *interpersonal communication*. The effect of both of these sources upon environmental imagery will be assessed.

The importance of various information surfaces to children's views on the environment

Goodey's (1971) model provides a useful framework for our discussion. In Figure 3.1 the individual (or child) is shown at the centre of a microarea, labelled personal space. This is the environment that a child knows best. For most children it will include their furniture, room, home, immediate home site and those friends and relatives that live nearby. From this area the child will move, with varying regularity and competence, to other parts of the environment: journeys include day-to-day visits to friends, school, play areas and shops, and more occasional excursions, such as holiday trips. Direct transactions of this kind provide an experiential basis for environmental knowing. In addition, children's views on the world about them will be shaped by messages received both from the media and from their conversations with others. Taken together, these indirect sources comprise what Gould (Gould and White, 1986) has termed an invisible, but real, information environment.

Although this model distinguishes between direct, sensory experiences and

55

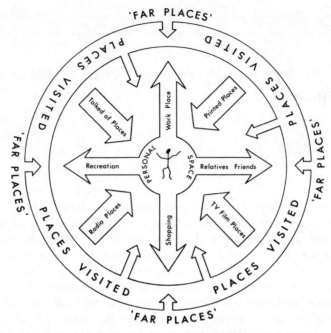

Figure 3.1   Sources of environmental information (Source: Goodey, 1971)

mediated communications about the environment and events, Burgess (1990) argues that we must be careful not to assume that media incursions are of secondary importance. For as Williams (1962) suggests,

> we have been wrong to take communications as secondary. Many people seem to assume . . . that there is, first reality, and then, second, communications about it . . . We need to say that what many of us know from experience . . . that the struggle to learn, to describe, to understand, to educate, is a central and necessary part of our humanity. The struggle is not begun, at secondhand, after reality has occurred. It is, in itself, a major way in which reality is continually formed and changed. (pp. 11–12)

In other words, we must not presume that reality exists as something separate from the individuals who receive information about it, 'this is an erroneous distinction' (Burgess, 1990, p. 143).

The extent to which children draw upon and are affected by this information surface has been examined by Gould (1972). He looked at how children living in Jönköping, south-west Sweden, acquired information about their country. He likened these children to 'little black boxes sitting in Sweden receiving information signals and storing some of them away for future recall' (Gould and White, 1986, p. 133). To untap their geographic information the children were asked to write down all the places they could think of in a given time. The results are shown in Figure 3.2. For 7-year-olds, their information surface was

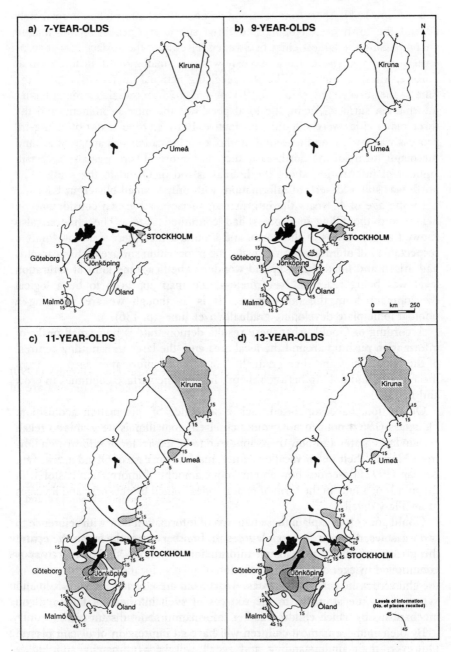

Figure 3.2   Information surfaces of Swedish schoolchildren (Based on: Gould and White, 1986)

at a very low level. Apart from 'a strong dome' of local information immediately around the town of Jönköping and three subsidiary 'peaks' of information encompassing the largest cities of Sweden, elsewhere the surface was at zero-level or only just above it. An anomaly was the 'small mound' in the north at Kiruna, where a miner's strike was receiving national media coverage at the time of the survey. The results for 9-year-old children revealed a much higher information surface. Again, the local peak was the most prominent, and the three major cities were still quite distinctive. Between them a sort of 'filling-in' process was evident and a second 'hump' of information was apparent around the major towns of the north-east, such as Orebro. There was also a certain amount of information about the holiday island of Oland to the south. The north was still a 'desert' of information, with only 'a small blister' at Umea.

By the age of 11 years the information surface had grown considerably in height and the filling-in process had continued apace. The children also showed an awareness of the north, and around Umea there was now 'quite a respectable hill of information'. Lastly, the information surface of 13-year-olds had arisen and filled again. Gould wonders whether some kind of saturation level was being reached. Nevertheless, the map appeared to be a logical development from the other three. 'It is as though we are watching a photographic plate developing gradually over time' (p. 136).

According to Gould, what these results demonstrate is how small peaks of information push up around the local area and 'the large transmitting centres' of the major cities and then gradually 'corridors of information seep out from these nodes and link up between them'. In time the surface continues to grow and in-fill.

Others too, have supported such a sequence of information acquisition. Douglass (1969) noticed how young children from Illinois were able to recall certain large states and how there appeared to be a corridor of information flow from Florida, their major vacation centre, just like the case of Oland in Sweden. Kaplan (1972) describes how an enormous amount of information is stored in the minds of adults in the form of major nodes, joined by networks and linkages of ancillary detail.

Gould goes on to explain these patterns of information flow with reference to two variables, distance and population size. In other words the larger the centre the greater its ability to transmit information of various kinds; receptivity is conditioned by age, but is also a function of relative location or the distance of the child from the generating nodes. Apart from these observations, Gould and White give little attention to the sources of such information flow and the mechanisms by which children gather information about distant places.

By their mid-teens most children will have an impression of distant places. However, their understanding and recall will be very patchy and highly selective. Their knowledge will rarely reflect direct experience and instead will be based almost entirely on communication flow. An informative study on how older children view the world was carried out by Saarinen (1973). Groups of high school students, aged 16 and 17 years, from the United States, Canada, Finland and Sierra Leone, were asked to sketch a map of the world, labelling places they considered to be interesting or of importance. From the results Saarinen was able to identify a number of factors which were important in shaping students' views. These included *proximity* – near countries were more likely to be mentioned than more distant ones; *size* – large countries were recalled more readily than small ones; *shape* – countries with distinctive shapes, such as the boot shape of Italy, were more often drawn than those with difficult or complex boundaries, while landlocked countries frequently had low image-ability; *current events* – recent newsworthiness heightened awareness; and *culture* – countries linked by politics or with similar levels of development with the homeland were frequently included, but so too were countries which stood in sharp contrast in terms of their patterns of living. What these results suggest is that children's knowledge of distant places is largely dependent on secondary experience. At the world-scale children's imagery reflects pulses of communication flow and the intermittent diffusion of information. Accordingly, Saarinen suggests that much of what is recalled has a temporal bias, so that at different times it is very likely that different places will be highlighted.

Mass communication and environmental imagery

Burgess (1990) highlights the importance of the mass media to environmental knowing. Just in terms of sheer numbers, the amount of people who consume different media products on a day-to-day basis is staggering. In the United Kingdom, for example, 98 per cent of households have at least one television set and just over half own or rent a video; the average adult viewing time in 1988 was over 25 hours per week, whilst children watched approximately 18 hours per week (BBC, 1988). The total number of people purchasing a daily newspaper exceeds 10 million, and this is a considerable underestimate of who actually reads them. According to Burgess, 'reality is constructed through shared, culturally-specific, symbolic systems of verbal and visual communications, including those of the media' (p. 143). Like Hall (1977), she recognizes the powerful effect media sources have in shaping our views of the world. Four different ways in which the media have progressively 'colonized' the social and cultural sphere of people's daily lives are pinpointed:

1. The selective provision of social knowledge about the lives, landscapes, and cultures of other groups.
2. The classification of the plurality of difference in the 'world-as-a-whole'.
3. The production of consensus about the 'natural order' of things.
4. Redefinition of ideological legitimacy.

In these ways the media are instrumental in influencing the *meanings* people (including children) attach to the environment.

Gold (1980) points out that the selectivity which is always present in spatial information when presented by the mass media usually falls into one of three categories:

1. *Deliberate manipulation*, whereby the content is 'massaged' to produce a specific message, whether of a positive image, such as in promotional literature which is designed to encourage movement of some kind, or of a negative image, such as in the reporting of the so-called 'inner city riots' of the early 1980s in which the inner city was 'mythologised' into 'a discrete, hostile and alien place' (Burgess, 1990, p. 148).
2. *Incidental manipulation*, in which spatial bias results as a by-product of other aims. A good example of this can be seen in the Underground Map of London, where topological transformation designed to give passengers a clear idea about route interconnections and destinations is frequently misinterpreted as a source of information on locations and distances.
3. *Inadvertent manipulation*, or the unintentional bias that results from the limited world view of the communicator.

When looking at how children 'construct' their images of distant places it is useful to distinguish between *popular media* (comics, newspapers, television, radio, films) and *educational media* (maps, textbooks, charts).

Popular media

Tajfel and Jahoda (1966) have argued for some time that young children are capable of absorbing attitudes and prejudices imparted by the media (and through conversations) about other nations, well before they are able either to recount where these places are located or before they have any factual information about them. The young child is highly receptive to socially communicated values and will actively seek, select, receive, sort and remember information in ways that are often supportive of pre-judged categories (Tajfel, 1981). Empirical support for some of these observations comes from a study by Johnson *et al.* (1970) who investigated children's preferences for and knowledge about other nations. They found that children who read war comics 'shared a pattern of national preferences more congruent with the alliances of World War Two' (p. 238) and this was in contrast to other children. Also, middle-class children had, on average, a knowledge of other countries approximately two years ahead of working-class children, although the amount of knowledge a child had about another country was not a reliable indicator of place feelings.

Saarinen (1976) observes that every nation harbours images of other nations, largely promulgated by the mass media. An early attempt to investigate how nations see each other was carried out by Buchanan and Cantril (1953). They carried out a 'cross-national' survey in nine countries, shortly after the Second World War. In each nation respondents were asked to select from a list of words those they thought best described the characteristics of people from a list of other countries. The consistency with which various words were selected suggested to the authors that stereotyped views of certain people are commonplace in Western culture 'rather than the effect of bilateral national outlooks that differ from one country to another'. In particular, Russian stereotypes were largely negative, with descriptions of one's own country invariably flattering. Comparison of the results of this survey with similar scores made earlier revealed some marked shifts in the nature of stereotypes for various nations. For example, in 1942 Americans had a positive stereotype of the Russians which, by 1948, had become consistently negative and 'hostile'. When White (1965) carried out a similar investigation in the Soviet Union some years later he found confirmation for what has been termed 'the mirror-image effect' (Bronfenbrenner, 1961). Soviet citizens perceived the Soviet Union to be 'peaceful' and 'peace-loving', compared to the rather 'threatening' image held of the United States.

The susceptibility and responsiveness of children to societal stereotypes and media messages of this kind are demonstrated by the following examples. Consider the results of a survey of 16-year-old American children's views on Africa undertaken during the late 1960s (Hicks and Beyer, 1968). Predominant images included wild animals, jungles, witch doctors and 'Daktari', a popular television programme on big-game adventure. About the same time Murphy (1968) undertook a comparable study with seventh and eighth graders. He was forced to the conclusion that 'Tarzan evidently has been a heretofore unrecognised great teacher, as a very high percentage of students indicated that through books and movies about him they had gained a great deal of knowledge of Africa' (Goodey, 1971, p. 49). Compare these images with the views of children elicited in the mid-1980s (Hibberd, 1983). Predominant words now included 'poverty', 'malnutrition', 'unequal distribution of wealth' and 'low life expectancy'. These results illustrate the power and significance that mass communication has upon the developing child.

So, too, does the study by Webley and Cutts (1985). They were able to talk to schoolchildren in Britain and Argentina immediately after these nations had been at war. Children were asked to draw maps, select pictures to represent the Malvinas/Falklands and discuss the origins of war. Clear national differences were apparent: the British children stressed the issue of principle, whereas the Argentinian children argued the need to recognize territorial rights. The authors claimed that these results showed that even the youngest children in the survey, 7-year-olds, had learnt the respective rhetoric of their own countries.

Lambert and Klineberg's (1967) study provides some interesting insights into the development of stereotypes about foreign peoples. They interviewed over 3,300 children aged between 6 and 14 years from eleven countries. They found that 6-year-olds responded less frequently than the older children when questioned about other countries. Their responses tended to be non-evaluative descriptions of facts or general references to the 'good' or 'bad' qualities of these nations. The older children revealed a larger repertoire of evaluative distinctions. The content of the descriptions shifted from physical features, clothing, language and habits, to personality traits, politics, religion and material possessions. In other words there was a shift from 'comparison of observable and tangible characteristics to more subtle, subjective features'. The authors concluded that children apparently come to think about foreign peoples in an increasingly more stereotyped manner between the ages of 6 and 14 years. At the time of writing a news item has just broken about a leaked document, discussed by the British Cabinet, on the so-called traits of Germans. These are supposedly, 'angst, aggressiveness, assertiveness, bullying, egotism, inferiority complex and sentimentality' (*The Guardian*, 16 July 1990). One wonders whether such stereotypes, now disclosed, will affect the views of society!

Educational media

The importance of schooling to the development of children's attitudes, concepts and beliefs of the world about them has been demonstrated by Hess and Torney (1967). They surveyed over 17,000 elementary schoolchildren in the United States in order to establish how images of 'the world system of nations' develop. A major conclusion was that 'the school stands out as a central, salient, and dominant force' in the socialization of the young child. Hess and Torney go on to describe the strong positive attachment children develop for their home country; this is essentially an emotional tie which is highly resistant to change. Understanding about the concept of the nation comes about in three stages: first, the child focuses upon national symbols, such as the flag and the Statue of Liberty; secondly, the abstract concept of the nation is understood; lastly, the nation is seen as part of a larger organized system of countries. In this process children become imbued with a common cherished heritage, which Gottman (1952) has termed as their 'iconography'.

Instrumental in shaping children's views of the world are global maps and atlases. Saarinen (1988) documents how different map projections have been popular at different times and how each projection creates a different image of place. An implicit part of map-making on a world scale is the centring of a projection. Peters (1983) points out that the centre of the first global maps was the area in which the map-makers lived. However, since the mid-sixteenth century, with the advent of the Mercator projection and the spread of European colonial power, the most commonly presented world image has been a map centred on Europe (*Eurocentric*). Of course, other centring is possible. For example, in China *Sinocentric* maps have been common for over four hundred years, and in America US centred maps have been published since 1850 (*Americentric*). In order to examine the pervasiveness of these different global images, Saarinen (1988) examined 3,863 sketch maps of the world drawn by students in seventy-one sites in forty-nine countries. The set confirmed the three main types of centring, but by far the most common (more than 80 per cent) were Eurocentric maps, centred on the Greenwich meridian. The main deviations from this mode were drawn by students from countries that would have been on the edge of a Eurocentric map: thus, students in East Asia and Oceania often chose Sinocentric perspectives, while on the West Coast of North America they chose the Americentric map. Saarinen suggests that the overwhelming preponderance of Eurocentric imagery is a lingering effect of European colonialism. He points out that the tradition in many Asian educational systems of using Eurocentric maps is strong. Although the educational systems of India, Pakistan and Bangladesh, could just as effectively use Sinocentric maps that would place their countries in central positions in relation to the rest of the world, there is a seeming reticence to abandon their European educational heritage. Even more indicative of the hold of European educational values were the results for such places as Hong Kong, Singapore, the Philippines and Thailand, where most students sketched Eurocentric maps even though such maps placed their countries in peripheral positions.

Saarinen's findings illustrate the power of educational media on mental imagery. Equally, his study shows how geographical education can play a key role in helping to modify old Eurocentric world views. For example, up until the 1960s Eurocentric maps dominated classroom texts in Australasia. However, at this time an Australian publishing house printed their first set of a Sinocentred school atlas. Twenty years on, most of the students who took part in the survey in Australia, New Zealand and Papua New Guinea presented their maps in this way.

The importance of school textbooks to image formulation has been discussed by Elson (1964). Looking at American schoolbooks of the nineteenth century, she noted that America was represented as a country of simple, honest people engaged in useful occupations, while Europe was depicted as aristocratic, and class-ridden. Pictures of the races clearly communicated the superiority of whites over blacks. Elliott (1979) suggests that until the mid-twentieth century this type of geographic writing was the rule rather than the exception. Even as late as the the mid-1960s Pratt (1972) was noting 'inaccuracies', 'omissions' and 'biases' in many Canadian textbooks. Canadian texts informed the student that black immigrants were turning much of Britain's cities into slums and words like 'backwardness' and 'savages' were frequent descriptors of African societies.

Such blatant bias has been greatly remedied in modern schoolbooks. However, Wright (1979) suggests that through the inadvertent selection of visual stimuli in contemporary texts strong and potentially evaluative images of places are still subtly conveyed. Reviewing visual images portrayed in current textbooks on Africa he noticed few contained pictures of industrial activities, while photographs showing farming, often by traditional methods, were commonplace. Visual images of this kind produce penetrative and lasting impressions for pupils and authors and editors should attempt to provide a balance between 'traditional' and 'modern' images of places.

However, increases in carefully chosen and well-balanced information in the school may not be sufficient to break down common, societally-held prejudices generated by popular culture. This can be shown with reference to a study by Stillwell and Spencer (1974). They believed that one of the principal sources of information for children in the development of their attitudes about other nations was the formal and informal curriculum of the school. In order to confirm this belief, they investigated 9-year-old children's uptake of inform-ation from wallcharts and poster displays. The week-long exhibition showed visual images of four target countries: India, Germany, the United States, and the USSR. Children were interviewed before and after the display. In the subsequent interviews, all children showed a significant increase in information about all four countries, which supported the research hypothesis on the role of the curricula; the effect, however, was not uniform. Prior to the display the children had been 'strongly pro-American, anti-German, with India and Russia being just on the positive side of neutral'. Afterwards, 'America remained popular, Germany moved to a strong positive, Russia remained relatively neutral, and India moved to a negative preference.' The authors conclude that education, in providing more accurate and unbiased information, need not necessarily increase understanding and acceptance. Seemingly, in this case children's negative re-evaluation of India arose because the visual stimuli heightened awareness of the differences between the sub-continent and Britain. In consequence, children resorted to preconceived value-systems and labelled Indian society as definitely 'not like us'.

Interpersonal communication and environmental imagery

Interpersonal communication, too, offers a means by which spatial information is imparted. Spatial information in interpersonal situations may be directly elicited, for example by asking directions, or may be the result of chance or incidental remarks, such as when a person adds spatial details to a narrative to provide a frame of reference. Little attention has been given to the diffusion of spatial information by conversational behaviour. An exception is the work of Williams (1977). He suggests three areas in which interpersonal communi-cation has a significant role:

1. As an important informational source in the learning process whenever a person searches for a suitable solution to a locational problem.
2. As an instrumental means of conveying socially accepted standards about the use of space.
3. As a significant part of the process by which socio-cultural attachments to space are passed on from one generation to the next.

However, it is naive reductionism to assume that those who *encode* information impart a clear, unambiguous message which is uniformly absorbed by all (Burgess, 1990). Instead, it is more likely that the different groups who consume these messages create their own discourses, through their own, equally selective, *decoding*. Jaspers *et al.* (1983) have shown that children tend to be most receptive to content that reinforces or elucidates their existing views and outlooks. Klapper (1960) describes three 'self-protective' measures by which individuals 'defend' themselves from 'unsympathetic content': first, *selective exposure*, whereby a person, consciously or unconsciously, chooses to attend or subscribe only to those media that concentrate upon those areas and places considered to be of interest; secondly, *selective perception*, whereby a person may fail to perceive content that does not accord to already acquired spatial knowledge; and thirdly, *selective retention*, whereby a person will forget unsympathetic content more quickly than that which reinforces personal preconceptions about places.

Summary

Spatial information derives from two principal sources (see Figure 3.3). Much comes from *direct* sensory experiences, which constitute *primary* sources of spatial information. These include the senses of sight, sound, smell and

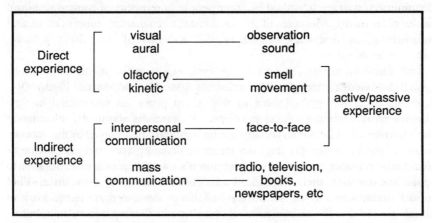

Figure 3.3   Sources of spatial information

movement (Banz, 1970). Primary spatial information is an outcome of the concerted operation of all these senses. This is not to say that each sense plays an equal part in the acquisition of environmental knowledge. Skurnik and George (1967) suggest that the detection ranges of individual senses vary considerably, with only sight, hearing and smell, 'the distance senses', being able to receive information from parts of the spatial environment beyond the tactile zone. Of these, smell has the most restricted range, with odours rarely

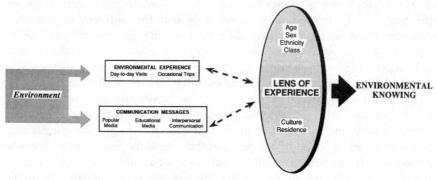

Figure 3.4   Circuit of environmental knowing

carrying for more than a few hundred metres, whereas vision permits stimuli to be received over large distances. Dodwell (1966) claims that sight is the most important source of spatial information, with over 90 per cent of human knowledge about the environment being received through the eye. The senses of sight, hearing and smell are themselves enhanced through an individual's movement through space: kinetic experience contributes to the child's growing repertoire of place. Also, a considerable amount of spatial information is communicated to an individual by other people (interpersonal communication) or the mass media. Messages of this kind constitute *secondary* sources of spatial information, in that they consist of the accounts of the direct sensory experiences of others.

Individuals contribute, to a greater or lesser extent, to the acquisition of their spatial knowledge through their active or passive experiences. Figure 3.4 attempts to draw together some of the salient processes recognized in this chapter on how children develop a sense of awareness about places far from their home area. The model recognizes the important part played by the various forms of media in 'constructing' an image of distant places, but also suggests that such messages are mediated by children's own complex transactions with space and through their own social and cultural lenses of experience. The model attempts to capture the intricacy of this process, in that the child is not simply viewed as a 'black box' passively receiving in-flowing information, but is portrayed as an active being, capable of selecting, storing and interpreting messages of different kinds.

PART 2

Children's environmental cognition: Competing theoretical and methodological perspectives

Part One has examined how, through a combination of direct and indirect experiences, children come into contact with large-scale environments of different kinds. Transactions of this sort provide an important experiential framework for the acquisition of environmental knowledge. In Part Two we will examine a broad range of issues which relate to the capability and competencies of children to understand various concepts of space and place. Chapter 4 reviews competing theoretical perspectives on the development of children's environmental cognition. Apart from being of epistemological interest, these competing views give rise to contrasting expectations on the environmental capability of children, which have important developmental and educational implications. Related to this debate is the methodological issue of how best to explore children's understanding of the environment. The process of uncovering children's grasp of large-scale space is a difficult task. Recent work suggests that children's abilities can be moved *upwards* or *downwards* dependent on the nature of the exercise and its locational setting. In Chapter 5 the results provided by different stimulus techniques are compared and their implications are examined. A widely used procedure for gaining an insight into the mental maps of children has been free-recall map drawing, and within this chapter the different ways of coding, classifying, and analyzing children's cartography are discussed.

4

Theoretical perspectives on children's environmental capability and competence

Liben (1981) identifies three competing philosophical traditions which attempt to explain the development of children's spatial cognition. These can be neatly represented by three questions. Is spatial ability given innately, and closely aligned to language acquisition (*nativism*)? Is spatial ability built up empirically from sensations derived directly from experiences of different geographical environments (*empiricism*)? Or, is spatial ability constructed out of some sort of interaction between inherited and experiential factors (*constructivism*)? In essence, these three fundamental positions define a continuum stretching from, at one extreme, those theories in which knowledge and behaviour are seen to be entirely determined by external environmental forces and experiences, and, at the other extreme, those theories which explain knowledge and behaviour as products of hereditary and biological forces. In this chapter our attention will be upon explanation rather than evaluation: in Part Three, we will review a range of empirical studies which provide evidence for and against each of these competing perspectives.

Empiricism

The philosophy of empiricism contends that behaviour in general, and knowledge in particular, is shaped and controlled by the external environment. Environmental knowledge is considered a product of successions of sensations arising from experience and impressed upon a *tabula rasa*, a blank slate. Such ideas form a central part of contemporary learning theory. According to Langer (1969), 'the child is born empty of psychological content into a world of coherently organised content . . . like an empty slate he is written upon by external stimuli: like a wax tablet he stores the impression left by these stimuli' (p. 51). These views depend upon the notion that the environment has a *real*, objective existence independent of the observer; whilst the central nervous system is viewed as little more than a 'black box' that cannot be investigated directly. The assumption is that the child is born dependent upon the environment which provides 'the necessary stimulation to provoke him to respond if he is to survive and adapt' (Langer, 1969, p. 64).

With respect to environmental knowing, three sub-classes of learning theory can be recognized. The first is based upon the extreme *stimulus-response (S-R)* tradition of Watson (1913) and Skinner (1938; 1974). Stea (1976) has reinterpreted these ideas into a seven-stage model of environmental learning:

1. The environment constitutes a complex of stimuli.
2. These stimuli press upon an individual (organism).
3. In turn, they trigger a cognitive process within the brain.
4. A response is learnt.
5. This response is either negatively or positively reinforced.
6. The individual (organism) is predisposed to make this reinforcement effective.
7. The result is that learning can be said to have occurred.

Environmental determinism of this kind presumes that behaviour and knowledge are solely determined by external reality.

More moderate in their accounts of environmental learning are the views of the mediational S-R theorists (Osgood, 1957) and the cognitive behaviourists (Tolman, 1973). Both schools of thought recognize the importance of some form of *covert representation* mediating between the stimuli and the organism, and these mediating representations are regarded as important determinants of behaviour. For Osgood they took the form of 'mediational reactions' and 'expectancies', such that the organism behaved in ways that would take into account subsequent events. Tolman, on the other hand, recognized the importance of *cognitive maps* as mediating influences. The brain was compared to the central office of a map-making agency, and the stimuli that entered within were 'not connected by just simple one-to-one switches to the outgoing responses', rather they were 'worked over and elaborated upon in the central control room into a tentative, cognitive-like map of the environment' (Tolman, 1973, p. 31). It was this cognitive map, made up of routes, paths and environmental relationships, which finally determined what responses would be made. Later, Tolman (1952) elaborated upon his notion of a mental representation of the environment by suggesting the concepts of *behaviour spaces* and *belief value matrices* as mediating factors. A behaviour space is defined as a psychological space of objects related by distances and directions, as perceived at a given moment; whereas belief value matrices are learned differentiations and categorizations related to objects in behaviour space. Thus, Tolman effectively sees individuals possessing a mental image of the environment, which is a product of previous learning, and which increasingly mediates between stimulus and response.

However, the empiricist tradition has been criticized on a number of accounts, first, for its over-reliance on observations based upon animals (Watson and Skinner experimented extensively with animals and Tolman's initial propositions were based on work with rats); secondly, for its preferred methodology, that is, small-scale laboratory experiments, divorced from the real world; and thirdly, for its dependency on mechanistic metaphors, which inevitably reject the view that children create their own reality rather than simply learning an environment.

Nativism

In contrast to the empiricist position stand the ideas of the *rational nativists*. For them, knowledge is given as an innate quality, before experience: 'it is a basic act of pure thought that opens up reality to us' (Moore and Golledge, 1976, p. 13). Accordingly, sensations are seen as little more than images of objects, whilst designation arises not through sensory experience, but by innate structures which are an implicit part of 'our inherent powers of intellection'. Although nativism recognizes an external reality, the form and meaning of reality in general, and of the environment in particular, are determined by genetic and biological factors, which, in effect, precede and determine sensory information. Nativism assumes that children are born with predispositions to react to the world about them in predetermined ways. Knowledge is, therefore, innate and simply opens up and unfolds with biological maturation.

Stea (1976) suggests that the skill of cognitive mapping is *evolutionary adaptive* and that 'a sense of place' is a vital part of human survival. He cites anthropologist Hewes (1971) who writes, 'a greatly improved sense of control and processing of environmental information must have accompanied hominisation ... we must suppose that a critical dependence on "geographic awareness" ... was part of the hominoid biogram' (Stea, 1976, p. 108).

Others, too, share these instinctivist ideas. Edney (1976a, 1976b), for example, claims that humans are biologically predisposed and equipped to develop close relationships with the environment. Human territoriality is seen as an important way of organizing behaviour and this operates at three levels: *the community, the small group* and *the individual*. At each level the main purpose of territoriality is to provide order and regularity to an otherwise random complex of space and place. Thus, territoriality at the level of the community encourages group identity and bonding, at the level of the small group it ensures congruency between behaviour and environmental setting and at the level of the individual it offers security, identity and stimulation.

Kaplan's (1973) propositions provide a bridge from these evolutionary ideas to neurophysiological explanations. He agrees that environmental information processing was a necessary adaptive skill, but goes on to suggest four major types of knowledge, and four types of responses, required for survival:

1. Where one is (perception and recognition).
2. What is likely to happen next (prediction and anticipation).
3. Whether it will be good or bad (evaluation and generalization).

4. Some possible next steps (action and innovation).

The fact that humans are able to recognize, anticipate, generalize and innovate ensures their survival. Taken together, these types represent an innate ability, both to cope with *specific* information (relating to objects in an environment), and to abstract *generic* information (which provides a way of coming to terms with new environments based on previous experience). Kaplan (1976) saw a neurophysiological basis to these mechanisms. He suggested, like Hebb (1966), that there are structures in the brain (*neural nets*), whose function is to handle and process environmental information. These neural nets are made up of sets of elements that correspond to real world elements, and these are linked in such a way that arousal stimulates mental representation. For Kaplan, 'man must be born with a tremendous propensity to make and extend maps ... the very possibilities for elaborate and extensive representation ... require a strong bias against too much internal rumination' (Kaplan, 1973, p. 77).

Two variants of nativism, which deserve more detailed attention, are provided by the works of Gibson and Blaut. To some extent, the categorization of either author within this school of thought is somewhat contentious. For example, we shall see that Gibson pays particular attention to the import of environmental stimuli in shaping environmental perception. By the same token, Blaut recognizes the role of socio-cultural systems in the formulation of children's mapping behaviour. However, what links both Gibson and Blaut, albeit rather tenuously, with nativism is their belief in innate mechanisms which are part of children's response repertoire from birth. Whether measured in terms of perceptual capability (Gibson) or mapping acquisition devices (Blaut), children are seen to be predisposed towards particular patterns of response, which develop independently of learning contexts. Subsequent interaction between children and their physical and social environments may heighten environmental knowing, but both authors propose a universality of environmental abilities unfettered by mediating cognitive processes and phylogenetic in origin. As Blaut (1987b) points out, stances of this kind must not be confused with the notions of '*reductionism* involving an intra-organismic, individual-psychological prime cause' (p. 300).

Gibson and the ecology of perception

Gibson's contribution to how children perceive their environment is 'compounded by the fact that the body of his work reflects a slowly evolving system of ideas' (Heft, 1988, p. 326). In his early writing (1950; 1958) Gibson argues that environmental perception is a direct product of the stimulation that reaches the child from the environment. Equally, he proposes that the world of the neonate is not one of total incoherence. Instead he suggests that the perceptual system is attuned from birth to respond to relational information and that this ability is not dependent upon the construction of cognitive structures. All the information a child needs to perceive the environment is already contained in the pattern of stimulation that impinges upon him/her from the environment. The child is predisposed to perceive directly the meaning that already exists in a patterned environment without the need for intervening processes of recon-struction and interpretation (Lombardo, 1987). Indeed, experiments with the newborn have revealed an incipient capability to discriminate between simple spatial properties, such as a cross and a square (Antell and Caron, 1985). Gibson postulates the presence of an innate component or *analog*, which he terms the *rigidity principle*. He argues that children are equipped with an inborn ability to establish primitive spatial coordinates for positioning things outside of themselves. The differentiation of outside from inside from surface is a slow process, but it begins before birth and it seems to incorporate an awareness of a global or environmental reference system.

In later years Gibson's (1966; 1979) views underwent significant changes, which are best illustrated through his initiation of the study of ecological optics. This is the analysis of light as available information for perceiving. At any point in space a child is surrounded by the reflection of light from environmental surfaces. This reflected light is structured by the characteristics of these surfaces to give an *ambient optic array*. When the child changes his/her point of view the structure of reflected light also changes. Such movements enhance perception in two ways. On the one hand, movement of this kind enables the perceiver to uncover the *invariants* in the ambient optic array; information that specifies the rigid or inanimate features of the environment by which body location can be oriented. On the other hand, there is a *flowing* or *streaming* of the array that accompanies the perceiver's movements, such as when walking along a path. This flowing perspective structure is visual information about locomo-tion (Heft and Wohlwill, 1987). In these respects visual perception becomes much more than just seeing, it incorporates movements of the eyes, head and whole body. Consequently, the act of picking up information about the environment becomes a continuous act, 'an activity that is ceaseless and unbroken' (Gibson, 1979, p. 240).

Heft (1988) describes these suggestions as truly revolutionary, running counter to the long-held 'causal theory' of visual perception which contended that perception was based upon visual stimuli initiating a series of mental events in a passive observer, resulting in a percept. Rather, Gibson rejects all varieties of stimulus-response-type accounts of perceptual processes in favour of a more 'functionally oriented, ecological approach to perceiving' (p. 330). For Gibson, perception is an *intentional, adaptive* activity carried out by individuals who are naturally inclined to explore an environment in order to detect its functionally significant features. In addition, Gibson argues that the relationship between the child and the environment should not be seen as one of dualism, that is, of two separate and unrelated entities. Instead, he proposes an alternative ecological perspective which characterizes the relationship as one of *fittedness and reciprocity*: each is functionally and structurally tied to the other. This sort of patterning is phylogenetically determined, in that the capacity of children to fit and harmonize with the make-up of the environment is due to evolutionary adaptation.

In his discussion on adaptation and exploration, Gibson introduces another instance of reciprocity, the concept of *affordances*. Affordances are what the environment or its facets functionally offer the child. This is a relational concept which focuses on the fit between environmental features and the perceiver. Affordances establish what behaviour is possible in particular places and as such 'they constitute, from a psychological perspective, the ecological resources of the environment' (Heft, 1988, p. 332). The notion of affordances draws attention to the continuous and changing relationship children have with their surroundings and highlights the importance of 'the adaptive behavior of animals in their econiche' (p. 332).

Because meaning can be perceived directly from the environment, Gibson is suggesting that many basic aspects of environmental perception do not have to be learnt, instead they are part of an organism's make-up from birth. This is not to say that ecological theorists entirely discount the role of environmental learning. Indeed, Gibson acknowledges that through environmental experience the perceiver learns to discriminate more important stimulus variables from less important ones. Thus, through learning the child is able to achieve a progressively more accurate picture of the environment. However, this tendency for exploration is, itself, a natural, adaptive mechanism.

Also, Gibson's functional ecology offers a reformulation of the traditional developmental view of the relationship between perception and environmental cognition. Instead of considering perception to be a lower-order process (Piaget, 1969; Wapner, 1969), which is subordinate to cognition, 'both can be seen as autonomous processes serving different complex functions in the environment' (Newtson, 1980). Both the environmental setting, or context of the activity, and the goals and purposes of the child, will condition whether perceptual or cognitive processes are required. For example, wayfinding and navigation can be regarded as forms of environmental perception, as they depend on the picking up of information over time. However, mapping tasks and inferential problems, such as imagining new routes, both rely on conceptual skills and hence cognitive processes. Despite the seeming potential of Gibson's work for environmental psychology, Heft (1988) points out that, as yet, it is an insufficiently explored resource. To date, too much attention has been focused on the perceiver and their mental representations of the environment and not enough consideration has been given to the form of the environment. In this capacity, Gibson's work offers a conceptual framework that recognizes *representative types* of environment–child transactions.

Natural mapping

A recent contribution to the nativist school of thought comes from the work of Blaut (1987a; 1991). He argues that 'map-thinking' (macroenvironmental cognition) is by no means a high-level intellectual activity, but a formal set of operations that evolves from very basic phylogenetic and ontogenetic roots. Mapping behaviour is carried out by all individuals, of all ages in every culture: it is a natural ability, akin to language behaviour, 'and perhaps equally primitive and basic' (Blaut, 1987a, p. 27).

Blaut cites the studies of Chomsky (1985; 1988), who argues that 'there seems to be an intellectual structuring ability, probably in part inborn, and certainly present in every infant of our species and ours alone, which emerges as basal linguistic competence . . .' (Blaut, 1991, p. 62). Blaut speculates whether this same structuring ability, which Chomsky refers to as the *language acquisition device* (LAD), also emerges as a *mapping acquisition device* (MAD). The LAD structure enables infants to tie signs and symbols together by means of basic syntactic rules and hence, the development of language is seen as a natural ability. By the same token, it is not unreasonable to infer

> the existence at birth of an awareness of place syntax, a device (the MAD) which gives the infant a readiness to assign primitive and tentative directions, distances, and meanings to parts of the world, to orient itself crudely to a global reference system (a terranium), to display primitive locative abilities (for example, pointing and finding hidden objects), and to map the world into both cognitive maps and material map-like models such as toy assemblages. (p. 62)

Indeed, Chomsky (1988) himself points out that children are able to point before they can speak. For Blaut, the young child's use of gestures and sounds, and then of symbols to represent the large-scale environment, corresponds to the structuring and syntactic processes of language acquisition. In this case, there is no difference between the *spatial* process of environmental mapping and the *temporal* process of oral–aural language, 'both are spatio-temporal' (p. 63).

Not all agree with Chomsky's claims about the existence of a LAD. Bruner (1986), for example, emphasizes the importance of social learning and the cultural development of *a language acquisition support system* (LASS). Blaut acknowledges these ideas by suggesting an equally active and culturally pervasive *mapping acquisition support system* (MASS). In both these cases, less weight is given to innate devices and more attention is paid to social interaction and social guidance as learning mechanisms, although both are seen to build upon extremely primitive inborn abilities.

The link between mapping and linguistic behaviour is further apparent when written communication is examined. Young children display a *natural* skill to represent the world by graphic symbolization, whether through drawing, painting, writing or mapping. Blaut suggests that these skills are phylogenetic, inherited by all human infants. He points out that graphic communication comprises of two- and three-dimensional signs, some iconic and others not, and that humans have been interacting by means of these symbols since at least the Palaeolithic period. Taken together, these observations lead Blaut to suggest that mapping behaviour is natural, and is derived from innate and prenatal components. Accordingly, even the very young have incipient environmental skills and capabilities, which are enhanced by enculturation and social guidance.

Although periodically written off, the ideas of Blaut in particular have revived the claims of the nativist school. Experimental work by Gibson and Walk (1960) and Bower *et al.* (1971) further suggest that the perception of distance and depth, two qualities which seem to have evolutionary significance, are present in even the youngest infants and so may well be innate. However, the nativist position is not without its critics. Many of their ideas are difficult to prove or disprove. For example, many of the so-called innate abilities may equally be the outcomes of very early learning processes, which commence even before birth. Blaut (1991), in fact, suggests that

> perhaps it does not matter, for a theory of natural mapping, whether the source of mapping abilities is primarily an innate place-structuring mechanism, a MAD, or primarily an early learning (enculturation) process in which experience and the social support system (the MASS) build upon extremely primitive inborn abilities, the latter including such elements as a readiness to be aware of verticality, externality, and (perhaps) object permanence, and a readiness to make cognitive maps. (p. 63)

Given the nativist assumption that there is no way to understand the nature of reality except through the actions of organisms, whether environmental behaviour is pre-programmed or learnt will continue to be a matter of much conjecture.

Similar doubt surrounds the location of these spatial impulses in the brain. It seems likely that the two hemispheres of the brain have different functions: the left hemisphere controls *propositional* functions such as language, writing and other linear processes; whilst the right hemisphere controls *appositional* functions such as perception, fantasy and spatial knowledge (Bogen *et al.*, 1972; O'Keefe and Nadel, 1978). Stea (1976) suggests that appositional functions are well developed and dominant among pre-schoolers, but as children mature there is a shift in dominance to propositional functions. Whether the acquisition of these skills and the shift in dominance is the result of enculturation, or the outcome of other causes, such as innate conditioning, has yet to be conclusively determined.

Constructivism and the legacies of Werner and Piaget

Moore (1976) describes constructivism (interactionalism and transactionalism) as an attempt to synthesize the two traditionally polarized positions of empiricism and nativism. Environmental knowledge is seen not simply as an outcome of sensation and reinforcement on a passive organism, nor as a product of a set of innate structures given before experience, but as a construction built out of 'intentional acts by an active organism from the interaction of sensation and reason' (Moore, 1976, p. 15).

According to Moore (1976) the constructivist position can be summarized by six general principles.

1. Environmental knowledge is constructed in that individuals create *structures* or mental models that enable them to understand and cope with the real world. This suggests that environmental learning is not just a matter of accumulating pieces of information, rather, individuals attempt to make sense of the world by identifying order and organizing frameworks. The structures which result from these processes determine how individuals construe reality. The suggestion that individuals construct their own realities implies that each person has their own view of the world. In practice, however, it is assumed that people from similar backgrounds will construct similar mental models.

2. Environmental knowledge is an outcome of interaction between factors internal to the individual (needs, personality, motivation) and the demands made on the individual by the situation (environmental constraints). This means that knowledge of place and space is constructed in a purposeful manner and that learning is most likely to be accomplished during the course of some effortful, goal-oriented activity (for example, journey-to-school, shopping). In turn, these activities are themselves constrained by factors such as, availability, accessibility, and personal, societal and cultural circumstances.

3. Humans are naturally inquisitive and adaptive. They actively seek out and assimilate environmental information beyond what is needed for everyday life and this further enables them to adapt to, and cope with, their surroundings.

4. Transactions with the environment are mediated and supplemented by previously constructed conceptions, such that cognition takes stock of experience. In other words, there is an element of learning in the processing of environmental information.

5. Environmental knowing proceeds in stages dependent upon an individual's intellectual development, with each stage represented by different structures. It follows that as children grow older their views of space will be *qualitatively* different to when they were younger. This point reinforces the notion that spatial learning is not just a function of acquiring more

information, it also involves deriving more sophisticated schemata with which to organize this information. Also, at each stage, these structures select and order the environmental knowledge that will be assimilated.

6. Any study of environmnetal knowledge must recognize the inception and development of these cognitive structures. Transformation of these structures can take many different forms. Two are especially important: *onto-genesis*, developmental changes associated with the life-cycle; and, *micro-genesis*, short-term adaptation to environmental change, which can take place as rapidly as a few days.

The importance of cognitive structures, of the sort outlined by Moore, to the development of environmental knowing, can be best seen by examining the contributions of Werner and Piaget. Their theories were developed as a result of extensive empirical study and through the systematic observation of children's behaviour and intellectual growth. Although these theories were primarily related to *microspace*, with little attempt to apply them to larger-scale environments, they have both been generally extended in this way. This discussion will only consider those ideas which relate to the acquisition and comprehension of environmental knowledge.

Werner's theory

Werner (1948; 1957) provides an *organismic-developmental* framework for understanding children's cognitive structures. Three stages of developmental progression are suggested.

1. *Progressive self-object differentiation.* During this stage the child learns to differentiate himself from the surrounding environment. This is usually achieved by the age of 2 years.
2. *Progressive constructivism.* This stage is usually completed after the age of 8 years. It is a period of increasing activity, when the child begins to construct a personal image of the environment.
3. *Constructive perspectivism.* This stage is characterized by an ability to adopt other people's viewpoints.

These three stages are paralleled by three levels of development, *sensorimotor*, *perceptual* and *contemplative*, and three types of spatial experience, *'action-in-space*, *perception-of-space*, and *conception-of-space'* (Hart and Moore, 1973, p. 255). In effect, what Werner suggests is that the development of environmental knowing is a process involving the increasing differentiation of the child and the environment, proceeded by a reintegration between the self and the environment.

Piaget's theory

The ideas of Werner are shared in a general way by Piaget, in the sense that both suggest the development of the child's concepts of space is the result of constructions derived by interaction between the child and the environment. However, Piaget (Piaget and Inhelder, 1956) identifies four periods of cognitive (intellectual) development and provides detailed descriptions of the criteria upon which these are founded. These stages are presented as an invariate sequence, which occur at more or less the same age among normal children.

The sensorimotor stage. This stage, which usually extends from birth until 2 years of age, marks a change from the *passive* to the *active* child. At first, children are capable only of reflex activity and limited thought. As their ability and confidence to move through space develops, so they begin to establish limited representations of the environment based upon their experience (*schemata* based on action). Near the end of this period, children will be capable of coordinated activity and internalized thought.

The pre-operational stage. This stage extends from about the age of 2 years to approximately 5 to 9 years. During this stage children develop an ability to conceive of space apart from their actions. At first, environmental knowledge will be based on simple mental constructs and symbols based largely upon personal experience, but with time these are supplemented, albeit un-systematically and often intuitively, with images derived from memory. Throughout this stage, children's thoughts are *egocentric*; they find a continuing difficulty in decentring from one aspect of a situation.

The concrete operational stage. This stage typically extends from the age of 7 to 11 years, and marks a significant turning point in intelligence. During this period children become capable of logical thought. The forms of thought developed in the pre-operational period become highly stabilized equilibra-tions, such that mental representations of the environment are no longer intuitive patterns but symbolized, systematic and coordinated abstractions. Children no longer confuse their views with those of others. They are now capable of seeing the world from perspectives independent of themselves, such that elements and relations are 'composable, associative and reversible' (Piaget and Inhelder, 1967). This progression from egocentrism to *relational coordina-tion* parallels the changeover from progressive constructivism to progressive perspectivism of Werner's theory.

The formal operation stage. This stage extends from about the ages of 11 to 13 years onwards. It is a period characterized by *reflective abstraction*, whereby children develop an ability to conceive of space entirely in the abstract, without the need for these representations to be based upon real actions, objects or spaces. Children are therefore released from having to rely on experience for knowledge. This stage marks the end of the structural aspects of intellectual development.

On the basis of this general theory of cognitive development Piaget postulates

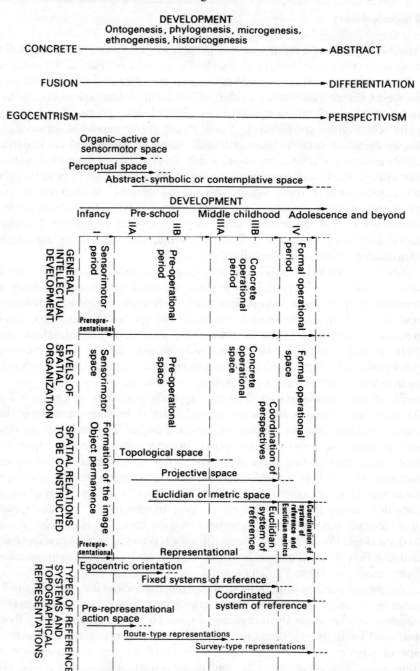

Figure 4.1   Cognitive development and environmental capabilities (Source: Moore, 1976)

a developmental sequence on the way children learn to construct spatial relations. This sequence corresponds to a particular type of spatial geometry, based on *topological, projective* and *Euclidean* principles. These ideas have been summarized by Moore (1976, p. 149) in Figure 4.1.

From the age of about 2 years, children gradually learn to master *topological* principles which relate to such qualitative relationships as proximity, separation, order, openness and closure. Shortly after, when they reach the age of about 3 years, children begin to develop a sense of *projective* space. This involves a knowledge of perspectives and of the interrelationship of objects as seen from different views. Initially, an understanding of projective space develops alongside that of topological space, although it is not until the age of 11 or 12 years that children fully learn how to coordinate perspectives. *Euclidean* principles emerge from about the age of 4 years and continue to develop for a further 10 years or so. Skills of this kind are based on a recognition of metric relations and properties, including distance estimation, proportional reductions of scale and rectilinear coordinates.

In effect, what Piaget suggests is that the process of environmental learning involves much more than just accumulating disparate pieces of environmental information. Instead, development is seen as proceeding from 'lower modes of biological and reflexive functioning, through action-oriented and perceptual functioning, to higher modes of conceptual and symbolic functioning' (Gold, 1980, p. 67). The key to this developmental sequence and to the learning process in general, is the concept of *adaptation*. Piaget proposes that adaptation is an intrinsic quality of humankind and adaptation to the environment is the basis of all environmental knowledge. In turn, the basis of adaptation is intelligence. However, intelligence itself cannot be inherited, only a mode of intellectual functioning composed of two *functional invariates*: *assimilation*, the incorporation of new information into existing frames of reference (schemata) in the mind, and *accommodation*, the readjustment of these frames of reference (schemata) to cope with assimilation. Kaluger and Kaluger (1974) show how these two functions are the essential ingredients of successful adaptation and how they work continuously to produce changes in children's conception of space and place (see Figure 4.2). When assimilation and accommodation are in balance a state of *equilibrium* is reached, which is desirable not only to safeguard children from being overwhelmed by new experiences, but also to prevent them from being over-reached in attempts to accommodate an environment which is changing too rapidly. In summary, Piagetian theory suggests that cognitive structures reach higher degrees of organization and allow more complex cognitive operations as a function of interactions between the child and the environment and as a function of the simultaneous assimilation of new information to the structure, while the structure accommodates to the new information (Moore, 1976).

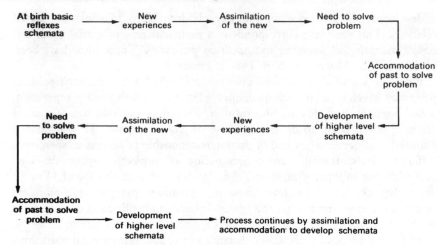

Figure 4.2   Piaget's theory of adaptation and equilibration: the development of
schemata (Based on: Kaluger and Kaluger, 1975)

Hart and Moore's theory

In an attempt to extend Piaget's ideas to cover how children come to terms with
large- as well as small-scale spaces, Hart and Moore (1973) hypothesized that
children's understanding of the spatial layout of the environment would also fall
into three stages, each associated with a particular type of reference system.
During the sensorimotor stage and for part of the pre-operational stage
children would be capable only of *egocentric orientations* in which the environment is viewed simply in relation to themselves and to their actions. With time,
this would be replaced by a *fixed system of reference* in which children would think
of the environment mainly in relation to familiar and known locations, such as
their home, school, houses of friends. Towards the end of the concrete
operational stage children would begin to develop an ability to comprehend
space according to a *coordinated reference system*, based on abstract geometric
patterns and cardinal directions. Hart and Moore argued that these three stages
would be systematically related both to Piaget's three principal stages of general
intellectual development (the sensorimotor stage is excluded as although infants
perceive and act in space, they have no real cognitive representation of space)
and to the three stages of fundamental spatial cognition. Accordingly, by the
end of the formal operations stage children would have developed a broad
range of spatial skills based on a coordinated reference system and a full set of
spatial geometric principles. These ideas are shown diagramatically in Figure
4.1.

However, as a result of further observations on the behaviour of children, as
well as adults, Moore (1976) subsequently rephrased these three stages into
more structural terms. The basis of his revision was that developmental analysis

of any human behaviour could be made along four major dimensions: (i) degree of differentiation and integration; (ii) degree of complexity; (iii) degree of abstraction versus concretization; and (iv) degree of relational coordination versus egocentrism. Taken together, these dimensions lead to the definition of three essential structures and levels of the organization of knowledge: Level I, *undifferentiated egocentric*, in which all information is assimilated according to one viewpoint and differences and variability in the subject matter are not recognized. Information is viewed in terms of its personal significance, with positions located mainly through egocentric, sequential and topological relationships; Level II, *differentiated and partially coordinated into fixed subgroups*, whereby the environment is seen in terms of groups or clusters of elements, but no coordinate system is used to link the clusters. Intra-group organization is seen largely in functional terms or topological proximities, and occasionally with regard to projective relations; and Level III, *abstractly coordinated and hierarchically integrated*, where the environment is no longer seen in terms of the subject's personal actions, but is referred to by a systematic, abstract reference system. Moore (1976) points out that this kind of intellectual functioning is not just limited to children, but will also come into play whenever adults are called to adapt to new environments or forced to respond to rapid environmental change.

However, Moore (1976) acknowledges that whilst children advance through a number of qualitatively different stages by which the world is organized, environmental understanding is not dependent on developmental progression alone. To comprehend how people come to know an environment and how they come to organize their knowledge of a place, 'it is necessary to understand the transactions of persons in environments and the interactions between intra-organismic variables, like values, aspirations, and socio-economic background, and external situational demands, like the cognitive demands of environments of different properties' (p. 163). In this way, Moore sets out a *transactional-constructivist* approach to environmental knowing, whereby experience and background are recognized to a greater extent than by the classical Piagetian/ Wernerian position.

Brunswik's probabilistic model of environmental perception

Brunswik's (1956; 1969) theory of *probabilistic functionalism* is strongly akin to the ideas espoused by Moore. Brunswik contends that environmental perception is a function of the active role individuals play in interpreting sensory information from the environment. He points out that in many situational contexts observers are presented with complex and often ambiguous cues about their surroundings. For example, a common perceptual problem is to decide whether an object is a large one at some distance away or a small one close at hand. Perceptual ambiguity of this kind can only be resolved by the observer making a *probabilistic* estimate about the nature of the environment.

In Brunswik's probabilistic model, the child plays an especially active role in the perceptual process. In order to cope with the complexities and inconsistencies of the sensory cues that reach the retina, the individual must build up a repertoire of probabilistic statements about the environment. These probabilities are derived through environmental transactions, but as the child can never sample all possible environments it is left to the individual to mediate and make reasonable assumptions. In order to improve one's skill at probabilistic estimation, the observer must learn how to order, hierarchically, environmental stimuli according to their relative trustworthiness.

The notion that individuals play an especially active part in perceiving stands in sharp contrast to the ideas of Gibson that we examined earlier. In essence, what Brunswik is suggesting is that the world each one of us knows is largely created from our own experience in dealing with the environment. Such a view is entirely consistent with the transactional-constructivist perspective propounded by Moore.

Despite widespread recognition and empirical support, there are a range of criticisms which have been made against these various constructivist stances. On the one hand, there are criticisms which are directed against the developmental theories on which they are based. For example, Piagetian theory has been attacked for the mechanical nature of its developmental sequences, for its over-reliance on adaptation, for its general underestimation of the spatial skills of the very young and for its tendency to base generalization on inappropriate and difficult laboratory experiments divorced from the world of experience. On the other hand, there are criticisms which arise from Moore's contention that children come to terms with large-scale environments in the same way as they become familiar with small-scale space. For example, critics point out that unlike micro-spaces, knowledge of large-scale environments depends not only on direct sensory experience but also on communicated information and secondary data. Similarly, feelings of attachment are likely to be very different for micro and macrospaces, such that large-scale environments will be seen in much less personal terms. Furthermore, Moore's contention that adults will follow the same general progression as children when learning about a new environment is also seen as unlikely by some, especially given their greater inferential ability.

Summary

These competing theoretical perspectives give rise to different expectations about the spatial capability and environmental competence of young children. On the one hand, there is the Piagetian school of thought. For them, cognitive structures are seen as resulting from the unfolding of different kinds of thought processes through successive stages. By the adaptive mechanisms of assimilation and accommodation a child will acquire an evolving understanding of space, which although not entirely age-specific is characterized by sequential patterning. This approach is *structuralist*, in that it assumes environmental understanding is dependent on the level or stage of development, which itself is determined by the evolving structure of the brain. On the other hand, there is the *incrementalist* position, defined, at first glance, by the seemingly contrasting stances of the nativists and the empiricists. Although these two traditions disagree about the way in which children acquire spatial reasoning, that is, through either innate structures which are opened by experience or environmental learning, none the less, they are united in their belief that environmental knowledge is an outcome of the piecing together of bits of information in an incremental way over time. Such a perspective anticipates a more or less linear relationship between environmental knowing and age, and this stands in sharp contrast to the staged progressions of the constructivists. Furthermore, it gives rise to the assertion that the environmental potential of young children should not be underestimated.

5

Methodological issues: Uncovering children's environmental capabilities

Mapping children mapping space

A common problem when studying young children is to find suitable methodologies with which to examine their knowledge and awareness of large-scale environments. Siegel *et al.* (1978) have laid particular emphasis on the methodological difficulties of working with such subjects. They point out that the process of revealing a child's true environmental competence is a complicated affair, since performance cannot be divorced from the situational context. Accordingly, like White and Siegel (1976), they suggest that competence levels can be moved *upwards* and *downwards* depending on the load or difficulty of the task. As Neisser (1976) points out, young children may well have developed considerable environmental knowing long before they can recount where they have been or how they got there. Ideally, a situation is sought where any method of assessment would provide a view of cognitive competencies which is unbiased by intervening performance factors. Hart (1979) and Spencer and Darvizeh (1981a) argue that much of the younger child's apparent difficulty in externalizing about space is occasioned by the test material. Considerable debate exists as to what techniques and approaches can be regarded as suitable. In this chapter we will review a broad range of studies which have attempted to uncover children's environmental capability.

Several reviews of environmental methodology exist (Golledge, 1976; Evans, 1980; Downs and Siegel, 1981; Newcombe, 1985; Spencer *et al.*, 1989). What is apparent from these examinations is that all methods have their strengths and weaknesses, but that specific tasks make particular demands on the subject's abilities, frequently calling for different forms of spatial processing. A distinction can be made between those studies which have examined children's environmental abilities in the laboratory, frequently employing small-scale tests and those which have focused on how children respond to large-scale environments, which form part of their world of experience.

| | TYPES OF ENVIRONMENTAL INFORMATION | |
	SURVEY	SEQUENCE
RECALL (unstructured)	**GRAPHIC CONTINUOUS** Free-recall sketching, e.g. Home area maps	**GRAPHIC CONTINUOUS** Free-recall sketching, e.g. Journey-to-school maps
	VERBAL CONTINUOUS e.g. Spoken description of the home area	**VERBAL CONTINUOUS** e.g. Spoken description of a route
RECOGNITION (structured)	**ICONIC CONTINUOUS** e.g. Recognition of features on aerial photograph or on video film	**ICONIC DISCONTINUOUS** e.g. Recognition of a series of slides or photographs taken at intervals along a route
	GRAPHIC CONTINUOUS e.g. Recognition of features on a large scale map/plan	**GRAPHIC CONTINUOUS** e.g. Recognition of a route on a map
		GRAPHIC DISCONTINUOUS e.g. Identification of streets or features directed on a map
	VERBAL DISCONTINUOUS e.g. Names or descriptions of places written on cards are selected	**VERBAL DISCONTINUOUS** e.g. Routes are described by sequencing names of places/ streets, etc., written on cards

(Left side vertical label: TYPES OF TECHNIQUES)

Figure 5.1   A classification of methods of stimulus presentation

Laboratory methodologies

A classification of laboratory methods of stimulus presentation is provided in Figure 5.1. This typology recognizes that methods not only vary in what sort of environmental information they seek to test, but also in what skills they demand of the child. For example, environmental information can itself be classified into knowledge of an area (survey knowledge) and knowledge of a route (sequence knowledge). In addition, methods of testing differ according to whether they demand recall skills, mostly employing unstructured techniques relying upon *recall memory*, or whether they employ recognition exercises, mainly using structured procedures depending on *recognition memory*. Figure 5.1 further distinguishes the techniques according to whether they rely on continuous spatial information or whether they are presented in spatially differentiated parts, often with secondary controls (discontinuous). Within these categories, different modes of stimulus presentation are recognized: iconic, whereby the actual form and relationships of objects are maintained but at a reduced spatial scale; graphic, based upon maps and mapping tasks; and verbal, including both spoken and written exercises. To these can be added 3-D scale modelling, whereby children are asked either to reconstruct novel or familiar environments, or to place items within a scaled-model of the environment, and experimental procedures like distance estimation both in terms of time and space, rank ordering of paired locations and compass orientation exercises.

It has been suggested that the choice of technique for eliciting young children's knowledge of the local environment is critical in providing an assessment of their true environmental skills, capabilities and competencies. Early attempts to uncover cognitive maps relied largely on spoken reports and free-hand sketching (Piaget *et al.*, 1948; 1960; Piaget and Inhelder, 1967; Appleyard, 1970). However, a number of more recent studies (Brown, 1976; Goodnow, 1977; Kosslyn *et al.*, 1977) contend that as means for assessing environmental skills these methods are flawed, in that children's varying verbal and graphical abilities intervene between their knowledge of the environment and its depiction. This view is not shared by all: incrementalists, like Lemen (1966) and Goodnow (1977), are less critical of 'actual respondent cartography', arguing that graphic responses are closely related to cognitive abilities and reflect truly visible thinking. None the less, researchers have turned to other methods in order to gain an insight into the world inside children's heads. For example, Siegel and Schadler (1977) got young children to reconstruct, from memory, models of their classroom. But reconstruction of this kind is not without its problems. Siegel and Cousins (1985) identify two difficulties: first, the method assumes that children understand that a model is a replica of reality; secondly, the problem of translating spatial information from large-scale to small-scale is a confounding one for young minds (Siegel *et al.*, 1979). In an attempt to overcome the problem of scale translation, Herman and Siegel (1978) used a model construction task in which the model and the original environment were experienced and reconstructed at the same spatial scale. Even this method is not problem-free, since children's performances have been shown to vary according to the environmental context and reconstruction of this kind can never replicate the full complexity of real, large-scale environments.

Some of the strongest claims for young children possessing relatively sophisticated spatial skills have come from geographers like Blaut *et al.* (1970) and Blaut and Stea (1971) who have used aerial photographs to examine children's environmental cognition. They have shown that children, sometimes as young as 3 years of age, who have never before seen a vertical aerial photograph and who have had little contact with large-scale environments, can nevertheless carry out simple recognition and mapping tasks using this medium. Blaut and Stea stress the role of toy play in explaining these capabilities, in that play of this kind gives the child experience of vertical viewpoints they would otherwise seldom encounter. Others have used 'oblique' photographic simulations of journeys to assess children's environmental recall and understanding of routes (Allen *et al.*, 1978, 1979; Siegel *et al.*, 1979; Cornell and Hay, 1984), whether by slides or video sequences.

Children's ability to use maps has been explored in a number of studies. Most have involved 'treasure-hunting' games, whereby children are asked to find a piece of treasure which has been previously hidden and to locate it on a specially prepared map (Bluestein and Acredolo, 1979; Walker, 1980; Blades and Spencer, 1987a). The success of very young children, often no more than 3 and 4 years of age, to use maps in this way has led Walker to suggest that games of this kind could be usefully incorporated into the primary school curriculum.

The variability of children's performances using these different spatial media has been noted by Siegel et al. (1978, p. 228). They assert that if children fluctuate so widely in their levels of spatial ability dependent on the methods of stimulus presentation, it becomes 'critical to measure a child's performance in several conditions or situations before reaching conclusions regarding that child's competence'. Two recent studies are of interest in this context.

The first was undertaken by Spencer and Darvizeh (1981b). They compared a range of techniques for eliciting the route-knowledge of twenty children aged 3 and 4 years in a city environment. Four recall techniques, verbal description, drawing and modelling in 2- and 3-D were compared alongside a recognition technique, which required children to sort and arrange photographs taken of the route. A series of walked routes in the area around the nursery school which the subjects attended formed the basis of the experiments.

Spencer and Darvizeh found that descriptions elicited by graphic and verbal methods were incomplete and partial. For example, verbal reports were typically very brief, even given gentle prompting, and highly fragmentary. Most included little more than initial orientations accompanied by the name of a major road and only some included descriptive elaborations such as the colour of a door seen along the way or an address near the end point. However, Spencer and Darvizeh note that despite their obvious difficulty in giving a verbal account of a route, all children understood something of what was required. Children's maps were even more rudimentary and primitive in form. These mainly consisted of a wandering line, with a building at both ends. The level of building detail depended on the child's graphic competence. If based on these techniques alone, children's environmental competencies would be described as low-level, largely egocentric, and lacking in any objective spatial frames of reference. However, Spencer and Darvizeh contend that these conclusions are misleading and entirely the outcome of the techniques themselves. At these ages young children simply lack the motor skills and semantic abilities to provide clear route descriptions by graphic and verbal recall, but when using alternative methodologies a very different picture of children's environmental competencies emerges.

Children's environmental abilities were seen to be considerably improved when employing modelling and photo-recognition techniques. In one experiment, Spencer and Darvizeh provided their subjects with a set of felt pictorial symbols depicting features that they would have encountered on their trips, including cars, houses, public buildings, trees and roads. Using this medium, all children managed to represent the environment in a spatial form, with some providing a complex array of buildings, structured along road symbols, which could easily have been used as a basic map. In a further experiment children were provided with a 3-D environmental modelling kit in an attempt to add even greater realism to the task. This technique produced some of the most complete representations, with some children employing between thirty-five and forty-five models, aligned along a passable road layout, with a good orientation of pavements, buildings and junctions.

Recall of any kind inevitably suppresses true environmental understanding. In an attempt to overcome this difficulty Spencer and Darvizeh asked their subjects to recognize and correctly arrange ten colour photographs of places and buildings taken along a once-travelled route. Most of the photographs were taken at a node, a choice point where several paths joined together. The results revealed that all children found recognition easier than correct assemblage, but that two children were able to order all ten photographs correctly and a further twelve children were able to put the first four photographs and the last photograph in the right place. On a second task, identifying the route taken at each choice point, most children were able to recall all choices correctly; 'surely a striking result for a once-travelled novel route' (Spencer and Darvizeh, 1981b, p. 282).

What these results suggest is that by using inappropriate methods there is a great danger of underestimating the spatial competencies and environmental skills of the very young. Spencer and Darvizeh conclude that environmental performance is improved with decreasing reliance upon graphic and verbal representation and with increasing realism in the provided elements.

I carried out the second study (Matthews, 1984b; 1985a; 1985b), in four junior and infant schools in Coventry. I was concerned with the ability of children aged between 6 and 11 years to represent two familiar environments, their journey-to-school and home area, by means of free-recall mapping, verbal reporting, and the interpretation of large-scale plans (scale 1:1,250) and vertical aerial photographs (scale 1:4,087). I found that whilst children's ability to understand and represent space improved as they matured, generalization was difficult as children's place descriptions varied not only according to the method of stimulus presentation but also with the nature of the environment. For example, like earlier studies (Spencer and Darvizeh, 1981b), verbal reporting was seen to inhibit, severely, the environmental skills of young children, inevitably suppressing an understanding of their actual ability. Young children's verbal descriptions were typically inaccurate and unreliable, with only hazy references to directions, meaning that locations were difficult to pinpoint. When describing their home area distant places were not clearly remembered and responses were characterized by a paucity of environmental detail.

The results derived by free-recall sketching revealed a wider appreciation of place although the environmental context was important. When recounting their journey-to-school by this method, children of all ages were able to recall

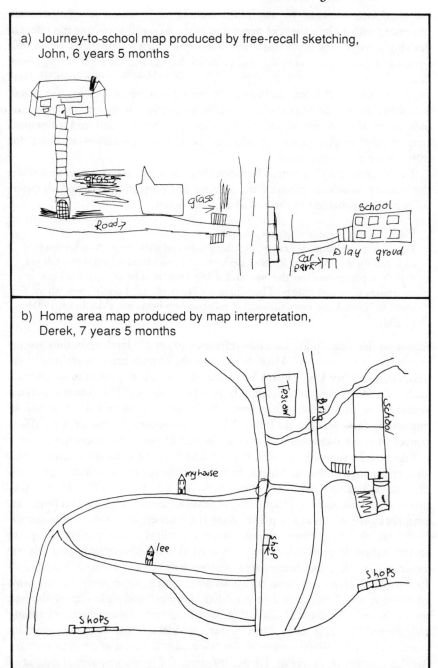

a) Journey-to-school map produced by free-recall sketching,
    John, 6 years 5 months

b) Home area map produced by map interpretation,
    Derek, 7 years 5 months

Figure 5.2   Young children's free-recall maps

more information than by any other technique. It would seem that when presented with a plain sheet of paper and asked to recall a journey the effect of drawing a route may be to jostle the memory in such a way that a reasonably structured image appears in the child's mind, building upon what has just been drawn. However, the home area maps were not as rich in environmental detail as those produced from the more structured stimuli, nor were far places accurately drawn. In terms of spatial comprehension, however, some 7-year-olds were able to reveal an appreciation of simple Euclidean principles, suggesting that this method could not be entirely dismissed as being too difficult for the young mind.

To illustrate the differences between these two techniques when describing the journey-to-school compare the amount of information revealed in Figure 5.2 with that provided in the verbal account below.

> Mike, 6 years 4 months, journey-to-school:
> I come out of my house, straight, look both ways and walk across. You see loads of cars and motor bikes and loads of conkers . . . I can't think of anymore. Oh yes, there's a playground on the way and a big church. The playground's got an enormous slide and swings. Then there's a big road, but I don't know where it leads to. Then I just cross the road. A lollypop lady helps me. (Matthews, 1985b, p. 231)

Although this description contains reference to certain landmarks they are not recalled in any sequence. Mike would pass the church prior to arriving at the playground. Other key features he would pass on the way seem to be omitted, such as a shopping parade and a large petrol station. The journey is not a straight one and yet no directional indicators are provided. It would be impossible for a stranger to follow Mike's instructions. Consider, too, Mike's concern for the incidental, his account is rich in personal experience.

Figure 5.2a shows how John, 6 years and 5 months, recalls a journey of a similar distance to that of Mike's, by free-sketching. The resultant map would provide a stranger with a better guide to the route, although no road intersections are shown. Orientation is possible, however, as certain important landmarks are drawn at key points along the journey, and in correct sequence.

By far the best environmental representations were produced by the interpretation of large-scale plans and vertical aerial photographs and this was especially so for the home area descriptions (see Tables 5.1 and 5.2). Performance levels on these occasions were much higher than by any other procedure, which suggested to me 'that these methods allow even the very young to get near towards disclosing their true environmental understanding' (Matthews, 1985a, p. 275). Places some considerable distance away from the home were correctly recounted and relationships between and within environmental clusters were grasped from the age of 7 years onwards. Compare a typical verbal report describing a 7-year-old's home area with another derived from map interpretation (Figure 5.2b).

Keith, 7 years 6 months, home area:
You come out of my house and see a telephone box and a bus stop up the road.
You see an estate and you might see over the fence . . . the school. Down the road
is the church . . . go down the road by a lamp post, go in there and there is a bit of
a brook. Go right up a big hill and go along and down a big ramp and and you see
all the brook and you are in . . . playground. I go over the road to play with my
friend, that's just over the road and you are in Mark's and you go right along and
you are by Greg's house. And you turn round and you go straight back by Lee's.
Cross the road and you are back in my house again. (Matthews, 1985b, p. 232)

This account, although by no means the longest report, highlights the difficulty
that young children encounter when attempting verbal description of an area.
Places away from the home are mentioned, but recollection is haphazard and
largely unsystematic. Personal transactions are emphasized at the expense of
order and coherence.

Figure 5.2b, on the other hand, reveals that children of the same age can
structure their knowledge of places into a reasonable map when prompted by
structured stimuli. Furthermore, it suggests that children with little previous
experience of printed maps can use these media in a successful manner.
Derek's description is well presented and full of identifiable landmarks, which
could be used by others as points of reference when walking around his home
area.

I compared further these four techniques by examining how they affected
children's awareness of place. Two measures of comparison were employed:
the standard distance statistic, which was used to summarize the spatial spread
of environmental information correctly identified around the home (the larger
the radius of the standard distance the more dispersed and further spread the
environmental detail) (Table 5.1); and the mean furthest distance of places
away from the home (Table 5.2). The results are of interest on two accounts.
First, although both measures confirm a growing awareness of space with age,
verified by Pearson's correlation analysis, even the youngest children were able
to show a grasp of complex spaces a considerable distance away from their
home, ranging from a mean of 193 metres in the case of verbal reporting to a
mean of 415 metres with the aid of an aerial photograph. Secondly, the findings
add further support to the assertion that the method of stimulus presentation
has an important influence on the ability of children to represent familiar
places.

Children's performances by age group were very uneven, suggesting that
levels of environmental knowing 'are intricately interwoven with the externalizing technique' (Matthews, 1985a, p. 269). In this instance, children of all ages
showed a much broader conception of space when using structured media and
this was especially so for those less than 9 years old. Like Spencer and Darvizeh
(1981b), I maintain that young children's lack of verbal and graphical skills
severely limits their ability to describe places.

In addition, my findings have a bearing on attempts to explain how young

Table 5.1 Awareness of place: information surfaces around the home (area bounded by standard distance circle, km²)

	Age group					
	6	7	8	9	10	11
Free-recall sketching	0.1	0.2	0.1	0.8	0.8	2.4
Air-photo interpretation	0.9	0.9	1.1	2.1	2.4	3.3
Map interpretation (1:1,250)	0.7	1.4	1.8	2.2	2.9	3.4
Verbal reporting	0.1	0.1	0.2	0.6	0.7	1.8

Source: Matthews (1985a)

Table 5.2 Awareness of place: knowledge of furthest places away from the home (mean distance of furthest point from home, metres)

	Age group					
	6	7	8	9	10	11
Free-recall sketching	210	329	260	505	530	556
Air-photo interpretation	415	420	508	592	610	748
Map interpretation (1:1,250)	366	448	521	595	618	803
Verbal reporting	193	227	271	411	508	540

Source: Matthews (1985a)

children acquire environmental and spatial skills. My results have shown that performance not only varies according to the method of stimulus presentation but also the rates at which children develop an appreciation of the environment seem dependent on the technique (Figure 5.3). For example, the results of free-recall mapping produced a stage-like sequence of spatial acquisition; strong similarities were apparent between the abilities of the 6-, 7- and 8-year-olds, in turn these were differentiated from the maps drawn by the 9- and 10-year-old children, which themselves were sharply different from those compiled by the oldest group. In contrast, whilst the results provided by air photograph interpretation confirmed a strong correspondence in the images of children in their early school years, they also suggested that there is likely to be a continual growth of environmental information with age, quickening between the ages of 8 and 10 years, and slackening thereafter. The pattern produced by those using large-scale plans contradicts the notion of similarity between age groups, instead a pronounced and steady learning curve was revealed, which implies a progressive and consistent acquisition of spatial knowledge with age. By far the poorest results were derived from children's verbal accounts. These were often hazy, regardless of age, locations were difficult to pin-point, and directions were only offered in the vaguest of terms. None the less, an age-related progression was discernible. Up until the age of 8 years most children found verbal reporting difficult and unrewarding, from thereon more environmental detail was recalled, such that by the ages of 10 and 11 years some children were able to talk about places in a reasonably structured and coherent manner.

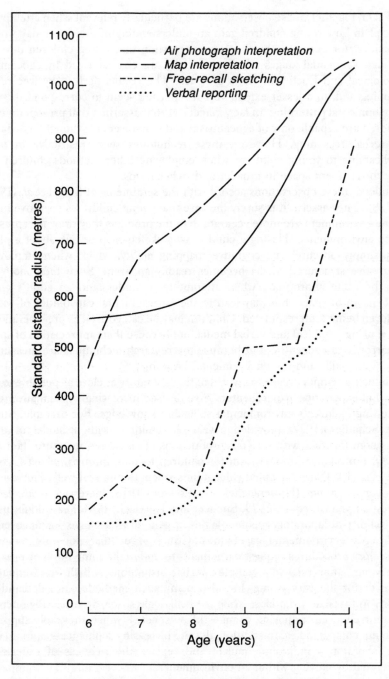

Figure 5.3   Awareness of places around the home: the influence of stimulus
techniques upon environmental recall

Taken together, these observations are particularly relevant when attempting to explain how young children gain an understanding of their everyday world. Consider, for example, the Piagetian suggestion that young children develop through sequential stages which essentially are characterized by egocentric, topological and Euclidean views of space. The results derived by free-recall mapping and, to a lesser extent, verbal reporting seem to correspond to such developmental patterning. In fact, Piaget's (1968) assertion that pre-operational children are capable only of egocentrism and non-reversible thought was based on verbal reasoning. However, these techniques seem restrictive in their applicability to young children; when employing other methods children are able to represent space in broader and richer terms.

Indeed, these observations accord with the sentiments of Siegel et al. (1978, p. 228). They assert, 'it is surely the case that young children's cognitive maps of the environment are more accurate than the products they draw to represent these environments.' Having a child draw a sketch-map or talk about a place may simply obscure true cognitive mapping ability, which when employing alternative structured media becomes readily apparent. Such methodologies may be quite appropriate when attempting to understand an adult's comprehension of space, but may lead to the environmental capabilities of young children being underestimated. Children may be categorized as pre-operational when using graphical and verbal media, not because their appreciation of space is narrow and egocentric, but because the research techniques are measuring only these skills and not environmental knowing.

In their attempt to make the world of the laboratory as close as possible to the world of experience, experimenters have devised increasingly imaginative ways of testing children's environmental skills and knowledge. For example, Siegel and Schadler (1977) provided 5-year-old children with a model of their classroom together with scaled reproductions of classroom furniture, Herman (1980) built a small model town for children to walk through, whilst Cornell and Hay (1984) used detailed video-film sequences of a real walk. However, a number of studies (Huttenlocher and Presson, 1973; Hardwick et al., 1976; Bluestein and Acredolo, 1979; Spencer and Darvizeh, 1981a) cast doubt upon the validity of laboratory methodologies in general as a means for uncovering children's environmental capabilities. Critics argue that not only do most laboratory procedures request participants to undertake some novel or unusual behaviour, after relatively complex verbal instuctions, which are frequently difficult for the very young, but also many such methodologies demand an ability to translate from large-scale to small-scale space, an especially onerous task for children, requiring changes of perspective which inevitably suppress absolute competencies. In addition, despite increasing sophistication, in no way can laboratory conditions simulate and replace the richness of experience generated by moving within an environment.

Real-world methodologies

Some of the most convincing evidence of young children possessing complex spatial comprehension comes from work which has taken place outside of the controlled laboratory environment. Yet, unfortunately, fewer studies of this kind have been carried out. The convenience and ease of setting up laboratory procedures have outweighed the undoubted benefits of studying children's interactions with place at first hand. Hart's (1979) study of children in a New England community, 'Inavale', is outstanding in this context. Unlike most laboratory studies where the experimenter spends only a short time with each child, Hart spent two years in close collusion with his subjects, following them on local trips, observing them whilst at play, and recording their feelings and attitudes about their outdoor worlds. What Hart's work confirms is that many of the experiences which are highly significant to children simply cannot be reproduced in the laboratory.

Indeed, Cornell and Hay (1984) have demonstrated that children's environmental capabilities differ significantly according to whether they were tested by laboratory methods or in the real world. For example, Cornell and Hay asked 5- and 8-year-old children to view a route by either watching a video-film, by looking at a set of photographs taken along the way, or by actually walking it. Children were tested by the same stimuli they used when learning the route. At each choice-point along the route they were asked to indicate which way they should turn. Those children who walked the route significantly outperformed the others, which suggests that laboratory procedures may seriously underestimate the true environmental potential of the very young.

The work of Darvizeh and Spencer (1984) further illustrates the value of real-world studies, especially with the very young. They were interested in the navigational capability of a sample of twenty 3-year-olds. One of the tasks involved Darvizeh escorting each child on a 15-minute walk along a novel route. She explained the walk as a game that they were going to play together and that a few days later she would ask the child to take her back over the same journey, as if she was a stranger. During the walk, Darvizeh pointed out eight salient landmarks, each located at choice-points and considered to be useful for subsequent route orientation. When children were later asked to retrace the route *all* managed to complete the walk successfully, with every child capably following the same succession of roads, paths and crossings, without the need of directional prompts by the experimenter. This study is interesting not only because it demonstrates that even the very young have considerable environmental acumen, which laboratory experiments have frequently failed to uncover, but also as it shows that 3-year-old children are capable of learning novel routes after only a single walk, evidence which flies in the face of Siegel and White's (1975) assertion that preliminary landmark knowledge is needed before route learning is possible. In fact, much of Siegel and White's claims are based on laboratory studies and a presumption that efficient spatial cognition only develops after about 6 years of age (see Chapter 7).

An example of the sort of imaginative study that can be achieved with time and patience, in a real-world setting is Golledge *et al.*'s (1985) intensive examination of the capability of a single 11-year-old boy to navigate a defined route over five successive days. He was first taken over the route in a forward direction and then asked to navigate the route on his own. Upon completion, he was taken back to a mobile laboratory and asked to describe his strategy for route learning, to draw attention to those aspects of the route that he particularly remembered and to generate a set of verbal directions that would allow another child to get from the beginning to the end of the route. By examining his responses Golledge *et al.* were able to develop a conceptual model which informs about how children are likely to acquire spatial knowledge of large-scale environments (see Chapter 7).

Summary

Researchers have employed a variety of methods to investigate the nature of children's knowledge of spatial information and their memory of places. At first, most studies relied upon laboratory-based techniques which required individuals to produce spatial representations of 3-D environments in 2-D form. Because individuals were found to differ in their graphic, verbal and motor abilities and because rescaling of this kind was seen to be a particularly onerous problem for young children, increasingly ingenious and sophisticated tasks have been devised in an attempt to uncover children's true environmental capabilities. However, despite a growing call for ecological validity (Newcombe, 1985) few studies have, as yet, examined children's understanding of spatial relationships and comprehension of large-scale environments in familiar, real-world places. Those which have, suggest that very young children have skills and competencies well beyond those anticipated by theoretical propositions derived by examining children in small-scale settings. It would seem that unless more studies are carried out with children in their everyday world of experience there is a danger that performance requirements will interfere between knowledge and its representation.

Children's cartography

A basic difficulty when studying the acquisition and development of cognitive mapping is the externalization of the cognitive map: 'getting the spatial knowledge out in some public medium' (Siegel and Cousins, 1985, p. 349). The term 'map' in this context is no more than a metaphor, since it is not known whether environmental information is stored in such a spatially coordinated reference system within the brain (Downs and Meyer, 1978). In effect, these externalized products are no more than 're-representations' (Downs, 1985), two levels removed from the actual spatial experience and so need to be regarded with some caution. For example, in the first instance, the real world is experienced by the child, cognitive maps are the outcome of these transactions, and only through subsequent representation is a public image provided.

The process of translating spatial information held in the mind into a tangible map or drawing is highly complex, and according to Beck and Wood (1976b) involves eight key elements: *synchronization*, the integration of sequentially experienced geographical data into a coherent framework; *rotation*, the transposing of the world of experience into a two-dimensional system of spatial coordinates; *scaling*, the representation of the environment at a scale other than the one which is experienced; *generalization*, the summarizing of complex environmental data into a few manageable propositions; *symbolization*, the selection of appropriate symbols with which to represent different parts of the environment; *verbalization*, the labelling of features with place names; *representation*, the visualization of an image by the mapper of what is to be drawn; and *externalization*, the process of producing a sketch map or a spatial product of reality.

Given the complex nature of this externalization process, Siegel and Cousins (1985) suggest that we are faced with a dilemma. Whilst the concept of a map, 'the map as a model', is a useful way of thinking about a child's representation of space, the production of a map, 'the map as a technique', is problematical as a method for studying children's images of the environment. Downs (1985, p. 334) identifies three difficulties which are of particular concern:

1. A sample of children's maps, drawn by approximately the same age group, will reveal considerable variation not because of differences in spatial competence but as a result of variance in manual graphic ability.
2. The resultant maps are difficult to handle, score, code and analyze.
3. Often children's maps do not look like adult maps, children are unfamiliar with mapping conventions and symbolization and their drawings do not evoke a reality that is acceptable to the conventional wisdom of adults.

To these can be added a fourth set of related problems: (Pocock, 1976a; 1976b):

4. By asking children to map an environment, a general filter is inevitably placed over their information store. In short, children's responses are constrained to 'physical attributes of the environment, and even then, annotation apart, to those items which are *mappable*' (1976b, pp. 493–4). Moreover, although the technique minimizes intrusion by the researcher, it is important to realize that the instructional set determines which aspects of the mappable information are elicited or provided. Even the size and shape of the paper can induce bias to the results.

However, Downs argues that we should not be discouraged by such problems. Difficulties of a similar kind have not deterred linguists from studying the evolution of language and, indeed, instead of being viewed as confounding problems they should be regarded as viable subjects for further enquiry. Like Treib (1980), who sees 'maps as the projection of experience' (p. 22), Downs (1985) contests that maps are neither mirror nor miniature, they are 'models of the world . . . carefully controlled symbolic abstractions' (p. 325) and, therefore, are legitimate sources of data in their own right. In the previous section, we have seen that there was a strong feeling that we should ask better questions in order to gain a clearer insight into the environmental acquisition process. What is being suggested here is that we should also find better ways of answering them (Downs and Siegel, 1981; Siegel, 1981). For the rest of this chapter I shall examine attempts to make sense of these external products of children's cartography.

The most common way of uncovering children's environmental images has been through sketch maps. I suggest two ways of analyzing children's sketch maps (Matthews 1984a). The first attempts to measure *quantitative* details recorded about the environment; the second attempts to discern *qualitative* differences in the ability of children to externalize, or put down on paper, their views on space and place.

Quantitative aspects of environmental knowledge

Under this heading it is convenient to distinguish between those studies and methods which have focused on *designative images* and those which have been concerned with *connotative* or *appraisive images*.

Designative imagery

Designative images are those which refer to the content of the map and include measures which attempt to assess *information on place* and the spatial spread of these information surfaces or *awareness of space* (Matthews, 1984a; 1984b; 1984c). The simplest way of measuring *information on place* is to count the amount of data correctly recorded on a child's sketch map. For example, I employed a measure termed 'mean information on place' to categorize my sample of children's maps on Coventry. This procedure is aided if the recorded environmental detail can be coded into different types of information.

Lynch's (1960) pioneering study of urban imagery is especially valuable in this context. As part of his investigation Lynch asked residents of Boston, Jersey City and Los Angeles to draw a sketch map of the central area of their city, as if they were drawing it to help a stranger. On close examination Lynch was able to categorize the content of the maps into five major organizational elements: *paths*, which are channels of communication along which people customarily move (roads, footpaths, pavements); *nodes*, which are places that people can enter and/or act as focal points along journeys (bus stations, churches, major road intersections); *landmarks*, which are useful points of reference used to keep track of where you are in the city (prominent buildings); *areas* or *districts*, which are large tracts of the city, usually identifiable and homogeneous in character (high-/low-class housing, docks, shopping centre); and *edges*, which are boundaries or barriers separating one area of the city from another. These can either be natural features (river, parkland) or man-made (railway line, change in housing fabric). Lynch (1960, p. 8) argues that elements of this kind are used to interpret information, to guide action, to serve as a broad frame of reference within which a person can organize activity, belief and knowledge, to serve as a basis for individual intellectual growth, and to give a sense of emotional security.

The manner in which these elements mesh together provides what Lynch terms an expression of the *imageability* of an environment, that is, the extent to which the components of an environment make a strong impression on the individual. Most studies replicating Lynch's methodology have been with adults (Francescato and Mebane, 1973; Orleans, 1973; Walmsley and Lewis, 1984), although I (Matthews, 1984a) successfully coded children's journey-to-school and home area maps according to this schemata (see page 137), I found that when children recounted a habitual journey *paths* and *nodes* stood out clearly on their maps, whereas when drawing their home area children were more likely to use *landmarks* as mental anchor points.

Walmsley (1988) suggests that the value of Lynch's technique is that it not only provides information on the overall image of a place, but it also gives an insight into 'i) the sequence in which the elements were incorporated into the map; ii) gaps in an individual's knowledge; iii) mapping styles; and iv) scale distortions' (p. 43). However, Lynch's schemata is not without its problems. Often there is considerable ambiguity over some of the elements. For example, in my survey many children drew attention to a prominent local church. It was decided to classify this feature as a landmark rather than a node, mainly on the use to which it was put.

Another aspect of designative imagery is *awareness of place*. A basic problem when analyzing children's free-hand sketches is that they are frequently distorted, fragmented and incomplete. In consequence any attempt to measure their spatial extent by simple scaling procedures is fraught with difficulty. The standard distance statistic is especially useful in this context as it provides a means for summarizing the extent of the information field recorded on children's maps, without the need for contiguity in environmental recall. As a technique it belongs to a group of centrographic measures which seek to plot the centres of spatial (point) distributions and their degree of dispersion (Kellerman, 1981). I employed this procedure (Matthews, 1986a) to compare the home area sketch maps of children of different age groups. In order to use the method all the data recorded by each age group (6–11 years) on their maps was transformed into point locations. This was relatively easy for most of the information, such as buildings, shops and landmarks. Where particular districts or streets were indicated the centre of these areal and linear features were taken. Attention was confined to the extent of the awareness surfaces and so points were recorded as places away from the home, only distance and direction being collectively preserved. The procedure involved marking a central point on a sheet of tracing paper which was subsequently reoriented to correspond to the home of each respondent on a 1:1,250 Ordnance Survey base map. Features were identified from this site, regardless of their accuracy. A centimetre grid was superimposed onto this distribution for analyses.

This technique enabled me to describe an age-related sequence in environmental learning. I found a hierarchic accumulation of spatial knowledge with each circle building on the area recalled by the group before it. Such results suggest that 'knowledge surfaces grow outward from the well known and develop unevenly over space as a mosaic of places becomes familiar and pieced together in the child's mind' (Matthews, 1984a, p. 92).

Appraisive imagery

Appraisive images inform about an individual's feelings for an environment or their preference for different parts of the environment. Information which relates to such affective imagery can be gained both indirectly and directly from children's cartography. By studying the content of children's maps in general and noting what children draw gives some indication, albeit indirectly, as to what children regard as important to their world. For example, a number of studies have shown that young children portray markedly different features on their sketch maps compared to older children. Spencer and Lloyd (1974), in their 'draw me a map' exercises with infants in Birmingham, found that those under 7 years tended to see the environment in primarily human and natural terms, giving prominence to personal and often idiosyncratic details which older children ignored. In an attempt to capture some sense of how children of different ages appraise their everyday environments (Matthews, 1984a), I categorized the elements drawn by my sample into six types: functional, recreational, natural, personal, transportational and animal. I found that whilst on both the home area and journey-to-school maps functional elements, paths, roads, shops and buildings, were dominantly represented by all age groups, the significance of these features increased with age: three-quarters of all the elements depicted by 11-year-olds were classed as functional compared to only about 50 per cent of the features drawn by 6-year-olds.

In another survey Moore (1986) set out directly to uncover what children regarded as their favourite places in which to play. He asked his sample of children, aged between 9 and 12 years and drawn from three different urban settings, to draw pictures of where they most enjoyed playing after school and at weekends. From these results, together with 'turf maps' of where children played, he was able to come to some understanding of the valued environments of childhood, which he likened to a 'woven metaphor . . a cloth of varied solids and voids, arranged in an irregular geometric pattern' (p. 36).

The methodology which is most commonly used to investigate directly children's affective images was pioneered by Gould (Gould, 1966; Gould and White, 1986). In essence, this procedure requires children to indicate how much they would like to live in a number of different places, by rank ordering these locations in relation to each other. The data are summarized and scaled by factor analysis (0 = low desirability; 100 = high desirability) and contours of equal residential preference ('isopercepts') plotted on a location map. Gould's methodology has been successfully carried out in a wide range of places (Pacione, 1982; Walmsley, 1982). I asked (Matthews 1987b) a sample of children aged 11–15 years attending a comprehensive school in Leamington Spa to rank thirty places in the town according to levels of like and dislike. Scaling of the subsequent matrix of individuals against places revealed a strong affiliation with their own part of the town (home area), a strong preference for recreational and shopping places and a dislike of particular housing estates and the uniformity of suburbia in general. However, Gould's methodology is not without its critics. Three main criticisms are commonly raised:

1. The technique usually demands the handling of large amounts of data, which inevitably leads to problems of *intransitivity*, whereby places are scaled inconsistently in relation to each other.
2. Because most studies have concentrated on very large regions often it is patterns of ignorance which are being appraised not patterns of knowledge.
3. Related to the above, because respondents are being asked to appraise particular parts of an environment by a researcher there is no way of knowing whether individuals regard these places as significant to their world in the first place.

Qualitative differences in environmental cognition

The invitation to map leads to considerable variation in how well children are able to respond to such a request. Under this heading we will consider attempts to classify and order children's maps according to variations in qualitative ability, including measures of cartographic competence, levels of accuracy and mapping style.

Cartographic competence

I suggest (Matthews, 1984a), that children's maps can be grouped into three levels or grades of competence, each associated with different methods of representation and different abilities to see space in a two-dimensional form (Figure 5.4).

   Grade I, *pictorial and pictorial-verbal* forms represent the simplest form of 'map', whereby children simply draw a picture of their environment, sometimes embellished through labelling. These are really nothing more than embryonic

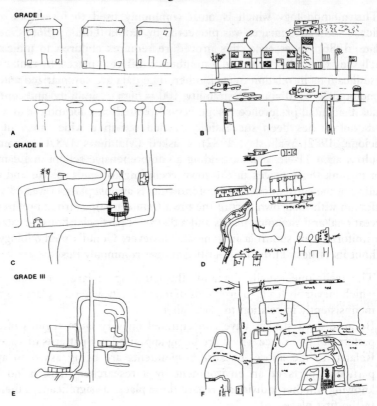

Figure 5.4   Grades of mapping ability

maps, with many of the features drawn as if 'lying down' along a street. Children who draw these maps lack the skill of rotation, which involves an ability to transform environmental information into an aerial view.

Grade II, *pictorial-plan and pictorial-plan-verbal* maps represent a mid-way stage in map development, with the result that horizontal and aerial perspectives are combined. These maps involve *some* rotation, symbolization and scaling. Symbolization is the process of selecting line, point or area signs to depict spatial phenomena, an essential aspect of drawing in plan form. Scaling is closely aligned to generalization and is reflected in the selection of mapped data.

Grade III, *plan and plan-verbal* maps represent the highest level of mapping competence and are based on an orthogonal transformation of space. These maps demand an appreciation of both representation, the act of visualization whereby the child retains in her head a mental image of what is to be drawn, and externalization, a conscious appreciation of all the operations already outlined so that an aerial plan is finally drawn. According to Gerber (1981b) this category of map depends upon a complex and interrelated set of sequences which he terms, sensation, classification, orientation and synchronization.

I used this technique to classify the home area maps drawn by my sample of 6–11-year-olds (Matthews, 1984a). I found a general trend, irrespective of age, for children to draw hybrid maps, combining both pictorial and plan forms: over 69 per cent of all maps were classified in this way. These results suggest that whilst the skill of rotation has been acquired by some children by the age of 6 years, not every 11-year-old has the ability to transform environmental images topologically. The most striking contrasts were found in terms of those children employing solely pictorial or plan maps. For example, 78 per cent of those drawing simple pictorial maps were aged 8 years or under, whereas very few children aged 10 years old and over drew in other than plan form. Furthermore, whilst children of all ages frequently resorted to some kind of additional labelling to clarify their sketches, most of the older children chose to embellish their drawings in a such a way.

These findings led me to suggest that not only does this typology provide an adequate means for organizing the maps of young children, but also it can be used to provide an insight into how children develop map-drawing skills. In this sample, both cartographic competence and mapping language were seen to be age-related and sequentially organized. Also, the observation that many 6-year-olds were sufficiently competent in the skill of rotation to draw part of their maps in plan form leads to the inference that such an ability is acquired or developed at a much earlier age.

Map accuracy
Successful map drawing does not just involve the ability to represent features symbolically, but also the capacity to arrange elements correctly within a spatial structure. In her studies with black adolescents, aged 12 years to 17 years, Ladd (1970) placed maps into one of four categories, dependent on their level of accuracy: *pictorial drawings*, which simply depicted a street scene, with no inherent spatial qualities; *schematic drawings*, which both named streets and areas, but in an unstructured and disorganized manner; *images that resembled a map*, which provided sufficient cues and spatial information to enable basic orientation and rudimentary wayfinding; *maps with specific landmarks*, which were sufficiently detailed to make an area clearly recognizable.

A more detailed method of assessment, which enables a score expressing map structure and accuracy to be ascribed to children's maps has been developed by Hart (1981). Hart suggests that any map can be broken down into groups or clusters of elements, which initially focus on children's homes and gradually take in parts of the environment located further afield. Once each cluster on a child's map has been identified, the clusters should be numbered from 1, the cluster of elements around the home, to 'n', the point at which all further clusters have been assigned a number. Within each cluster five levels of spatial organization are recognized and scored (Hart, 1981, p. 205):

1. *No spatial organization*, even though the elements may be logically classified.
2. *Linked*, that is, the elements are joined by a known route or path.
3. *Spatial proximity*, that is, the elements are juxtaposed according to their relative proximity to or separateness from each other.
4. *Spatial order*, that is, the elements are correctly related along a linear sequence.
5. *Positional*, that is, relative locations are accurate, front/behind, left/right.

In addition, each cluster can be scored in relation to each other by using the same five criteria. An 'integrated map score' is arrived at by multiplying the mean intra-cluster score with the inter-cluster score. However, Hart recognized that children are likely to draw maps of different sized areas when responding to the request to map a familiar location. Some children's maps may be extremely well organized, but cover only a small area, whereas other children may choose to map larger areas even though they are less familiar with the more distant places. In consequence, Hart further refined his index of spatial structure to provide 'a composite map score', which was obtained by multiplying the integrated score with a measure which expressed the 'extent of area'.

The advantage of Hart's classification is that it not only provides a detailed breakdown of the structure of children's maps, but also it offers a sound basis for comparison. Hart went on to extend this scoring system to cover the results of children who were asked to construct landscape models with paper and card. However, despite the sophistication of this methodology and the insights which it undoubtedly offers on how children depict their everyday world, Hart concludes that that there can be no substitute for ecologically valid research carried out in the natural settings of childhood.

An important note about Hart's five-point schema is that each position is not conceived as a stage or a level of development – taken together they simply relate to points along a continuum designed to express spatial organization. However, Moore's (1973) alternative classification is built around the assumption that children's understanding of and ability to depict a large-scale environment develops through three successive levels, each associated with progressively better appreciation of Euclidean relationships: these may be termed egocentric, objective and abstract stages of spatial comprehension. Accordingly, *Level I maps* contain unorganized elements or features arranged topologically from an egocentric perspective; *Level II maps* are partially differentiated with some degree of intra-cluster accuracy; and *Level III maps* demonstrate an awareness that all parts are parts of a whole, such that intra-cluster accuracy and the location of elements is high throughout the map.

I tested this technique (Matthews 1985a), with a sample of 6- to 11-year-olds, who had been asked to draw free-recall maps of their home area and journey-to-school. Children's spatial comprehension was seen to improve with age. The highest proportion of Level I maps were drawn by 6-year-olds, whereas by the age of 11 years most children were able to represent space in a highly organized manner, demonstrating a sound awareness of intra- and inter-cluster relationships. However, Euclidean accuracy was seen to vary with the environmental context, in that children frequently employed different frames of reference when describing different environments. Within individual variation of this kind has also been noted by Moore (1974) and Acredolo (1976). They have shown that in very complex environments children are likely to resort to simpler frames of reference, such as those defined by egocentric perspectives, even though they possess the ability to comprehend large-scale space in a more holistic manner. In my survey the tendency for children to draw simpler and less accurate maps when describing their home area may reflect the difficulty of summarizing, by memory alone, such heterogeneous places, whereas when describing a route, environmental structure and cohesion are more readily grasped.

Newcombe (1985) draws attention to other techniques of assessing spatial accuracy. These include correlating subjective with actual distances (Cadwallader, 1976; Canter, 1977), looking at the relationship between subjective and actual distances in order to assess whether respondents over- or under-estimate actual distances (Baird 1979; Magana et al., 1981), calculating the congruence between an overall map derived from subject's estimates by multidimensional scaling and a cartographic map of the area (Mackay and Olshavsky, 1975; Mackay, 1976; Kirasic et al., 1984) and performing analysis of variance of the degree of error in judgements (Liben et al., 1982).

With all these sorts of techniques and schemas there is an assumption that with age and/or experience of an environment children will become 'better' at mapping space in an accurate and spatially more correct manner. However, Downs and Siegel (1981) warn against the simple acceptance of such conventional wisdom. They contend that what these classifications are really measuring are children's capabilities to absorb adult values which they express through increasingly sophisticated adult modes of representation. In other words, children gradually learn to produce 'better' approximations to the products of adult thought. Adult modes of representation become desirable norms, and classifications, like those above, judge children's skills according to an 'adultocentric' set of values. Caution is needed when assessing environmental competencies in this way. Adult maps themselves are symbolic distortions of reality. Two-dimensional representations of 3-D surfaces inevitably involve subjective decisions which relate to simplification, selectivity and scaling. There is no 'perfect' mode or style of mapping. Furthermore, mapping 'accuracy', measured in terms of Ladd's or Moore's schemas, bears little or no relation to spatial behaviour. 'If we equate spatial behavior with the ability to navigate and move around a large-scale spatial environment, then we must conclude that spatial behavior is incredibly accurate and thus well adapted' (Downs and Siegel, 1981, p. 239). Children do not get lost with any notable frequency and they explore their world in increasingly confident and creative ways. It would seem that spatial behaviour is based upon models of the world that are not cartographic in nature and that *maps-in-the-head* are not stored in a cartographic manner. 'It follows that a cartographic map is not the best standard of accuracy' (p. 241).

What Downs and Siegel are suggesting is that we should view children's maps not as analogies of the real world, but as 'metaphors'. Representations are therefore no more than models, and we should be careful about the inferences that we draw from them. There is an important distinction between *competence* and *performance*. 'Good' and 'bad' fits between a child's drawn map and a professionally prepared plan need not inform about true spatial ability. For as Liben (1981) asks 'Who "has" Euclidean geometry?' (p. 14).

Mapping style

Qualitative structural differences in the way children represent the environment on free-recall maps have interested a number of researchers. An early attempt at distinguishing mapping styles was devised by Appleyard (1969a) from his study of Ciudad Guayana, Venezuela. His categorization was based on two key dimensions, the type of element emphasized and the level of accuracy. Appleyard found that respondents' maps either predominantly consisted of *sequential* elements, focusing on roads, paths or routes between places, or *spatial* elements, focusing on landmarks, or particular areas. In sequential-element maps the parts were more obviously connected and the connections were dominant. In spatial-element maps connections appeared to be incidental between parts, which were characteristically scattered over the map. A subdivision of each type was recognized according to the level of accuracy and sophistication, that is, the extent to which the drawn map approximated to the topographical map of the city. The eight idealized 'map styles' which were thus produced are shown in Figure 5.5.

Appleyard's schema has been reproduced in many studies elsewhere. For example, Spencer and Lloyd (1974) sorted 380 sketch maps drawn by children in Small Heath, Birmingham into these eight types and Goodchild (1974) found 'no great difficulty' in fitting sketch maps of Market Drayton into the same typology. However, Pocock (1976b) has questioned the applied universality of Appleyard's scheme, 'with its apparent invariance with regard to culture, scale and instructional set' (p. 496). He found that when he asked residents and tourists to draw a map of Durham that the results could not be fitted into Appleyard's scheme and a modified version had to be devised. Unlike Ciudad Guayana, which comprises a series of nine separate and distinct zones along a main highway, Durham is a unicentred city with a radial route pattern. Accordingly, Pocock's map-style categories attempt to accommodate variations of this general form. From a survey of 293 map drawings, Pocock classified 56 per cent of the total as sequential types. The most primitive of these was the *line* map, which was highly schematic in form, with very few lines and no lateral stems. Two kinds of *branch* map were recognized: the *branch-spinal*, which is a development from the line with the addition of lateral stems, and the *branch-focal*, which is no more sophisticated but the branches radiate from a central

TOPOLOGICAL

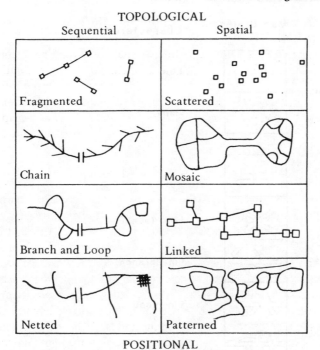

Sequential   Spatial

Fragmented   Scattered

Chain   Mosaic

Branch and Loop   Linked

Netted   Patterned

POSITIONAL

Figure 5.5   Methods of structuring maps (Source: Appleyard, 1969a)

point. The most popular form of sequential map was the *branch and loop*, which is distinguished by the extension of at least one lateral branch linking with the main spine. Completing the sequential category are two types of *net* in which a series of linkages constitutes a system or network of roads. These are subdivided according to whether the map does (*net-spinal*) or does not (*net-patterned*) show development from some main spinal route. In addition, net-patterned maps display greater overall accuracy.

The *mosaic* map is the most primitive form of spatial representation, simply showing broad zones or areas with little regard for other detail. Almost equally as primitive is the *scatter* map, on which are shown individual buildings and features but with scant regard to location. An advance on the above is the *scatter-link* map, which is characterized by a thin but schematically connected set of elements. The most sophisticated spatial maps are of the *patterned* type. 'An emphasis on spatial elements, with the actual outlines of many features, linear as well as spatial, are the distinguishing characteristics' (Pocock, p. 497). These are divided into those which resemble a sketch (*pattern-sketch*) and those which replicate reality in a near accurate manner (*pattern-map*).

However, whilst Pocock's typology is an undoubted improvement on Appleyard's for categorizing adults' maps of British cities, there is an implicit assumption in both schemas that maps can be readily sorted according to

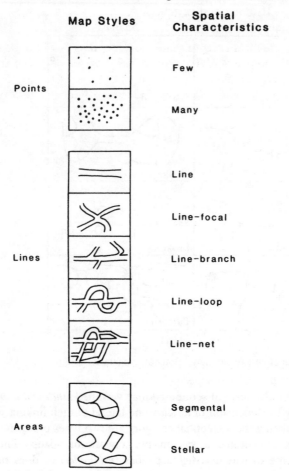

Map Styles   Spatial
                 Characteristics

Points   Few

                 Many

Lines   Line

                 Line-focal

                 Line-branch

                 Line-loop

                 Line-net

Areas   Segmental

                 Stellar

Figure 5.6   Characteristics of map styles

sequential and spatial elements and that there is no ambiguity in terms of how people represent space. However, through working with young children I found that they commonly combined many sorts of elements, causing difficulties in how their maps should be classified (Matthews, 1984a; 1986a). As a result it was felt that an alternative classification needed to be developed which would reveal the richness and diversity of children's responses and which would accommodate the hybrid nature of their mapping styles.

Cartographic language is characterized by line, point and area signs, and successful map drawing depends upon the mastery of such symbolization. The recognition of these three codes provides a means for classifying mapping styles (see Figure 5.6). *Point* maps are those which stress spatial properties such as individual buildings, landmarks, and nodes; *line* maps are those which emphasize sequential elements such as roads; *area* maps are those where districts or clusters of elements are visually important. Point maps are distinguished according to whether there are *few* features represented (P_1) or *many* (P_2). For line maps the simplest form is represented as a *single line* with no stems (L_1) grading in complexity to *line-focal* (L_2), *line-branch* (L_3), *line-loop* (L_4) and *line-net* (L_5). Area maps are classed as either *segmental* (A_1) or *stellar* (A_2) in form. Since children's maps seldom consist of one sort of element this typology enables maps to be classified according to the incidence of primary and secondary elements, and so combinations of point, line and area features are distinguished (in each case the principal characteristic is noted first). For example, a drawing classed as L_1P_1, would consist of a dominant, unbranching route, along which a few buildings would be located, whereas a L_5P_2 would represent a netted pattern of roads and a dense system of buildings and landmarks.

The children's maps in my sample were sorted using this technique, employing a double-blind procedure. The results yielded a 90 per cent concordance, suggesting that the classification provides a successful means for considering the style variations of children. Three further observations are of interest. First, like Pocock's assertion above, it would seem that the environmental context and the instructional set have a considerable bearing upon mapping style. With very few exceptions, when I asked my sample of 6–11-year-olds to draw a map of their journey-to-school most children responded by drawing line maps, whereas when recalling their home area, point maps were the norm. Few children relied upon areal representation as a primary ingredient. Findings of this kind run counter to the notions of researchers like Shemyakin (1962), who, in a formative paper on environmental cognition, argued that children of this age are capable only of route representation, with survey representation developing from the age of 12 years onwards (see Chapter 7). Shemyakin's contention was that a correspondence exists between the construction of external representation and the initial development of internal representation. In the light of my findings a more cautious conclusion appears appropriate. Children seem to be able to depict space in a variety of ways and this potential is already established by the age of 6 years.

Secondly, Shemyakin found that 6–8-year-olds represented a locality by tracing out familiar routes without recourse to any other roads. By the age of 8 years children showed other roads only as offshoots of their own routes, and it was not until the age of 12 years that they interconnected them. The results of my survey do not support such sequential development. For example, I found that even among the youngest children a wide variety of line elements were employed and nearly a third of 6-year-olds were able to draw branch and loop maps. However, only those aged 10 years and above were able to draw netted arrangements. In essence, within-sample differences were sufficient to obscure the progression suggested by Shemyakin.

Thirdly, the results of my survey suggest an age-related progression in terms of mapping style. Older children, whether employing line or point elements, are more capable of depicting space in a complex and integrated manner. On the other hand, a third of all 6-year-olds in this survey were sufficiently competent in cartographic skills to represent the environment in other than the most simplistic of ways.

Summary

In this section we have examined only some of the principal ways in which children's cartography have been analyzed. Pocock (1976a), for example, devises methods to assess how children orient their maps and how they are inclined to transform space topologically in order to create idealized representations. However, as Downs (1985) contends, the thrust of our discussion is to suggest that we should not just treat children's graphic representations as artefacts. By careful scrutiny of how children map their everyday worlds we can begin to uncover how the very young see and feel about large-scale spaces and to this end, children's cartography can be viewed as a legitimate data source. Maps make real what was intangible. They demand from children manipulative mental skills such as 'rotation, extrapolation and interpolation' (Downs, 1985, p. 341) as well as the need to understand 'relationship, continuity, coherence, and scale change' (p. 341). High-level spatial skills of this kind mitigate against the performance of the very young, none the less, by the age of 6 years there is considerable evidence to suggest that children of this age are already capable mappers, able to display a broad range of cartographic skills. The work of Goodnow (1977) on children's art provides a model for the analysis of child cartography. She writes about children's drawings,

> they may be regarded as expressions of our search for order in a complex world, as examples of communication, as indices of the type of society we live in, as signs of intellectual development, as reminders of our own lost innocence and verve.
> (p. 10)

The same could be written about children's maps. We should not make the mistake of seeing them as imperfect replicas of adult representations, instead they should be viewed as data sources in their own right. To paraphrase Goodnow, children's maps contain much beneath the surface, they tell us not only about nature and thought and problem-solving in general, but also about children themselves and what matters to their world.

Summary

Whilst the pessimism about the use of sketch maps and spatial modelling tasks as indicators of environmental competence may have been overdone, in her review of methods for the study of spatial cognition, Newcombe (1985) suggests that an 'empirical gap' remains in our attempts to understand how children make sense of large-scale environments, which largely corresponds to a continuing failure to study children in their everyday settings. She argues that researchers interested in spatial knowledge need to get beyond the idea that spatial representation is 'a thing in the head' (p. 297), more or less well externalized by any given methodology. Claims for 'ecological validity' of this kind have been made for some time (Bronfenbrenner, 1977; Cole, 1984). However, others ask 'what is a natural environment?' (White, 1980). School-aged children live and perform in a variety of behavioural settings, which include the home, the school, the shopping centre, and so on. Siegel and Cousins (1985) speculate on whether we should regard some of these settings as more natural than others. Although there are obvious advantages of working with children in their daily worlds of experience, many of the difficulties that such studies encounter can at least be controlled in the laboratory.

In addition, Golledge (1976) points out that we need to be much more aware of the artificial, and hence difficult, nature of many of the tasks used to assess children's spatial comprehension. He highlights three possible distortions that have afflicted many studies in the past: first, whether behaviour is natural or experimenter-controlled; secondly, whether behaviour is reported by the subject or interpreted by the observer; and thirdly, whether spatial representations are directly produced by the subject, or inferred by indirect judgement tasks. Newcombe further contends that we should ask, 'Does the task require rescaling? reorientation? the use of metrics? the use of symbolisation? knowledge of mapping conventions such as an aerial view? What degree of contextual support . . . is provided?' All of these 'dimensions' are likely to interfere with and distort children's attempts to convey their true understanding of space and place.

Part 3

Children's environmental competence

In Part Three attention shifts to the competence of children to understand large-scale space. An attempt is made to distinguish between what Liben (1981) has termed *spatial storage* and *spatial thought*. Chapter 6 reviews a broad range of studies which have examined those factors which affect children's environmental cognition and hence their storage of environmental information. The remaining chapters examine the abilities of children to comprehend and solve environmental problems of different kinds and those factors which are likely to impinge upon performances. Chapter 7 focuses on their ability to to solve everyday locational problems, such as searching, wayfinding and distance estimation, as well as their capability to make sense of large-scale environments in general. Chapter 8 considers children's capability to use spatial information presented in the form of maps. In Chapter 9, particular attention is given to the debate on whether gender variations in environmental experience induce sex contrasts in the spatial abilities of young boys and girls. Chapter 10 attempts to summarize the salient observations on how age-related factors influence children's environmental performance by examining recent empirical studies which cast further light upon the contrasting expectations of the constructivist, nativist and empiricist schools of thought. Cognitive mapping is not just about how children structure and organize space. Children's 'maps' include a wealth of information on how children feel and think about places. In consequence, in Chapter 11, I consider children's connotative images of place. Studies of this kind reveal the kind of environments that children consider enriching or boring and suggest ways in which the habitats of children could be improved.

6

Factors affecting children's environmental cognition

This chapter highlights how children's transactions with place and space are likely to affect their environmental cognition. In particular, attention focuses on the importance of activity patterns and the interplay of cultural, social and environmental factors to children's environmental awareness. At the outset we need to be clear about the specific focus of this chapter. When discussing environmental cognition we are concerned with children's understanding of environmental layout, including knowledge of spatial configuration, routes and places and their 'ability to store and access information about different environments' (Golledge, 1987, p. 131).

A central concept in this area is the notion of a *cognitive map*. Tolman (1973) introduced the concept of a cognitive map in order to explain the spatial behaviour of rats in maze conditions. In recent years the concept has gained considerable prominence with the development of cognitive psychology as an important research discipline. However, the concept of a map should be seen as no more than a convenient metaphor, used to summarize the extent of a person's environmental knowledge. Three confusions may result from the unqualified use of the label *map*. First, the term has been used as a 'catchall', a construct used to describe any environmental product derived from people's memory: these have ranged from free-recall drawings of a neighbourhood to views of the world. Secondly, the frequent use of the term map leads to the impression that there really is a *map* in the head, and this can act as a barrier in attempts to understand mental representations of the environment. Thirdly, constant reference to mental mapping has led many researchers to compare a person's description of reality with *actual* reality as reproduced by formal plans. This is an unfortunate practice in that it fails to recognize that formal plans are little more than interpretations of reality themselves (Spencer *et al.*, 1989). Indeed, there is an ongoing discussion as to whether cognitive information is not better described as being stored as 'holistic images, propositional strings, analogs or (in) other storage devices' (Golledge, 1987, p. 144). In the context of this chapter, the process of cognitive mapping will be regarded as 'a means of structuring, making sense of, and coping with the complexities of environments external to the mind' (p. 144).

The importance of activity-in-space to environmental awareness

Personal transactions with large-scale environments include both passive and active experiences. In this section we will review those studies which have considered the relative importance of activity-in-space to the acquisition of environmental knowledge.

Adult-related studies

Cohen and Cohen (1985) draw attention to a number of studies with adults which highlight the importance of activity to the acquisition of spatial knowledge. Three factors are identified as significant: environmental conditions, length of residency and person-related variables.

Environmental conditions
Various physical factors which influence activity have been shown to affect how adults learn about places. *First*, mode of transportation. The way a person moves through the environment greatly influences what they see. Pedestrians are close to the environment: smells, sounds and the feel of the pavement all contribute to a sense of immediacy. A person moving slowly through space has more time to discriminate between the surroundings. When travelling by car a person gains a completely different view. Carr and Schissler (1969) describe how cars enclose the driver and the passengers, isolating them from direct exposure to the world through which they are travelling. People in a car have less opportunity to stop, explore and linger than a pedestrian, but their increased speed does compensate for some of these other sensual experiences. Appleyard *et al.* (1967) have shown that between one-half and two-thirds of all sightings made by the driver or front-seat passenger in a car were of landmarks located directly ahead. Even during periods of wide scanning, the driver's attention regularly returned to the road itself, focusing on the foreground at points of decision. The driving experience has been summarized as 'a sequence played to the eyes of a captive ... but partially inattentive audience, whose vision was filtered and directed forward' (Jakle *et al.*, 1976).

People's views on space are likely to differ as a result of their different transportation experiences. For example, mass-transit passengers draw less accurate maps and make more mistakes on paired comparison distance estimations than more active travellers (Appleyard, 1970; Beck and Wood, 1976a; Golledge and Spector, 1978). However, Carr and Schissler (1969) report that recall of landmarks along a Boston expressway was not affected by being a driver or a passenger.

Secondly, environmental structure. The complexity and nature of an environment will influence activity and subsequent recall. Sadalla and Staplin (1980b) found that when respondents were asked to estimate the distance from a shopping mall to two equidistant places, the location viewed as closer had fewer intervening junctions, less traffic and took less time to reach. A number of studies have shown that the city centre or 'downtown' parts of urban areas loom large in the minds of those who frequent them. For example, Karan *et al.* (1980) in a study of Patna, India, found that adults exaggerated the size of the central area at the expense of outlying residential areas. In a similar vein, Klein (1967) working in Karlsruhe, West Germany, found that residents elongated the city centre towards their place of residence.

The opportunity to view an environment from single vantage points will also have a bearing upon how individuals learn about places. Evans *et al.* (1981) compared the mapping performance of a group of students visiting Bordeaux, France, with a group entering the University of California at Irvine. The subjects were tested after two weeks and ten months. It was found that the students at Irvine showed better configurative and environmental knowledge earlier in their residence and showed little improvement over time, whereas those at Bordeaux showed a marked improvement in their recall at the later testing. The authors suggest that these differences arose because Bordeaux was a city which required multiple views to see its entire space, whilst Irvine could be scanned as a whole from a variety of situations.

The distance between locations is a further environmental consideration. Karan *et al.* (1980) found that respondents who travelled furthest to their place of work drew the most extensive and comprehensive maps. Furthermore, the closer a place is located to an individual's activity space between home and work, the more accurate are distance estimates to it (Golledge and Spector, 1978).

Thirdly, local weather conditions. Devlin (1976) compared the place images of navy officers' wives who had moved to Idaho Falls, Idaho, either in September or December. In the first two to three weeks there was no difference in the number of streets both groups were able to recall. However, after three months, those who arrived in the winter, somewhat surprisingly, recounted more than twice the number of streets than those who came in the autumn. The authors surmise that this difference arose because the September arrivals experienced the weather as increasingly more severe over time and so were more likely to curtail their local explorations. On the other hand, the December arrivals experienced relatively constant weather conditions and so felt less restricted in their spatial activities.

Length of residency
The amount of exposure to an environment is an important factor in the acquisition of spatial knowledge. With time, an individual's opportunities to explore and interact with the locality increase, and through these transactions comes a developing sense of place and space. A number of studies, both with temporary and long-term residents, support the contention that activity-in-

space improves performances on tests of spatial capabilities.

Beck and Wood (1976a) examined the maps drawn by a group of adolescents on their first visit to London after three, five and six days. Without exception, all respondents were able to produce better organized, more accurate and integrated maps by the end of their stay. These findings were supported by Evans *et al.* (1981), who tested students visiting Bordeaux after two weeks and ten months.

Two campus studies are of further interest. Schouela *et al.* (1980) tested freshmen across a 24-week period. Like other studies, the authors noted an improvement in both landmark and route knowledge over time. However, when Herman *et al.* (1979) examined the environmental recall of freshmen entering the University of Pittsburgh after three weeks, three months and six months they found that whilst landmark and route knowledge improved between the initial testings, little additional improvement had occurred by six months. Also, some configurative appreciation was already apparent by three weeks and only 'fine tuning' took place from there on.

A cross-sectional study of residents of Ciudad Guayana, Venezuela after periods of less than six months, less than one year, one to five years, and greater than five years, was carried out by Appleyard (1970). He found a general increase in mapping accuracy and a consistently better recall of environmental detail over time. Similar findings have been reported by Milgram *et al.* (1972) in New York City, Devlin (1976) in Idaho Falls, and Golledge and Spector (1978) in Columbus, Ohio.

An exception to these general findings was noted by Ladd (1970). Working with black youths in Los Angeles, she found that performances on tests of spatial ability were not related to length of residency. In this case the effects of ethnicity were apparently more important.

Person-related variables
These variables relate to an individual's opportunity to carry out a range of activities in an environment. Of especial interest is Murray and Spencer's (1979) study of three groups distinguished by their levels of mobility: a high mobility group of domestic airline pilots, all male, aged 38 years or over, based in the San Francisco area; a medium mobility group of male amd female students, aged 18–20 years, from a Community College in San Jose, California, and from Sheffield University; and a low mobility group of South Yorkshire miners, all male, aged 40 years or over. The respondents were asked to draw five sketch maps: immediate locality, town, route map of journey from home to workplace/campus, region and world. The authors found that the most mobile group were significantly more likely to draw maps which were complex, more organized, and whose features were better represented than were the medium mobility group, who in turn drew superior maps to those in the low mobility group. These results support the hypothesis that wider experience in general enables the development of better mapping strategies. The main exception to

this relationship was found with the route map, where low mobility groups were at no disadvantage. The repetitious nature of this journey led to a very economic style of mapping for all.

These findings lend support to Beck and Wood's (1976a) earlier claim that general experience in a variety of cities facilitates more rapid mastery of a novel city. Others, too, have demonstrated the importance of potential mobility to environmental learning. For example, Walsh et al. (1981) revealed that healthy males in Long Beach, California, drew more accurate maps than elderly residents; whilst in Rome, Francescato and Mebane (1973) found that maps drawn by a mobile group aged under 30 years were more integrated and netted in form compared to a less mobile, older group whose maps were based largely on landmarks.

Kozlowski and Bryant (1977) suggest that an individual's expectation can significantly determine performance on a variety of spatial tests. They found that adults who considered themselves to have a poor sense of direction performed less well when confronted with the task of learning a new environment than those who judged themselves to be good. As both Acredolo (1982) and Bronzaft et al. (1976) suggest, the belief that one is poor at navigational and mapping tasks leads to avoidance strategies, which increasingly limits the opportunities to solve spatial problems.

In conclusion, there is ample evidence to suggest that adults' activity-in-space provides environmental opportunities which are likely to heighten spatial knowledge. We will now go on to examine whether this relationship holds for children.

Children-related studies

Cohen and Cohen (1985) recognize that 'from a variety of theoretical perspectives active locomotor movement within a large-scale environment presumably leads to a more accurate and flexible spatial representation than physically passive experiences' (p. 213). Activity-in-space brings the child into contact with multiple views of the environment and 'facilitates the integration of views and the coordination of precepts with motor experiences'. However, whilst there is general agreement with this claim, evidence suggests that the nature of the activity, the child's control of the activity and the purpose of the activity, all condition the child's response.

Active and passive exploration

From observations of 2- and 3-year-olds Hazen (1982) classified children into active and passive explorers of novel spaces. She found that in two different environmental settings (a museum room and a laboratory) active explorers developed a better spatial knowledge. Cornell and Hay (1984) have shown the importance of active exploration to route learning. Five- and 8-year-olds viewed a route either by a slide presentation, a video-recording or by walking the route with an instructor. When asked to indicate their way back to the start, children who had walked the journey out-performed those who had engaged in the more passive experience of viewing. Gale *et al.* (1990) exposed 9–12-year-olds to two routes through an unfamiliar suburban neighbourhood, with five learning trials undertaken on each route. One route was acquired by actual field experience, while the other was acquired by viewing a videotape. Mode of experience was found to have little effect on recognition performance; however, navigation performance following five video trials was inferior and approximated to that of children with only one trial of field experience. In a similar vein, Herman *et al.* (1982) compared the reconstruction of a mock town by kindergarten children following either standing and observing the town, riding through the town, or walking through the area. Children who walked or rode were more accurate than those who stood outside.

Hart's (1979) New England study provides abundant evidence on the importance of children's experience of place to their environmental recall. In a later review of his own work (1981) Hart writes,

> the development of children's spatial activity in their everyday geographic environment, and variations in the freedom of this spatial activity, are the most important forces influencing the quality, as well as the extent, of children's ability to represent the spatial relations of places in the large-scale environment. (p. 207)

He found that even the youngest children (under 7 years) were able to draw survey maps around their home and that the ability to coordinate larger and more distant places was clearly linked to broadening environmental transactions. For Hart, the extent of a child's range and such factors as the mode of locomotion through the environment were of overwhelming importance to the construction of environmental knowledge.

In another large-scale setting (Matthews 1987a), I examined the relationship between children's home range behaviour and their environmental capability across a variety of tasks. Working in suburban Coventry with a group of 6–11-year-olds, I gathered information on three home range conditions (free range, range with parental permission, range when accompanied) and examined children's ability to describe their home area using three different methods of environmental recall (free-recall mapping, air photo interpretation and map interpretation). The results were examined for information on place, measured by the mean number of elements clearly identified by children in their recall exercises, and awareness of place, the spatial spread of all recorded detail, which was summarized using a standard distance statistic. The results are shown in Table 6.1. For the first of these (information on place), I found that for each range condition and for all methods of stimulus presentation, strong significant correlations with high percentage explanations were evident. Such values suggested that environmental experience considerably influences children's ability to represent familiar places. Those children who roamed well

Table 6.1 The relationship between environmental experience and knowledge of place: correlation coefficients (*r*)

	Information on place	Awareness of place
Free-recall mapping		
Free range	0.88	0.73*
Range with permission	0.89	0.65*
Range when accompanied	0.87	0.68*
Air photo interpretation		
Free range	0.94	0.95
Range with permission	0.94	0.95
Range when accompanied	0.90	0.95
Map interpretation		
Free range	0.95	0.89
Range with permission	0.92	0.94
Range when accompanied	0.94	0.92

Notes:
  significant at $p = <0.001$
*significant at $p = <0.02$

Source: Matthews (1987a)

away from their home recounted most environmental detail. Conversely, children with limited home ranges showed proportionately less information on their maps. Furthermore, in all instances, home range and awareness of place were significantly related. Those children who travelled most widely within their home area showed the broadest representations of space.

I also requested these children to recount their journey-to-school using the same media presentations. My findings were consistent with an earlier study (Matthews, 1985b; 1986a), which revealed that children appear to recall their home area in greater detail than their trip to school. It was suggested that an explanation for this difference was the way in which children come into contact and interact with places. Play activities around the home call for more active responses on the part of the child than habitual travel along a familiar route. In consequence, free-play transactions are those most likely to develop environmental understanding and influence recall abilities.

In an earlier study (Matthews 1980a; 1980b), I showed how the views of a group of 11–18-year-olds towards their city centre changed with growing environmental experience and through more active, self-directed contact (see Figure 6.1). Eleven-year-olds had a narrow view of the city centre, focusing upon the shopping precinct where they regularly escorted their parents, often reluctantly, on shopping trips. Their views of the city were made up of scattered buildings and landmarks. They found it difficult to locate paths and roads and their maps revealed little sense of relatedness. In consequence, their maps were often confused and distorted and highlighted personal transactions, such as a street chessboard. With time and experience, children's knowledge of Coventry's urban form improved; place relationships became clearer and an under-

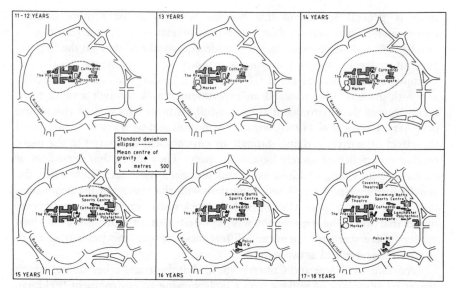

Figure 6.1   Spatial representations of a city centre: the mental territories of
Coventry schoolchildren

standing of routes and linkages was developed. A sense of place was seen to be
particularly heightened after the age of 15 years, when trips to the city centre
became largely self-motivated.

Schaefer and Sclar (1975) suggest that the onset of mass car ownership, with
children passively chauffered from place to place, has had a marked impact on
their comprehension and image of the environment. Some support for this
comes from Maurer and Baxter's (1972) study of 7–14-year-olds in Houston,
Texas. They found that those children travelling to school by car or bus
emphasized pathway elements in their images, whereas those walking to school
made greater reference to natural features like trees, grass, sky, sun and animals
and were more capable in completing mapping tasks. Furthermore, Lee (1963),
in a fascinating study of the effects of busing on children in Devon, found that
children younger than 8 years of age were unable to incorporate their school
bus journey into topographical representations of their local area. Most
children quite arbitrarily placed the school at the end of a short section of road
that began wherever the child boarded the bus. Hart (1981) suggests that bus
trips of this kind offer little opportunities for observation and reflection because
of high bus windows, crowding and socially complex conditions.

The nature of the activity
Most research on the importance of children's activity-in-space to environmen-
tal capability has been concerned with walking as an environmental experience
(Siegel *et al.*, 1979; Herman, 1980; Cohen and Weatherford, 1980). Whilst

there is general agreement that walking is likely to yield more detailed environmental information than more passive experiences, the results of a number of small-scale experiments provide equivocal evidence on the importance of active as opposed to passive contact to environmental recall. For example, Herman and Siegel (1978) report that kindergarten children, second and fifth graders, who watched an experimenter walk through a mock town reconstructed the environment as successfully as those who walked around the periphery. Cohen et al. (1980), working with third and sixth graders considered the effect of actively walking through an environment compared to the more passive experience of merely looking at space. They found that regardless of motor activity young children estimated distances most accurately when the activity of the response task was congruent with the activity of the acquisition task. Also, Herman et al. (1982), in their mock town experiment noted above, found that when the experiment was repeated with an older group of third graders there were no significant differences between the performances of passive observers and active movers.

According to Cohen and Cohen (1985), what these and other studies which report no advantage of walking over simply viewing an environment (Feldman and Acredolo, 1979; Cohen and Weatherford, 1981) have in common, is that they were 'large in size but ... small in scale'. In consequence, in all of the above the entire area could be viewed from a single vantage point. This conclusion is similar to the finding of Evans et al. (1981), reported earlier, when comparing the students' views of Bordeaux and Irvine. It would appear that the advantages of walking are therefore greatest when an individual is required to integrate multiple views of space. This is particularly so for young children as they mostly lack the experience and capability to organize and coordinate space through other means. In order to test this suggestion, Cohen and Weatherford (1981) compared the performances of third and sixth graders in small- and large-scale settings. Participants were asked to walk or view a novel environment. The environment was presented either with barriers, in order to impede an overall viewing, or without. Sixth graders estimated interlocation differences equally well whether walking or viewing, for both small- and large-scale environments. However, third graders were much more accurate in their estimates for the large-scale environment when actively walking, especially when the barriers were in place; these children performed equally well whether viewing or walking in the small-scale setting.

Control of the activity

A number of studies have suggested that environmental learning and recall depends on the level of control a child has of the activity (Acredolo et al., 1975; Acredolo, 1976). For example, Griffin (1973) contends 'it is common experience that in a strange city, we remain much better oriented if we find our own way about than if we cover the same ground in the company of others' (p. 299). In order to test such an assertion, Feldman and Acredolo (1979) examined the effect of active exploration upon memory for spatial location with children aged 3 and 4 years and 9 and 10 years. All the children took a walk along an unfamiliar hallway in search of a hidden object which they were later asked to relocate. Half the children were accompanied by an adult holding their hand (passive, controlled search), while the others proceeded on their own (active, self-directed search). They found that active exploration significantly improved the performance of the younger children whilst not affecting the performance of the older children. Across all conditions the 3- and 4-year-olds were significantly less accurate than their elders. These results provide support for the hypothesis that self-directed activity serves to increase the attention of young children, whilst older children, because of their greater environmental experience, demonstrate increased capacity efficiently to encode spatial information regardless of the mode of exploration.

Not all studies have arrived at similar conclusions (Poag, Cohen and Weatherford, 1983) and so the importance of control is largely unproven. For example, Herman (1980), in contrast to above, working with kindergarten children and third graders, found that children whose movements were controlled by an adult reconstructed an environment more accurately than those who encountered space through self-directed activity.

Purpose of the activity
Spencer *et al.* (1989) suggest that when children actively explore a route or a large-scale space, information which is related to an immediate purpose is more likely to be remembered than information which is not goal-related. To demonstrate this Gauvain and Rogoff (1986) introduced a group of children to a novel environment. One set of children were instructed to focus on route learning, whilst another set were told to concentrate upon general survey layout. When asked to recall the environment the two groups performed differently: the route-focused children recalled much less information on places off-route.

Summary

Most evidence suggests, whether indirect (adults) or direct (children), that children's activity-in-space is important to their construction of environmental knowledge. In particular, motor activity appears highly important to young children who are still learning to establish spatial frames of reference. Older children are more capable of handling a variety of spatial sources, whether passively or actively derived, and demonstrate greater flexibility in their acquisition and use of spatial information.

The importance of ecological factors to environmental awareness

In addition to activity-in-space, children's experience with place depends upon where they live. Two spatial scales are important: in the first instance, children are brought up in different cultural and societal settings, and secondly, within society they will belong to particular groups defined in terms of either social or environmental characteristics. In this section we will explore the significance of such ecological factors on environmental cognition.

Culture

Few studies have examined the effect of culture on children's environmental cognition. However, there is evidence to suggest that cultural differences are important to how children recall their everyday worlds. For example, Dart and Pradham (1967) asked Nepalese and American children to draw free-hand maps showing their route from home to school. The Nepalese children made maps which depicted the house and school as pictures and 'the process of going from one to the other, not the spatial relationship of one to the other' (p. 653). In contrast, the American children used abstract symbols to represent their homes and school and there was 'a clear effort to show spatial relationships and to provide needed spatial clues' (p. 653). These functional differences were attributed to differential exposure to Western-style maps, although the question of whether or not the Nepalese navigate quite well within their environment and culture was not raised.

In another study, Spencer and Darvizeh (1983) compared 3- to 5-year-old Iranian (n = 20) and English (n = 20) children's knowledge of their local neighbourhood, by semi-structured interviews, drawing tasks and actual route-finding performance. They hypothesized that whilst 'cultural differences may be found in the children's *descriptions* of routes, no such differences are to be expected in their *performance* on the routes' (p. 27). The results showed that in describing routes, by either verbal or graphic means, the Iranian children were apt to give a more personal and often more vivid and richer description than their counterparts, but one which contained fewer indicators of direction and less key landmarks. Some of the Iranian accounts were 'closer to stories about what the child likes to see on the journey, than a set of rules for another person to follow to complete the route' (p. 28). However, despite these differences in the style of route and place descriptions all children, in both cultures, were able to perform 'adequately' a navigational task, which involved the escorting of an experimenter to two specified local target places. These findings suggested to Spencer and Darvizeh that whilst culture was important to children's *expressive style*, fundamental differences in *cognitive style* were unlikely. They reasoned that such expressive differences are cultural artefacts, present among adults and older children, and when a young child is asked to 'tell a stranger how to reach a certain destination, he produces an account which selects out of his total cognitive map those features he is accustomed to hearing others give when giving directions' (p. 31). However, Spencer and Darvizeh acknowledge that no published data exists on the style and content of adults' route maps in Iran.

More recently, Matthews and Airey (1990) have compared the place and route descriptions of Kenyan and British children. Our sample consisted of an age- and sex-matched group of 7–13-year-olds, who were tested by graphic and verbal techniques. Cultural differences in *expressive* style were found to be statistically significant. For example, Kenyan children were more likely to draw fragmentary maps, full of idiosyncratic detail and value-laden observations about their surroundings. 'Dangerous places' were strongly demarcated, as well as favourite haunts and play spaces. Religious places were frequently given prominence, and often drawn out of proportion to their surroundings. Even the oldest Kenyan children drew maps which retained some pictorial element and geometrical accuracy was low in nearly every case. Like Iranian children, their verbal accounts seldom contained directional information and were usually presented as series of unfolding events, interrupted by colourful anecdotes about places and people. Non-geographical features were more likely to be used as key landmarks by the Kenyan children, whereas the British sample showed a greater awareness of the functional interconnectivity of the environment. Yet, there is nothing to suggest that Kenyan children do not find their way effectively about their home area, nor get frequently lost on their way home from school!

In summary, the limited evidence which is available supports Evans' (1980) observation that it is 'difficult to demonstrate cultural differences *per se* in environmental cognition'. Those differences which have been observed relate largely to expressive style and to the nature of the environment under description, rather than supporting developmental differences in cognitive ability and spatial representation.

Social characteristics

Cognitive maps mirror closely the spatial patterns of regular activity, often defined by social group membership. For example, Orleans (1973) has shown that knowledge of urban form and structure reflects the spatial mobility and behaviour of different socio-economic groups. He questioned three different groups resident in Los Angeles and from their responses constructed composite maps in order to compare their knowledge of urban space. The middle-class, white residents of Westwood had the most detailed and richest knowledge of the sprawling city, whilst the black residents of Avalon, near Watts, had a much more restricted view. Their knowledge largely comprised of fragmentary information about other districts, which were vaguely 'out-there-somewhere', and some understanding of the main roads that linked their community to the city centre, but they showed a very poor grasp of interstitial detail. However, even more limited were the views of a Spanish-speaking minority of Boyle Heights. Their collective map showed nothing more than their immediate neighbourhood and the bus depot, which acted as the entrance and exit to their limited urban territory.

Children's images of an environment not only reflect their surroundings, but many aspects of themselves and their lives. Ladd (1967) asked a number of black children living in the Mission Hill district of Boston to draw a map of their area. She found that most drew only their black neighbourhood, with the adjacent white residential areas constituting *terra incognita*. As an example she refers to the map drawn by Ernest. All of the detail is of the area around his home and school. Ernest also draws in Parker Street which divides his neighbourhood from the white Mission Hill project. Quite unconsciously, he uses a quarter of his sheet of paper to show this road, which suggested to Ladd the magnitude of this local socio-psychological barrier.

In a similar vein, Maurer and Baxter (1972) found that in a study of white, black and Mexican children's views of Houston, Texas, the effect of ethnicity was very strong. White children's images were considerably more extensive, while those of the black children, in particular, emphasized the home. Maurer and Baxter suggested that these differences were a reflection of the socio-economic consequences of varying migrational and travel mobility and outcomes of cultural division. Likewise, Stiell (1989), working with working-class Indian and white children, aged 6 to 11 years, in an ethnically mixed neighbourhood in Birmingham observed pronounced differences between the environmental cognition of the two groups. Not only were the maps of the Indian children more limited in extent compared to their age- and sex-matched counterparts, particularly those of Indian girls, but also they highlighted different facets of their locality. For example, content analysis revealed a keen appreciation of cultural artefacts by Indian children. Retail outlets, clubs and religious buildings serving the local Indian community were emphasized, elements which were largely ignored by their white neighbours. Stiell proposes that despite the physical propinquity of these two groups their maps suggest the coexistence of two socially discrete worlds, whose boundaries seldom overlap.

Environmental characteristics

A number of studies suggest the importance of environmental setting to children's imagery of place. Bar-Gal (1984) asked fifth-grade children attending a village school and an urban school in northern Israel to draw maps of their 'home town'. The urban children drew houses, streets and cars, whereas the rural children drew houses, trees and flowers and were more inclined to

Table 6.2 *Core items* mentioned by children living in three different areas in Venice (item/total items)

Core item	Historical centre	Areas Lido	Mainland
Bridges	.38		
Water	.15		
Trees	.23	.20	
Houses	.35	.79	.38
School		.25	
Cars		.41	.25
Friends/relatives		.19	.15
Streets			.28
Gardens			.21

Source: Axia and Nicoloni (1985)

embellish their drawings with people, butterflies and birds. Barbichon (1975) noted a similar response: his urban sample focused almost entirely on commercial buildings, compared to the more personalized accounts of rural children who presented houses and people. These sorts of differences have been reported among adults as well. Haney and Knowles (1978) found that when they examined adults' sketch maps and descriptions of their neighbourhood, suburban residents were inclined to emphasize the friendliness of neighbours, whereas inner city residents focused on their proximity to shops, churches and schools. Axia and Nicolini (1985), working with kindergarten children in three different parts of Venice, found that children as young as 5-years-old were sensitive to their surrounding environment. They asked children to talk about and describe their city. A qualitative analysis was undertaken to find out which elements children mostly used to represent Venice. Each element was assigned a score by dividing the number of times it was mentioned by the total amount items. The elements which reached the highest scores were considered 'core items'. Table 6.2 shows that although functional and natural features were largely recalled, irrespective of place of residence, children in different areas chose different core items to represent their city.

Devlin (1976) suggests that in addition to exposure to an environment, children's cognitive maps will be affected by their attitudes and feelings towards places. Schouela *et al.* (1980) also report that locations which are *important* for an individual are likely to act as 'anchor points' for the articulation of other parts of the developing image. Wood and Beck have explored the significance of affective imagery (Beck and Wood, 1976a; Wood and Beck, 1976). They devised a mapping system, *Environmental A*, to capture the affective qualities of city images. Their sample was a group of 15–19-year-old American tourists visiting London, Paris and Rome. After generating a skeletal base map of the areas they had visited, respondents were asked to reveal their subjective feelings about different parts of the city using a set of cartographic symbols derived from the vocabulary of *Environmental A*. These symbols largely comprised descriptive pictograms which attempted to express different qualities of place: for example, a skull and cross-bones stood for danger, and a closed eye for restful. Their results confirmed both the value of the methodology and the importance of attitudinal imagery to environmental learning. For each city, the maps of the adolescents centred around areas of interest, excitement and danger. Spencer and Dixon (1983) later employed this approach to examine how newly arrived residents learnt about their locality. They found that impressions gained within the first three weeks were highly significant in determining environmental imagery. There is ample evidence from the studies outlined above that emotional experiences of various kinds are equally likely to be instrumental in shaping children's impressions of place.

Summary

This chapter has shown the importance of children's varying transactions with place to environmental cognition. Tuan (1979) suggests that experience is a cover-all term for the various modes through which a person knows and becomes acquainted with reality. Accordingly, experience embraces not only activities of various kinds, but also the surrounding cultural, social and environmental milieux which enshroud the child as soon as he/she is born. In time, experience becomes compounded with feelings and emotions which tint all transactions (Tuan, 1979, p. 8). We have seen that a child may regularly come into contact with an environment, but unless the senses are awakened that place may lack sharpness and imageability. However, whether experience alone leads to environmental knowing or whether it simply contributes to an on-going repertoire of cognitive structures by which children come to organize their world is discussed further in Chapter 10.

7

Children's understanding of large-scale space and place

In Chapters 2 and 3 we saw that the acquisition of environmental knowledge by children is a product of both indirect and direct experience. Indirect environmental experience may be provided by a variety of media sources, but direct experience of large-scale environments usually comes from physically moving through them. However, how children come to understand large-scale places is a matter of much conjecture. According to Gärling *et al.* (1984a; 1984b) the acquisition of environmental information requires effortful processing, particularly at the initial stages of learning a new environment. Likewise, Downs and Stea (1977, p. 9) suggest that the process of spatial understanding demands a series of 'psychological transformations by which an individual acquires, codes, stores, recalls, and decodes information about the relative locations and attributes of phenomena in the everyday spatial environment'. In this chapter we will focus upon the strategies which children employ to make sense of their surroundings. The chapter is presented in a number of sections. First, we will examine the strategies used by pre-school children when learning spatial information. Secondly, we will identify the components which comprise large-scale spatial knowledge, discuss competing theoretical views on the manner in which children acquire such knowledge and review empirical studies which have examined the process of acquisition. Thirdly, we will consider the acquisition process in relation to the particular spatial task of wayfinding. Lastly, we will look at the ability of children to estimate distances.

Early spatial learning strategies

Wellman and Somerville (1982) suggest that young children's search behaviour is a useful expression of early spatial processing and environmental competence. Searching in this context refers to activity which involves bodily movement rather than visual scanning or an internal cognitive search. Cohen and Cohen (1985) point out that this class of problem involves (i) the recognition of a need to search; (ii) an identified object for search; (iii) a search space (environment); (iv) information about both the object and the search space; and (v) strategies of search. Children commonly employ three different types of search strategy, each of varying efficiency and effectiveness: *spatial associative search*, a procedure based upon visiting places in some way linked with the object; *comprehensive search*, an exhaustive search of all possible locations; and *selective search*, whereby only those sets of locations that suit the immediate task are sampled.

From an early age children are capable of performing simple search strategies which demand some grasp of spatial reasoning, albeit at a small-scale. For example, a variety of studies have shown that 8- to 12-month-old infants will search for a totally hidden object concealed whilst in view, although most are unable to organize, plan or execute a successful search and their behaviour is quite inconsistent (Wellman and Somerville, 1982). Sophian and Sage (1985) explain early failure not in terms of Piaget's assertion that children of this age are unable to distinguish the object from their own actions and so are incapable of understanding the relationship between objects and space, but by suggesting that errors arise simply through inattention and lapses of memory. Indeed, when only a little older, 12 to 18 months, success at recovering a viewed object that is hidden greatly improves. In addition, infants of this age are quite successful at finding a hidden object not in view. For example, Wellman (1985) records that if an experimenter conceals a toy with his/her hand and then hides the toy in a container, most infants of this age will start their search with the correct container. However, it is not until the age of 18–24 months that invisible displacements are mastered, whereby the toy is not only concealed, but also invisibly moved to another hiding place.

From the age of 2 years onwards, children are capable of both selective and comprehensive searches when moving around real large-scale environments, although the age of the child and the nature of the task will affect what strategy is used. In the first instance, young children are more likely to use simpler strategies which involve associative reasoning and the rudiments of a travel plan. With age, more efficient logical search procedures increase, especially as the child's memory improves. However, Wellman *et al.* (1979; 1981) have shown that 2-year-olds are capable of complex strategies, providing the physical demands of the task are not too great. For example, a comprehensive search is required when no information is available to limit search space: 2-year-olds are quite capable of understanding this requirement, although their performance is hampered by difficulty in remembering which locations have already been searched. Three-year-olds are much more successful at carrying out non-redundant, comprehensive searches. Equally, 2-year-olds will undertake selective, logical searches when verbally directed or when the object being searched for has a typical location (e.g. a fork in the kitchen). Hazen (1982) has also shown that young children are able to make logical inferences about locations from their search behaviour. She taught 2- and 3-year-olds a route through three small rooms. When moved to a new starting position or asked to make a detour, none of the children resorted to backtracking and many 3-year-olds were efficient at minimizing route length.

School-aged children are considerably more resourceful in their search strategies. Kreutzer *et al.* (1975) note that fifth graders, when compared to kindergarten children, are able to generate more sophisticated searching procedures and are more consistent in their performances. Cornell and Heth (1986) have shown that 6–8-year-olds, when carrying out search-and-hide tasks, demonstrate not only an awareness of the spatial layout of large-scale spaces, but also are able to use this knowledge to plan efficient strategies which minimize unnecessary and ineffective effort.

In summary, effective searching demands a range of spatial abilities which contribute to environmental competence in general. Considerable evidence suggests that skills of this kind do not suddenly appear in the middle years of childhood. Instead, from an early age, children can be seen to be logical, deliberate and intelligent searchers (Wellman, 1985) sensitive to the spatial organization of places and capable of inferential thought.

Children's acquisition of large-scale spatial knowledge

As children's activity-in-space grows, so their exposure to large-scale environments increases. In so doing, children come into contact with more complex spaces.

Components of spatial knowledge

The components of spatial knowledge have been distinguished by many studies (Golledge *et al.*, 1985; Gale *et al.*, 1990). In general, three major components have been identified: these relate to *landmark, configurational and route knowledge*. At the simplest level, an individual must have knowledge of important objects and/or places, commonly referred to as landmark knowledge. Such knowledge includes an ability to state that a place exists and to recognize it among others with some degree of certainty. This ability is essentially *declarative* in nature. Spatial knowledge also includes information on the relationship of places and this is often of two kinds. On the one hand, individuals possess knowledge of the position of places, together with information on the relationships of these places with each other, differentiated by distance and direction within a coordinate of space. Like landmark knowledge, spatial structures of this kind are also declarative in form, although more elaborate in nature. On the other hand, knowledge of places further involves *procedures* for moving from one location to another and an understanding of the layout of routes which enable such activity. Wayfinding ability, which can be taken as an example of a high-level spatial problem, demands both declarative and procedural skills and knowledge.

Theoretical perspectives on the acquisition of spatial knowledge

A number of competing theoretical perspectives on how children acquire spatial understanding has been proposed. Whilst there appears to be broad agreement of a general progression from landmark to route to configurational knowledge, and of a relational sequence which progresses from topological to projective to metric properties, the manner in which knowledge acquisition comes about is contested. Three different views are distinguished below. There is also a contrary position which contends the sequence outlined above.

The first viewpoint has been expounded by Siegel and White (1975). They suggest that the development of environmental understanding in children conforms to a *linear sequence*, and mirrors the construction of spatial knowledge by adults. First, landmarks are noticed and remembered. Children act in the context of these landmarks and in the course of these transactions paths and routes are established between these landmarks. Spatial knowledge along these routes develops from topological to metric properties. With experience, landmark and route sets are successively formed into clusters. At first, whilst there is a high level of coordination within these clusters, the clusters remain uncoordinated with each other. Lastly, an overall coordinated frame of reference arises, such that within and between clusters accuracy is accomplished. The sequence outlined above is a process going 'from association to structure and of deriving simultaneity from successivity' (Siegel *et al.*, 1978, p. 226).

A second perspective is offered by Piaget and Inhelder (1967) and Hart and Moore (1973). To them, environmental understanding represents more than just a process of knowledge accumulation. They suggest that a child's knowledge of the environment is both a function of environmental experience and of general cognitive capacity. Accordingly, a *hierarchical process* of understanding is postulated, whereby environmental understanding comes about in ordered stages. Three stages or levels of understanding are suggested. These stages correspond to Piaget's theory of cognitive development which has been discussed in Chapter 4. First, at the lowest level, the young child is capable only of landmark knowledge, associated with places of activity and emotion. Views of place are essentially egocentric, uncoordinated and topological in nature. As the child's cognitive capabilities develop, landmarks are pieced together into routes and the projective properties of places become understood. Environmental understanding is now characterized by differentiated and partially coordinated sub-groups. During this stage there is a shift from egocentric to allocentric frames of reference. Lastly, the child develops an ability to both coordinate and integrate space in an abstract, hierarchical and metric manner. In essence, what this approach suggests is that environmental understanding develops from a low-level, primarily enactive landmark-based plan of an intimate locality to a higher level, coordinated and configurational view of place.

A third perspective draws upon both viewpoints outlined above. Golledge

(1978) proposes an *anchor point theory*, whereby a hierarchical ordering of place comes about through a system anchored by primary, secondary and tertiary nodes and the paths that link them. Primary nodes are those places which are first understood. In general, these relate to the child's home and to other familiar environments within their immediate locality. Primary nodes serve as anchor points from which the rest of the hierarchy develops. As interaction takes place along the paths between primary nodes there is a 'spillover effect', in the course of which other places around the primary nodes become known. In turn, these additional places become secondary nodes and in this sequential manner tertiary nodes become fixed to the system. Continued interaction among these nodes and paths heightens environmental understanding and brings about a highly coordinated view of place.

At variance to all these views is Lynch's (1960) contrary suggestion that people rely on paths for frameworks in early learning and that an awareness of landmarks develops only with familiarity. According to Lynch, paths are channels for customary or occasional movement. People observe the landscape as they move through it and along these paths other environmental elements become arranged and related. With experience, landmarks frequently become relied upon to provide 'clues of identity and even structure', but their use and recognition depend upon patterns of movement.

Empirical studies of the acquisition of spatial knowledge

Although there are competing theories on the child's acquisition of spatial knowledge, these theories represent general positions rather than formal models (Golledge *et al.*, 1985). To date, most empirical studies on the acquisition process are limited in scope and not explicitly tied to any formal model. Instead, empirical studies have tended to focus on several issues relating to landmark, route and configurational knowledge.

A basic element of most children's cognitive maps is landmarks. Of fundamental concern is the question of which characteristics and features of objects and locations cause them to be selected as landmarks. Appleyard (1969b) has shown that for adults the most easily recalled and recognized buildings are those with high use and important symbolic functions. Physical features such as bright surfaces, contrasting size and sharp changes in gradient also influence memory, although a number of studies (Sieverts, 1967; Goodey *et al.*, 1971) have shown that architectural distinctiveness is not very memorable in itself. Studies of children's landmark selection reveal a concern 'of the minute and detailed and of the incidental as compared to the adult world' (Pocock and Hudson, 1978). In Harwich, for example, the notable landmark of the lighthouse was much less important than the public toilets located at its base (Bishop and Foulsham, 1973). In Coventry, 11-year-olds frequently recalled a street chessboard located within the city centre at the expense of surrounding urban detail (Matthews, 1980a). Maurer and Baxter (1972) recount how children in Harrisburg, Texas, omitted prominent buildings and factories from their sketch maps and included drawings of dog houses and trees. Spencer and Lloyd (1974) in their 'draw me a map' exercises noted that young children tended to see the environment in primarily human and natural terms. However, I found little support for this observation working with 6–11-year-olds in suburban Coventry (Matthews, 1984a). When asked to sketch their home area a strong functional bias was evident, with shops, buildings and pathways characteristically represented. Nevertheless, the younger children frequently personalized their 'maps' by drawing pictures of animals in nearby fields, moving cars, 'lollipop ladies' (road-crossing wardens) and friends and relatives. Features clearly insignificant to their elders were often given prominence: a favourite climbing tree, a special site for playing, or, as many 6- and 7-year-olds described, a tree known locally as 'the moth-hawk tree' because of its attraction to moths in summer. Such results emphasize that the way in which children use, move around and observe the environment is very different to how adults come into contact with space.

Another issue relates to the importance of landmarks as components of routes. Recent studies by Allen and his colleagues (Allen, 1981; 1985; 1987; Allen et al., 1978; 1979) have shown that children of a variety of ages are more likely to understand route configuration in the presence of scenes with high landmark potential. Distance judgements for low landmark potential scenes were considerably inferior. Also, Allen suggests that children are unlikely to remember routes as just strings of landmarks. In tests with second and fifth graders he showed that children frequently subdivided routes into sections bounded by particular environmental features. This finding, that route knowledge may involve higher-level organization, such as sub-divisions and discrete loci, lends support to those who argue above (Piaget and Inhelder, 1967; Hart and Moore, 1973) that landmark selection is a far less developmentally demanding task than route construction.

This last observation leads on to a further issue, of whether landmarks precede routes as children's initial pegs for understanding space. This issue corresponds to the debate between Lynch and the others outlined above. Most published results seem to support the importance of landmark acquisition (Acredolo, 1976; 1977; Acredolo et al., 1975; Beck and Wood, 1976b; Cousins et al., 1983; Darvizeh and Spencer, 1984). However, recent evidence suggests that children are capable of responding in different ways to different spatial problems, and observations upon environmental capability should not be divorced from the nature of the test conditions. Spencer et al. (1989) observe, 'impressions from walking routes with children would incline one towards accepting the primacy of landmarks as pegs for routes. However, if an experimenter were to work solely in the laboratory a different conclusion may be reached.' For example, Darvizeh and Spencer (1984) escorted a group of 3-year-old children, one at a time, along a novel route. They found that young

Table 7.1 Children's views on place

	Element composition (mean frequency per map) Age groups					
	6	7	8	9	10	11
Journey-to-school[1]						
Landmarks	0.5	0.4	0.9	0.7	1.3	2.2
Nodes	0.5	0.8	1.7	2.0	2.4	1.8
Paths	1.6	1.7	2.3	3.1	3.0	3.5
Districts	0.04	0.8	1.1	1.4	1.6	1.7
Total elements	2.64	3.7	6.0	7.3	8.3	9.2
Home area[2]						
Landmarks	2.0	1.8	2.2	4.2	2.2	3.3
Nodes	0.3	1.2	1.2	1.7	2.1	2.0
Paths	0.9	1.2	1.8	2.4	2.4	2.5
Districts	0.3	0.8	1.0	1.8	2.2	1.3
Total elements	3.5	5.0	6.2	10.1	8.9	9.1

Notes:
1. Figures do not include home, school, or route
2. Figures do not include home

Source: Matthews (1984a)

children, either when learning a route or retracing it, made use of landmarks from the outset. In addition, analysis of children's verbal accounts of these trips indicated extensive use of a broad range of landmarks. However, when they used a set of two- and three-dimensional mapping symbols for 3-year-olds to construct maps of the novel routes that they had just learned, many children began by fitting together the entire road structure before labelling it with landmarks, whereas others used roads and landmarks together to unfold their maps.

In a similar vein, I concluded that children may learn about different environments in different ways (Matthews, 1984a). I asked my sample of 6–11-year-olds to draw maps of their journey-to-school and of their home area. The results were classified according to a fourfold schema and are shown in Table 7.1. On the basis of these findings I suggested that when faced with a linear journey, the route itself becomes a well-remembered construct, but when describing an area spatial properties are more likely to be remembered. Also, children's varying transactions with the environment are likely to affect their comprehension of place. For example, the habituation involved in repeated travel from abode to school provides a different mental imprint to the behaviour experienced in exploring places around the home. Thus, whereas the former provides an awareness of sequential elements, the latter demands an appreciation of points of reference and orientation, as provided by landmarks, with only a rudimentary understanding of routes.

However, studies by Spencer and Weetman (1981) and Byrne (1982) suggest that these sorts of differences may be an outcome of the instructional set. They have shown that individuals switch between sequential and spatial mapping styles according to the particular task at hand. For example, if an instructor places emphasis upon drawing a route then the map, perhaps not surprisingly, is likely to be more sequential than spatial in form.

The development of route knowledge to survey and configurational knowledge provides another issue of investigation. Both theoretically and empirically there is support for the notion that environmental knowledge progresses towards a more coherent, spatially integrated and structured form. For example, Shemyakin (1962) asked children to draw sketch-maps of their neighbourhoods. Young children (6–7 years) drew only landmarks and those routes along which they frequently travelled: few drew the whole street or added information about adjacent streets. The maps of these children were largely inaccurate and subsequently classed as 'low-order', route-style representations. Older children (9–10 years) produced more complex drawings: branches along the main routes to other streets were now appended, although these links were seldom interconnected. By the age of 12 years children presented the locality in the form of a netted and 'closed aggregate'. According to Shemyakin, these maps were of a 'higher order' and could be described as 'survey maps'. Shemyakin's empirical description of the development of spatial representation lends support to Piaget's theoretical expectations on the capability of children to handle spatial information. Although we shall argue later that Piaget tends to underestimate the environmental skills of the very young, what is important in this context is the suggestion that as children become more acquainted with an environment, procedural knowledge accumulates and both distance and directional information become more precise.

The nature of how this transition from landmark and route knowledge to survey knowledge takes place has not been clearly established. Both Garling and his colleagues (Gärling et al., 1981; 1984a; 1984b; Gärling and Böök, 1981) and Rieser (1983) suggest that the ability to piece together seemingly disparate pieces of environmental information into an organized whole demands an effort of imagination which they term *inferencing ability*. Gärling argues that young children are capable only of comprehending the position of visible reference points. The acquisition of spatial information about non-visible reference points, especially in large-scale environments, requires both effortful central processing and deliberate attention processes. Inferencing ability of this kind emerges later in childhood. Successful inferencing depends upon such factors as the complexity of the environment; on the extent to which reference points are visible or not, particularly at points of origin, destination or where some spatial decision is called for; and on whether attention processes are undisturbed.

Rieser (1983) further proposes that the nature of spatial inferencing depends on three considerations: first, the functional purpose served by the inference, such as the extent to which the inference will help the observer make sense of places out of view; secondly, the capability of the observer to make use of different spatial frames of reference, whether egocentric or otherwise; and thirdly, the psychological process underlying the inference, that is, whether the inference demands *deliberate computational processes*, such as when an individual cognitively links together existing pieces of information to solve a spatial problem, or *relatively automatic perceptual processes*, as is the case when observers behave as if they seemingly comprehend some novel environments from the outset.

An alternative explanation is propounded by Chase and Chi (1980). For them, the progression from route knowledge to survey knowledge represents much more than just growing procedural competence. An integral part of this transition is a changeover from one-dimensional to two-dimensional knowledge which implies a qualitative difference in the way spatial information is coded and stored in long-term memory. Like Golledge (1978), they argue that such a progression can only be accomplished by the grouping and clustering of information around particular reference nodes. In due course, these nodes become the anchor points which provide the skeletal structure for the hierarchical organization of space. They believe that explanations based upon anchor points, unlike procedural hypotheses, at least offer an understanding of how children become much more efficient at using spatial information with growing environmental experience. In summary, empirical evidence provides qualified support for the developmental progression from landmark knowledge to configurational knowledge postulated by the Siegel and White and Piagetian frameworks. However, children's performances and their ability to recall large-scale environments cannot be divorced from the task demands.

Route-learning and wayfinding

Wayfinding describes a person's ability, both cognitive and behavioural, to reach a spatial destination (Passini, 1984). According to Passini, this ability is based on three distinct performances: decision-making, decision-execution and information-processing. Wayfinding, therefore, represents a spatial problem-solving exercise. In order to be successful at wayfinding, all of these decisions require environmental information, some of which may be *perceived* directly in the setting, some *retrieved* from previous experience and some *inferred* from previous experiences. As such, wayfinding inevitably relies on information reflecting locational references. In this section we will review three competing views on how children manage to cope with wayfinding and 'the dynamics of purposeful mobility'.

Most studies of children's wayfinding ability have been carried out in small-scale, impoverished environments (Pick and Acredolo, 1983). From their review of extant research and theory on the acquisition of spatial knowledge by children, Golledge *et al.* (1985) set out four issues which they felt defined the prerequisites for a computational model of wayfinding in large-scale settings.

These were:

1. Route-finding knowledge is largely based upon episodic experience, stored in long-term memory and processed and transformed during all spatial activities.
2. Spatial knowledge is made up of different components, such as landmark, route and configurational knowledge, and their different forms of representation, both declarative and procedural.
3. Children's knowledge of the environment is rarely complete, some portions of their cognitive maps are distorted by 'holes, folds, tears, and cracks' and can be represented only in topological terms, whereas other parts have full metric properties.
4. Children frequently make errors in task performances, some of which are products of the way in which previous information has been processed and stored.

Golledge *et al.* (1985) tested their model in relation to how a single 11-year-old boy learnt a novel route, over a 5-day period, in a moderate density neighbourhood in Goleta, California. They found that the model and the hypotheses which they derived from it supported their initial conceptualizations. A number of points emerged: knowledge of a route is focused on key choice points; these choice points serve to segment a route; with experience, these segments become increasingly differentiated and appropriately sequenced; routes appear to be hierarchically organized, both with respect to choice points and the segments which they anchor; errors occur most frequently where choice points are complex, and/or at lower levels of the hierarchy where understanding is less complete.

More recently, Gale *et al.* (1990), working with a group of sixteen children aged between 9 and 12 years, in another neighbourhood of Goleta, have added to our understanding of children's wayfinding strategies. They revealed that successful navigation does not require extensive knowledge about all scenes along a route. Instead, knowledge acquisition during route learning is a highly selective process, and much environmental information is ignored without adverse effects. Like Golledge *et al.* (1985), they found that the scene type which was selected and stored with the highest frequency was views at route intersections. Several reasons are suggested for this: first, in a specific navigational task what is learned is determined by the goal of the task. The goal in this case was successful route-learning and so children focused their attention on points where choices had to be made; secondly, views at intersections are important because they are the most complex and visually stimulating, providing a much larger spatial vista than a scene along a street; thirdly, views at intersections are the points at which new views are seen first. The novelty of a fresh view encourages a highly enactive response from the child, which in this case leads to a focusing of attention. In essence, what Gale and his colleagues are suggesting is that successful wayfinding depends on the goals of the task, the properties of the environment and the type of interaction.

Although such work is novel, in that it attempts to show how concepts relevant to non-spatial thought can be used to provide an understanding of spatial reasoning, specifically the concepts relating to declarative and procedural types of knowledge, both Golledge *et al.* (1985) and Gale *et al.* (1990) deliberately link their approach to the strictures common to the standard *constructivist* position of developmental psychology. For them, children's wayfinding ability is a function of environmental experience and of different cognitive strategies. In other words, sensory information derived from episodic environmental encounters is mediated and supplemented by existing knowledge structures to provide route and navigational skills.

In marked contrast to this approach are the *ecological* views espoused by Gibson (1979) and Heft (1983). Their ideas differ from the constructivist position in two major ways. First, they challenge the notion that environmental information results from temporally discrete and episodic transactions. Instead, they suggest that as an individual moves along a route successive vistas are opened up at successive vantage points and wayfinding becomes 'a sequence of transitions between vistas' (Heft, 1983). Environmental understanding therefore involves the coordination of information gained through the *perception* of successive information over time. Secondly, they challenge the notion that the environment as perceived is largely a mental construct. Both Gibson and Heft attempt to do without map concepts, their descriptions of wayfinding are based emphatically on visual cues and processes. As an individual moves through an environment, rich environmental information is given off, especially at transitions between vistas, which when taken together enable the observer to understand the extended layout of place. To demonstrate the efficacy of such an explanation of route-learning Heft (1983) carried out an experiment with three groups of subjects: the first set were shown a filmed series of transitions between different views along a journey; the second set were shown a complete film of the journey; and the third set were shown the complete journey, without the transitions. When tested on route knowledge, as Heft had hypothesized, no difference was found between the first two groups, and both outperformed the third.

However, Spencer *et al.* (1989) argue that given present knowledge ecological explanations appear incomplete. They cite the findings of Strelow (1985) who suggests that in most tasks involving movement through an environment both *perception* and *cognition* combine, to a greater or lesser extent. For example, in some cases, like obstacle avoidance by the sighted, perception is uppermost, whereas in others, such as travel by the blind, cognition is dominant. By the same token, successful wayfinding is an outcome of the same sort of interaction.

There is another view, which suggests that navigational ability may be an innate skill rather than one which is acquired. This kind of explanation, which is characteristic of *rationalism* and *nativism*, argues that knowledge, in this case wayfinding ability, is innate and precedes experience. For example, Baker

(1980; 1981) has suggested that humans have the capability to interpret the earth's magnetic field in such a way as to enable them to 'sense' the direction of travel needed in order to return to the place of origin of a trip. Such skill involves both *orientation*, knowing which direction is which, and *wayfinding*, knowing which direction to follow in order to return to the home base. Baker substantiated his claims by conducting a series of experiments whereby a group of students were blindfolded and driven around a rather circuitous route in a bus. At particular stops, students were asked to indicate the direction of the point of origin. A significant proportion were able to do this for displacements varying between 6 and 52 km. To confirm that navigational skills of this kind were magnetic in origin Baker repeated his experiments with half of his sample wearing magnets and the other half wearing brass bars: all subjects thought they were wearing magnets. The results showed that those wearing brass bars continued to make acceptable estimates of direction, unlike those wearing magnets. Baker explained this discrepancy by suggesting that the magnets had disrupted natural navigational ability.

More recently, Walmsley and Epps (1988), this time working in the southern hemisphere (Australia), have provided support for such claims. In similar experiments involving a group of thirty-five men, women and children, they tested directional accuracy at four points at distances up to 15 km away from the point of origin, while their sample were blindfolded and still in the bus. When the mean vector and the homeward component of that vector were calculated from the estimates, participants proved to be able to sense direction reasonably well. Interestingly, and like Baker, they found that females tended to have a better sense of direction than males. In addition, adults had no greater direction-finding ability than children. Whether such results are simply the result of chance or whether navigational ability is genuinely innate has yet to be firmly substantiated. Walmsley and Epps are suitably cautious in their conclusions. They write,

> it would be wrong, of course, to exaggerate the importance of magnetic sense of directions in humans. Magnetism is probably only really useful in giving the starting direction for a journey and, even then, it is only significant in the absence of both environmental cues (e.g. topography, sun, wind) and signs (either in the form of maps or in the form of indicators). (p. 40)

However, a number of questions remain to be answered. When, why and how might such a magnetic sense of direction have developed in humans? Is it something that may have helped the species in an evolutionary sense? If so, why do females outperform males? Why, too, do such results run counter to the findings of other psychological tests on women's spatial capabilities? Clearly, much work remains to be done.

Children's cognition of distance

Successful understanding of large-scale environments depends, in part, on acquiring four sorts of knowledge: knowledge of point, area and linear features; knowledge of the closeness of these features; knowledge of the relative location of these features; and, knowledge of how these features interlink with each other (Briggs, 1973). Each of these types of knowledge is itself dependent upon an appreciation of the distance separating the features from each other and from the individual. However, a number of studies have shown (Lowrey, 1970; Downs and Stea, 1977; Pocock and Hudson, 1978) that there is often a considerable difference between *objective*, real-world distances and the *subjective* distances individuals carry around in their heads. Downs and Stea (1977) draw an important distinction between *cognitive* distance and *perceived* distance. Perceived distance is the distance people judge to exist between themselves and a visible object, and depends on the accuracy of the individual's *perception* of the visible object. Cognitive distance, in contrast, involves the judgement of distance between oneself and an object which is out of view or not now visible. Here the accuracy of the distance estimation depends on the spatial information stored in the mind.

Initial interest in children's cognition of distance was largely based on the assumption that mental representations of space comprised information not unlike that contained in maps. It therefore followed that these schemata, like maps, would possess a *scale* by which the physical world was transformed for storage and retrieval in the memory (Canter, 1977). If these transformations could be uncovered an insight would be gained not only into the child's cognitive map but also into his/her general environmental competence.

Various methods have been used to investigate cognitive distance. Some studies have asked for direct estimates of physical distance (Lee, 1970; Matthews, 1981); others have sought the time taken to walk particular routes (Herman *et al.*, 1983); some have investigated shortest travel distances or 'crow-flight' routes (Briggs, 1973; Lowrey, 1970); whereas others have required children to make scaled assessments about a large-scale environment by placing markers at appropriate distances apart on a featureless model base (Anooshian and Wilson, 1977; Siegel and Schadler, 1977). Baird (1979) has used multidimensional scaling to explore the accuracy of distance estimation. He chose a set of target places within a large-scale environment, familiar to his subjects, and then asked his respondents to estimate the distances between all possible pairs of targets. Multidimensional scaling enabled Baird to convert the data into a two-dimensional map.

However, in the course of such experimentation there has been a growing realization that distance estimates are frequently subject to distortions and errors and as such constitute an imperfect means for exploring children's cognitive maps. The various factors which may be responsible for these distortions are only beginning to be systematically identified. They include not only methodological issues, but also characteristics which relate to both the environment and perceiver.

Methodological issues

A number of studies have shown that children's competence to judge cognitive distances depends upon the methodology employed. For example (Matthews 1981), I compared the ability of a sample of 11- to 18-year-olds to estimate the physical distance and walking time to nine well-known locations in Leamington Spa, from three different starting positions. In both test conditions, all age groups were able to reproduce the relative order of places with a high degree of accuracy, but the time estimates were much less accurate than those of physical distance. Patterns of overestimation were common. The general trend was for shorter distances to be greatly overestimated in relation to objective distances, and for the degree of exaggeration to diminish as real distances increased. Lowrey (1970) noticed a similar patterning with a sample of adults. He suggests that overestimation of such magnitude arises with shorter distances because of the efforts needed to start a journey and the problems individuals face in overcoming inertia. I also found that in the case of the physical distance estimates only, older children were significantly better than their juniors, which suggested a sharpening of environmental imagery with age.

Other methods, too, are problematic. 'Crow-flight' distance, for example, is an abstraction which individuals rarely experience, requiring a sophisticated grasp of spatial relationships, well beyond the capabilities of most children (Canter, 1977), while estimating shortest travel distance is not independent of mode of transport. For example, Herman et al. (1984) have shown that children often confuse duration estimates with distance cues. Spatial modelling also has its pitfalls. Changes of scale are especially onerous for the very young, often suppressing absolute competencies. For example, Cohen et al. (1979) asked children aged 6 and 11 years to estimate the distances between six items of furniture in an unfamiliar and familiar setting. The younger children could as easily reconstruct either setting as the older children, but they were significantly less accurate when the task involved rescaling. The importance of task demands on performance has been clearly demonstrated by Cohen et al. (1980). They noted that when the nature of the training and that of the testing procedures were not congruent, such as when the training involved walking and the testing did not, there was a greater tendency for younger children to overestimate distances.

Furthermore, Cadwallader (1979) has shown that an individual's ability to estimate distances not only varies according to the chosen methodology, but also is seldom consistent when employing a particular scaling procedure. In his tests, Cadwallader frequently found that distance judgements were subject to both *intransitive* and *non-commutative* errors. In the first case, he observed that his subjects were quite likely to assess that distance 1 was longer than 2, distance 2 was longer than 3, but distance 3 was longer than 1; whereas in the second case, subjects often estimated that the distance from A to B was different from B to A. These errors led Cadwallader to suggest that individuals' cognitive representations of large-scale environments rarely show the mathematical properties of metric space and as such constitute highly complex, personal geographies.

The diversity of methodology makes comparison of results very difficult. None the less, a number of broad hypotheses have emerged about the variables that shape cognitive distance in adults and children.

Environment-related variables

A factor which has been shown to affect performance is *directness*. Sadalla and Magel (1980) found that a group of young adults estimated a 200 ft path with seven turns to be longer than the same distance on a two-turn path. This difference could not be attributed to the amount of time subjects took to walk the different paths as there was no significant difference in travel times. In two further experiments, the subjects were asked to assess distances along a 185 ft path with two or seven turns and a 140 ft path with three or five turns. Even in this latter instance, where the paths differed by only two angles, subjects consistently estimated that the path with greater number of turns was longer. Findings such as these and by others (Thorndyke, 1981; Kahl *et al.*, 1984) on the *angularity effect* lend support to Sadalla and Staplin's (1980a; 1980b) concept of an *information storage model*. These authors reasoned that because paths through the environment with numerous attributes contain more information for potential storage in memory than paths with fewer attributes, distance estimates should increase as a function of the number of attributes. However, when Herman *et al.* (1986) tested the ability of second, fourth and sixth graders to estimate distances along paths with none, two, four and eight turns they found little support for this model. Distance judgements did not differ significantly for paths containing numerous turns relative to paths containing fewer or no turns. They concluded that the route angularity effect could not be considered a robust phenomenon and that more research on the subject was needed.

Apart from turns, others (Kosslyn *et al.*, 1974; Cohen and Weatherford, 1980; 1981; Newcombe and Liben, 1982) have shown how environmental barriers, such as walls and fences, distort children's and adults' distance estimates. For example, Cohen *et al.* (1978) noted how the presence of hills and buildings resulted in overestimated distance judgements for 9- and 10-year-olds and adults. When these features were absent an opposite effect was observed. Similarly, Herman *et al.* (1984) found that the number of objects encountered along a route, which they termed environmental 'clutter', had a tendency to increase distance estimates. These results suggest that the *functional distance* of places has a considerable effect on children's distance judgements.

An additional intervening factor is *direction*. From North American research it was found that subjects overestimated distances towards the city centre (Golledge *et al.*, 1969; Briggs, 1973). Curiously, this result has not been replicated elsewhere. Lee in Cambridge (1962) and Dundee (1970), Heinemeyer (1967) in Amsterdam and Lamy (1967) in Paris, all found that distances towards the central city were underestimated. Some explanation for this may be found in another hypothesis about cognitive distance, that is, distance estimates depend on the perceived *attractiveness* of a place. As Rapoport (1976) suggests, in North American society there is a tendency to think of the downtown area as a place to be avoided, whereas the city centre in European life is an area of positive attraction.

Person-related variables

There are a number of factors relating to the individual which influence distance cognition. *Age* is obviously important, particularly in young children where increasing age is reflected in more accurate distance estimation, as well as a growing awareness of a wider number of locations (Siegel, 1977; Cohen *et al.*, 1979; Matthews, 1981; 1984a, 1987a).

Less clear cut are the effects of *sex* on distance cognition. Few studies have compared boys and girls in distance estimation tasks. Instead evidence is based upon how boys and girls perform on spatial representation exercises in general. In this context, few sex contrasts are evident before the middle years of childhood (Saegart and Hart, 1978; Evans, 1980), from which time boys often outperform girls (Matthews, 1986b; 1986c; 1987a). These differences seem little to do with biological factors, but are more likely to be related to the growing home ranges and broadening environmental experiences of boys compared to girls (see Chapter 9). Equally tenuous is the effect of *socio-economic status*. Generally speaking, individuals from upper status, professional groups tend to show a better appreciation of distance than other groups, possibly because of their broader personal contacts and wider transactions with space (Orleans, 1973). However, even here the evidence is mixed. Appleyard (1976) has shown how, in Venezuela, the lower status groups have better city-wide knowledge than their upper status counterparts, because they travelled more than the well-off who tended to remain within their exclusive suburbs.

A person's *attitudes* and feelings towards an environment have been shown to influence recall. In studies with adults, Parr (1966; 1969) and Gustke and Hodgson (1980) noted that distances along routes considered to be pleasant and full of *interest* were judged to be shorter than distances along paths with fewer events. Cohen and Cohen (1982) have demonstrated a similar effect with children. They showed that the *type* of activity children engage in, as they walk a route, affects their estimates of distance. When children enjoy and see a purpose in an activity which involves movement through space their judgement of distance is heightened. In an 'interact-linked' activity undertaken along a novel route, whereby a set of items needed to write and post a letter were laid out in a linear sequence, children were better able to estimate distances than in a condition where the activity had seemingly no particular end purpose. Also, in situations where the acquisition task was passive, third- and sixth-grade children have been found to misjudge distances (Cohen *et al.*, 1980), especially compared to other similarly aged groups whose more active experiences apparently led to much closer estimations.

A further hypothesis relates to *familiarity*, whereby distance estimates are said to improve with length of exposure to an environment. Support comes from Anooshian and Siegel (1985) who showed that young children, resident in a test neighbourhood for at least six months, were more accurate in giving direction estimates requiring spatial inferences along a familiar route than along an unfamiliar one. Herman and Siegel (1978) and Siegel *et al.* (1979) have also shown that repeated exposure to an environment facilitates the acquisition of more accurate spatial knowledge. However, a number of studies cast doubt upon this relationship (Acredolo *et al.*, 1975; Anooshian and Young, 1981). For example, Cohen *et al.* (1979) compared the interlocation distance estimates of first and fifth graders in a novel classroom environment and a familiar school library. Although older children were the most accomplished in either setting, both age groups performed best across tasks when estimating distances in the novel context. These findings, taken together with those on the importance of congruent activity outlined above, lead Cohen and Cohen (1985) to suggest that familiarity of an environment may not be as critical to children's spatial construction as the type of interaction with a place.

In summary, as Cadwallader (1979) argues, it seems unlikely that there exists a simple relationship between subjective and objective distance. Instead, many factors contribute to distortions and errors in children's distance cognition. Spencer *et al.* (1989) point out that so much ingenuity and energy has gone into disclosing distortions and errors of various kinds, that researchers have seemingly forgotten to ask under what circumstances children make use of such estimates. They argue that in any navigational or route-following task, knowing whether a place is ahead or behind and its relative distance away, is probably sufficient information. Similarly, 'the child may in practice only need approximate and relative distance estimates in order to be able to make efficient choices between destinations to be visited' (p. 128). Accordingly, they suggest that distance estimate exercises are more interesting in terms of how they inform about processes of environmental learning rather than their products *per se*.

Summary

The nature of knowledge acquisition in spatial learning remains largely unresolved. Although there seems common agreement that the components of spatial knowledge comprise landmarks, routes and configurational properties, how children come to understand and use such information for route-learning, wayfinding and distance estimation has not been firmly established. However, from studies of children's searching capabilities it would appear that these sorts of skill do not suddenly spring up in middle childhood. From an early age children appear to be inquisitive about their everyday surroundings and keen to explore their broadening range of habitats. Environmental transactions of this kind provide a burgeoning store of experiential information upon which children can draw on future occasions. Cognitive psychologists frequently refer to spatial information stored in memory as *schemata*. Brewer and Treyens (1981) speculate that there are five ways in which schemata may influence environmental recall and memory for places:

1. They can determine what objects are looked at and encoded into memory.
2. They can act as a framework for new information.
3. They can provide schema-based information which becomes integrated with episodic information.
4. They can guide the retrieval process.
5. They can determine what information is to be communicated as output.

Minsky (1975) suggests that environmental learning is essentially a schema-based process occurring over time which involves collecting evidence, filling in details, deducing and interpreting on the basis of existing knowledge, expectations and goals. He hypothesizes that this complex process can take place rapidly because schemata develop in memory which correspond to common environments. *Information slots*, or variables in the internal structure of the schema which have not been filled with perceptual information, are filled by default assignments based on stereotypic expectations derived from past experience. Although supported by studies in room-sized environments (Kuipers, 1975; Brewer and Treyens, 1981), notions such as these have been largely untested in real-world, large-scale settings. It would seem that other than a common acceptance that environmental knowledge comes about through a complex interaction between organism and environment, how children become skilful environmental actors has yet to be conclusively explained.

8

Children's use of maps

A particular kind of environmental skill is the ability to understand space when represented in a two-dimensional manner or map form. In the context of this discussion maps are broadly defined to include all 'vertical' representations of large-scale space, whether cartographic in nature, such as plans and charts, or iconic in form, such as aerial photographs. By setting mapping in a broad base we are able to capture the essential function of a map, that is, 'rendering the experience of space comprehensible' (Downs, 1985, p. 325). Whatever its specific purpose, the map as a representation must evoke reality. In order to do so, for most map-making four questions need to be asked (Downs and Stea, 1977):

1. What are we interested in representing (*purpose*)?
2. What viewpoint or perspective are we taking (*perspective*)?
3. At what scale is the representation (*scale*)?
4. How do we construct the representations (*symbolisation*)?

Decisions on each of these four questions lead to a set of rules for map-making. Successful map interpretation, on the other hand, demands an ability to understand how space is reshaped by such decision-making. In this chapter we will examine three aspects of mapping ability: first, the remarkable skill of infants to comprehend various iconic media, despite having no previous experience of such stimuli and with only limited experience of large-scale environments; secondly, the genesis of map-using ability and map-reading; and thirdly, the capacity of children of different ages to learn about mapping skills.

Mapping ability of very young children

The work of Piaget and his fellow constructivists has had a considerable bearing upon contemporary educational practice, especially with regard to the way in which young children are introduced to maps and mapping tasks. We have reviewed Piaget's developmental framework in Chapter 4. In this section we will focus on the way Piaget's theory has been interpreted with regard to

children's mapping capabilities. According to Piaget, children's spatial development progresses through three distinct stages, with each stage associated with
particular mapping skills. This conclusion was derived through experiments
which tested the ability of children to see space from different perspectives. In
one of these, Piaget and Inhelder (1956) constructed a three-dimensional
model of three mountains, which they set on a table. A child was seated at one
side of the table and a doll was placed alternatively at each of the other three
sides. After each placement the child was shown a series of pictures representing the mountain as seen from a different viewpoint and asked to select the
picture that corresponded to the doll's view. Children between 4 and 7 years of
age typically attributed their own perspective to that of the doll; children aged 7
and 8 years appeared aware of perspectives other than their own, but operated
imperfectly on these; and children aged 9 and 10 years generally gave correct
answers. The errors made by children in the first stage were described as
'egocentric', and these tended to decrease with age. Evidence of this kind
suggested to Piaget and Inhelder that very young children were incapable of
seeing the world in other than egocentric terms and would not be able to
understand any perspective that they had not experienced. It therefore followed
that very young children, especially those under 7 years, would have difficulty
with maps, since these not only provide a non-egocentric view of large-scale
space, but also their aerial dimension was beyond the experience of most
children.

In another influential experiment Piaget and Inhelder (1956) showed
children a model-village, made up of an arrangement of streets, houses, a
church, trees, etc., and then asked them to reproduce it by either making their
own model or by drawing it. Children aged younger than 7 years were found
incapable of complete and accurate reconstruction by either means, most only
managing to reproduce small clusters of some of the elements. Between the
ages of 7 and 9 years, whilst children were able to replicate the model with
consistency, they frequently distorted the distances between elements. Not until
the ages of 9 and 10 years were children able to draw an accurate reconstruction. Further signs of 'Euclidean' development came at about 11 to 12 years
when many children capably made a small-scale plan of the overall
arrangement.

Taken together, the results of these and other similar experiments have had
far-reaching consequences, not only in relation to how children are introduced
to map work in schools, but also to educational research on spatial coordination
in general. These are itemized by Spencer et al. (1989):

1. There has been a profound reluctance to introduce map work to children
   aged less than 7 years in the primary school curriculum. Children of this age
   are regarded as being in the topological stage of development and so
   incapable of seeing the world in non-egocentric ways. In addition, concepts
   such as scale and grid-referencing are regarded as too difficult for the young

mind and so are reserved until children reach the Euclidean stage of development, usually coinciding with the early years of secondary schooling.

2. There has been virtually no educational research on the spatial skills of children aged less than 7 years simply because map work is regarded as inappropriate for children with little more than topological spatial understanding.

3. Work with older children has often been interpreted from a Piagetian perspective, with the consequence that their spatial skills and capabilities have frequently been underestimated.

There is now a growing body of opinion which is critical of Piagetian interpretation, although its full impact is still to be felt on the school curriculum (see Chapter 12). Critics of Piaget suggest that we should be extremely cautious in recognizing both stages and ages of development. One of the reasons for young children's underperformance of tasks of spatial comprehension is the way in which the test material has been presented. Researchers such as Huttenlocher and Presson (1973), Kurdek (1978) and Newcombe (1985) have all shown that by using altered methodologies, which are more appropriate to the everyday experiences of children, the very young do not necessarily view the world as egocentrically as Piaget suggests. For as Fishbein *et al.* (1972) point out, if young children find it difficult to deal with the world of the hypothetical and are more comfortable with the world of the concrete it seems unreasonable to ask them questions about how a doll would see a view or how a doll would take a photograph. Dolls cannot do either (!) and so any 'methods which employ dolls instead of people should prove more difficult for these children' (p. 32).

To get at the first appearance of cognitive mapping in children or to uncover its subsequent development are very difficult research tasks. We have seen already that many procedures unwittingly require young children to carry out tasks which demand motor-skills and levels of eye–hand coordination which they have not fully developed. As a result, these techniques of assessment have often, and unfortunately, intervened between environmental knowledge and its depiction. Yet, some of the most convincing evidence of very young children possessing relatively complex cognitive mapping skills has come from the work of geographers who have used aerial photographs to test spatial capability (Blaut *et al.*, 1970; Blaut and Stea, 1969; 1974). An aerial photograph is related to a drawn map in many ways. For example, they both share the same structure and function, and the operation of decoding is similar to map-reading. At the time of testing, these experiments flew in the face of conventional wisdom, in that it was firmly believed by educators that children would not be capable of aerial photograph interpretation before the age of 10 years.

Two findings are important in the context of such an assertion. First, Blaut and Stea have shown that children as young as 3-years-old are capable of interpreting aerial photographs and that the development of this ability seems complete before the age of 9 years. These skills go beyond just simple recognition and basic interpretation. For example, 'First-grade children can identify houses and roads, trace them, name the shapes drawn on the tracing (after the photo has been removed), color code the shapes, and finally, draw a pencil route over roads connecting two widely separated houses' (Blaut and Stea, 1971, p. 389). Photo-interpretation ability of this kind suggested to Blaut and Stea that young children must possess a broad range of spatial and mapping skills they were supposedly incapable of performing. These include rotation, perspective-taking, orientation, reduction from three-dimensions to two, an appreciation of scale and abstraction and symbolization (in that the features shown on the aerial photographs were in black and white). What is of additional interest, is that these are the key processes for map-reading and map-making outlined at the start of this section.

Secondly, photo-interpretation ability in children appears to be independent of culture, education or location. When Stea and Blaut (1973) tested a group of Puerto Rican children, they found a level of interpretation which was comparable to their mainland counterparts, despite a culture in which there was significantly less visual media. Also, Puerto Rican children did not perform any differently with photographs of their own community, nor did urban children perform better on urban images compared to rural children and vice versa.

Blaut and Stea explain their findings in the context of children's toy play. Between the ages of 3 years and 5 years, children show a growing interest in modelling the environment. Through their play with miniature cars and buildings and so on, they develop important experiences of seeing the world from above. As children move through and above their miniature world, they gain perspectives that would otherwise be impossible. Model play of this kind appears to be a universal source of enrichment, 'it is almost as if a *drive* exists for experiences related to cognitive mapping, which, in children, is partly satisfied by toy manipulation' (Downs and Stea, 1977, p. 192). Together with surrogates for direct experience, like television, magazines and story-telling, 'toy play provides "as if" experience for the child who cannot move rapidly around a town, nor climb into an airplane and actually view the world from above' (p. 192). Blaut (1991) proposes that young children's macroenvironmental mapping behaviour is best conceptualized as a natural ability, that is, a skill which emerges in infants without teaching. Young children appear to be ready to understand the geographical structure of their world and this readiness may be part of a much broader structuring process that either appears in the first months of life or is more likely to be innate. We will examine the efficacy of Blaut's model in Chapter 10.

Confirmation of the ability of very young children to interpret aerial photographs comes from Spencer *et al.*'s (1980) study of 3-year-olds attending a British nursery school. In Piagetian terms these children were in a pre-operational stage of development and yet few found problems in interpreting photographs comparable with those used by Blaut and Stea. In this study, all thirty children, without guidance or prompting, interpreted the photographs in environmental terms by referring to roads, houses and trees rather than geometrical patterns of lines and shapes. Children were also able to use recognizable features on the photograph, such as roads, as contextual cues to infer other elements, such as cars. Interestingly, many of the children referred to the railway lines on one of the photographs by the proprietory name of the toy tracks they played with at nursery school. This sort of evidence suggested to Spencer 'that Blaut and Stea may well be right to stress the importance of toy play in the construction of geographical images' (Spencer and Darvizeh, 1981b, p. 23).

Children's ability to understand satellite images as well as vertical aerial photographs has been studied in two New Zealand primary schools by McGee (1982). He found that when 6-year-olds were shown a Landsat photograph of New Zealand, over half were able to name their country and many were able to identify mountains on the image. When studying an aerial photograph of their city most children showed considerable ability at finding not only where their school was located, but also at locating well-known landmarks.

However, whilst this sort of evidence casts considerable doubt upon the efficacy of Piaget's developmental claims, others review these findings with caution. Piché (1977), for example, argues that most of the decoding tasks outlined above are relatively straightforward, based upon the principles of object perception rather than the higher-level skills of encoding and reconstruction, which are the basis of mapping. To Piché, children's ability to find their way in a neighbourhood does not mean that they have completed their representation of it. By the same token, the ability to recognize simple elements from a photograph, with no specific reference to place, does not mean that children have a complete grasp of spatial comprehension. Downs et al. (1988) make a similar observation following their questioning of forty 3–6-year-olds about the contents, functions and forms of a set of place representations, including aerial photographs and maps. The representations varied in familiarity of place, viewing angle, colour and symbolization. Whilst most children could confidently recognize a map in terms of its form ('that's a map') and general content ('states and stuff'), few children were able to characterize aerial photographs in other than content terms ('lots of buildings' but never a 'photo') (p. 687). Significantly, they also found that whilst both representations were understood as showing places in general, 'neither elicited uniformly reasonable understanding of particular places' (p. 687). Consequently, a road map of Pennsylvania was variously interpreted as 'part of Africa' and 'California, Canada, the West and the North Coast', whereas a black-and-white aerial photograph (1:12,000) of downtown Chicago was described as 'the USA' and 'the whole world'. In contrast to the work of Blaut and others above, the findings of this study suggest that the ability to understand the 'holistic' nature of iconic and graphic representations develops slowly and in complex ways. Children may be able to distinguish place elements on various kinds of media as young as 3-years-old, but they find great difficulty in piecing these components together to provide a composite understanding of place.

The genesis of map-reading and map-using ability

Despite a burgeoning body of evidence which has shown that children aged less than 7 years can make sense of iconic stimuli, relatively little work has been carried out with the same age group in order to establish their map-using and map-reading skills. A formative investigation on young children's understanding of maps was undertaken by Bluestein and Acredolo (1979). They asked a group of children aged 3 years to 5 years to identify and find a toy hidden in a room using a simplified map. Children were shown on the map where the toy was hidden. Children saw the map either in the room or outside of it and the map was either correctly oriented to the room or rotated relative to it by 180°. Of the children who saw the map in the room at the correct orientation, half the 3-year-olds, three-quarters of the 4-year-olds and all of the 5-year-olds, managed to find the toy. However, whilst the position of the map inside or outside the room did not affect performance, only those aged 5 years were able to use the map correctly when the map was rotated. When children were given an additional instruction with the map held vertically, few had difficulty in coping with this change of perspective.

These results suggested to Bluestein and Acredolo that the analysis of map-reading ability in young children is divisible into two parts. The first is the ability to differentiate and interpret cartographic symbols, and this skill was evident in all children. The second is the ability to superimpose a map on space and, in contrast to the above, this skill was found to develop rapidly with age. Taken together, what these results reveal is that even very young children are capable of rudimentary map-reading using graphic stimuli, and that this skill is already evident at the age of 3 years.

More recently, Blades and Spencer (1987a; 1987b) have carried out a series of experiments with a group of 3- and 4-year-olds in order to examine their map-use capabilities. In the first experiment they used a room containing a selection of furniture and six hollow bricks, which served as a hiding place for a small toy. Children were shown the location of the hidden toy in a scaled model of the room (a surrogate map) and asked to go into the actual room and find the toy. Each child was asked to go into the room on six occasions, always to a different hiding place. Out of a total of ninety-six trials, the children went straight to the hidden toy on eighty-three occasions. The few mistakes that occurred were largely blamed on overexuberance, with children running into the room without proper regard to the model. These results impressed on Blades and Spencer that young children seem to be able to use maps and models of small environments to locate a particular place, and they appear to find such 'treasure hunting' games comparatively easy and enjoyable.

These findings led Blades and Spencer to speculate that if young children could use maps to find particular places, they might also be able to use maps to follow a route. In order to test for such capability, the researchers set out a series of coloured buckets in the nursery playground. Maps at a scale of 1:50 were drawn of the layout and each map showed a route, either between bucket to bucket or along paths between the buckets. Children were asked to carry a map and walk through the playground following the marked route. Two groups of seven children with mean ages of 4 years 1 month and 4 years 8 months took part in the exercise. Blades and Spencer found a very significant difference in the performance of the two groups. Out a total of seventeen different routes, the younger children managed a mean success rate of 4.1, compared to the much better mean score of 13.7 for the older group. Blades and Spencer note that the younger children often seemed confused about the purpose of the map as a route-guide, most walking straight to the target bucket. However, the 'fact that older children were successful is an indication that map use is within the capability of 4-year-olds'.

In both of the experiments above the children could see the whole environment at the same time. In practice, maps are more likely to be used on occasions when a route is to be followed through an environment which is not completely visible. In order to see whether young children could use a map in this way Blades and Spencer designed a chalk maze which was 25 metres long, with screens strategically placed to hinder children's view across the total route. In addition, cardboard boxes, located behind the screens, served as 'roadblocks' and their position was chosen so that children would only see them after making a route choice decision at a junction. Six variations of the standard maze were designed. Maps were drawn at a scale of 1:100 to show the layout of the maze. A total of sixty children were tested, banded into five age groups spanning 3 years to 6 years (3.8–4.2; 4.4–4.10; 5.0–5.5; 5.6–6.0; all 6.2) and every child was asked to use the six different maps of the maze. None of the children had any previous experience of map work.

The children's performances were compared against chance. Each route involved three T-junctions and so in the six variations of the maze a child was scored out of a possible eighteen correct choices: a score of nine or less suggesting a high incidence of chance. Blades and Spencer found that only the youngest of the five groups performed no better than chance. The majority of children aged 4.4 years and above were able to use the maps effectively, most avoiding the paths that were blocked. In general, children's performances improved with age.

The results of these experiments provide further support to those who argue that Piaget's developmental sequence considerably underestimates the environmental potential of the very young. What Blades and Spencer have shown is that untrained children as young as 3-years-old can use maps to locate objects in small environments and that from about the age of 4.4 years most children can use a map to follow a route.

Research into older children's map ability has been more extensive. The concern has been to assess how children respond to various properties of maps rather than to map use in general. Walker (1978; 1980), for example, examined the ability of 100 children, aged 5 years to 9 years, to understand the concepts of relative length (scale), orientation and symbolization as represented on a map of their playground. He found that whilst 6-year-olds showed an understanding of map symbols, few managed to grasp the basis of orientation and scale. However, 8-year-olds were confident in all three skills and were capable of using a map to good effect in an outdoor setting. Gerber (1981a) has suggested that children appear to reach higher levels of achievement when the distinct elements of a map are introduced separately. They seem to be able to handle one element of a map at a time, but they have difficulty in dealing with several elements simultaneously. We will now review studies which have focused on how children respond to different mapping elements. An excellent review of children's map use is further provided by Spencer *et al.* (1989).

Orientation

The ability of 6- and 8-year-olds to orientate a map rotated at 90° and 180° to the landscape was investigated by Presson (1982). He found that children were much more successful at 90° degree rotations, whereas when the task became more difficult they tended to rely on landmarks for navigation. Piagetians would explain this type of error in terms of egocentrism. However, Spencer *et al.* (1989) suggest that difficulties of this kind are better explained in terms of children making a false assumption that the given maps were correctly oriented in the first place, an error of judgement which is more likely when a 180° rotation is called for. Levine *et al.* (1984) have noted that adults frequently make similar mistakes when attempting to read 'you-are-here' maps displayed for public view. When Blades and Spencer (1986) taught 4-year-olds how to orientate simple maps, the majority assimilated the skill with little difficulty and were able to apply the strategy to different situations.

Scale

The idea of scale appears more difficult for children to grasp. A distinction needs to be noted between awareness of relative sizes, which Walker (1978) and Gerber (1981b) indicate can be appreciated by 8-year-olds and the measuring of scale. Bartz (1970) and Carswell (1971), for example, have shown that correct scaling, whether drawing everything exactly in proportion or reading off a distance on a conventional map, is a problem that many 10- and 11-year-olds continue to encounter. A similar conclusion was reached by Towler and Nelson (1968). They showed a group of 6- to 12-year-old children a model farm. The children were then presented with a quarter-sized board representing the farm and a set of shapes representing the farm buildings. The shapes were produced at five different scales. Children were asked to select and place on the board the appropriate scaled shape. Only the oldest children managed successfully to complete the task, which convinced Towler and Nelson that children do not develop a full concept of scale before the age of 10 years. However, the fact that very young children can interpret maps and use maps for navigational purposes, as described above, suggests that even 4-year-olds have a basic understanding of reduction and relative proportion, which are an implicit part of scaling.

Coordinates

Until recently, the limited research on children's understanding of position and direction on prepared maps suggested that only children aged 10 and 11 years were capable of using all-figure grid-referencing (Catling, 1979a), although 7- and 8-year-olds could use simple letter–figure grids (Bartz, 1970). These assumptions were largely based on Piaget *et al.*'s (1960) experiments with young children. They provided children with two sheets of paper of the same size and a ruler. On one sheet of paper a point was marked. Children were asked to copy this point exactly onto the other sheet. Only children aged over 8 years were able to do this with any success. In this experiment no coordinate structure was provided and so children were left to locate the point through their own resources. However, in a similar test, in which a simple grid square system was provided, Towler (1970) was able to observe that children aged less than 8 years seldom used these reference lines in any case.

Two recent studies cast doubt upon the claim that young children are unable to grasp spatial coordinates. In the first, Somerville and Bryant (1985) showed children a solid square board that was then placed over two rods: one rod protruded from left to right on the underside of the board, so defining a horizontal coordinate, whereas the other protruded from top to bottom on one side of the board, so defining a vertical coordinate. Children were asked to extrapolate where they thought the rods crossed under the board, by choosing from one of four positions marked on the board's surface. It was found that children aged as young as 6.5 years performed the task with considerable success, and that even some 4.5-year-olds were able to make reasonable estimates. These findings led Somerville and Bryant to assert that children are capable of using spatial coordinates at a much younger age than Piagetians suggest, and that this skill is within the grasp of many 4-year-olds.

In the second study, Spencer *et al.* (1989) provided children aged 4–6 years with a board incorporating sixteen sunken squares in a 4×4 layout. Each square contained a picture, hidden by a cardboard cover. The board was covered by a simple alpha-numeric coordinate system, with numbers (1–4) defining the vertical coordinates and letters (a–d) defining the horizontal coordinates. The grid was arranged so that the points of intersection coincided with the midpoint of each cell. Children were given a grid reference (for example, 2a or 4b) and a copy of the correct picture and asked to uncover the appropriate card on the board to see if the pictures matched. Most 6-year-olds managed the task without difficulty, although 4-year-olds were less successful. However, when the alpha-numeric grid was replaced with a colour coded system, the grid reference in this case was a card with two colours on it defining the two axes of the grid, half of the 4-year-olds and the majority of the 5- and 6-year-olds completed the test successfully. This suggested to Spencer *et al.* that in the first experiment it was the numbering and lettering system which had held back performance, both demanding skills in which young children are rarely proficient, and not the concept of the grid. The results of these two studies are important in that they provide evidence which challenges the conventional wisdom of the classroom. Given appropriate methods and materials children as young as 4-years-old appear to be competent in tasks requiring spatial co-ordination.

Symbols

According to Catling (1979a), the fact that very young children can use a prepared map to find a hidden 'treasure' does not show that children have developed full mapping capabilities. Rather, all 'it indicates is that in a simple, practical situation, where the objective is clear, like finding a "treasure", they can use a map effectively, being able to note a symbol and locate the feature it shows' (p. 293). This is not the same level of skill as being able to identify 'a homogeneous grouping on a conventional map'. To achieve this, three levels of operation are involved: first, the symbols need to be perceived and understood, and recognized for what they represent; secondly, the specific elements within the map for which the search is being made need to be abstracted from the 'ground'; thirdly, the pattern that they form needs to be coordinated and their configuration appreciated (Catling, 1979a). Both Satterley (1964) and Heamon (1966) have suggested that these skills may well be beyond the capability of children younger than 10 or 11 years of age. Thus, Catling surmises, it is likely that younger children will find difficulty in extracting information from maps to which they cannot apply direct experience.

Even when given a map of a familiar place, Dale (1971) has shown that young children are often unable to recognize their own area. He showed forty children, aged 6 to 11 years, a map of their village, at a scale of 1:5,000. Only fourteen children were able to recognize its location. When provided with an aerial photograph of the village, at the same scale, children preferred the photograph to the map for simple recognition tasks. This suggested to Dale that young children's ability to observe detail more readily on a photograph than a map arose because the photograph retained an image of reality, albeit at a different perspective, which was obscured by the abstractly presented patterns and symbols emphasized on maps.

Yet, in contrast to Dale, Blades and Spencer (1987b) have shown that children as young as 4–6 years of age can readily understand relatively complex maps and cope with abstract symbols. They showed a group of 108 children a large map, drawn in colour, of an imaginary urban area. Altogether there were ten different symbols represented on the map (road, river, park, roundabout, bridge, school, church, railway, station and house), although there was no key to help decode the symbols. None of the children had been trained in map interpretation and none were familiar with mapping conventions. On testing, they found that 4-year-olds were able to interpret at least half of the symbols and that by the age of 6 years most of the children were able to identify the majority of the symbols. The results of this experiment led Blades and Spencer to conclude 'that young children can appreciate a view of the world from above even when, as in the case with a map, the view is one that is conventionalized and includes symbols' (Spencer *et al.*, 1989).

These differences between the findings of Blades and Spencer on the one hand, and Satterley, Heamon and Dale on the other, may well arise because of differences in the maps used. Blades and Spencer provided a specially prepared map of 48×46 cm in size, on which the symbols had been specially crafted for ease of interpretation; roads were shown in grey, rivers in blue, parks in green and so on, and overall, there was little visual clutter. However, the others relied on Ordnance Survey maps and it may well be that the style of representation, the selectivity and the level of detail shown on these maps combined to create distracting 'noise' for the younger child. The success of other simplified maps in practical test situations reinforces this assessment. Also, when Bluestein and Acredolo (1979) and Walker (1978) tested young children's map use they did so in situations which involved movement with a map. Active manipulation of this sort seems to heighten young children's awareness of the relationship between map symbolization and the real world.

Downs *et al.* (1988) suggest some caution with regard to symbols which encourage literal interpretation. In their study, whilst children correctly identified on a map a river as water because it was blue and a road because it was grey, they interpreted a yellow coloured symbol depicting a built-up area as 'firecrackers' and an 'egg'. Also, an airplane symbolizing an airport was seen as a single airplane and many children suggested that once that airplane had flown away the symbol would not be needed on the map. Clearly, many children aged 6 years and under find it difficult to distinguish symbolic and literal representation.

Relief

An understanding of relative relief is a concept which young children find very difficult to make sense of in map form. The symbolic representation of relief on most maps is usually in the form of contour lines. Few studies have looked specifically at children's ability to understand relief maps. Sandford (1979) suggests why younger children in particular may find symbolization of this sort difficult to grasp. From studies with primary and secondary school children he shows that the concept of contour understanding comes about in three stages. First, children are only able to perceive contour patterns as being widely or closely spaced; secondly, with experience and practice, children begin to interpolate mentally the space between the contours and to see across them instead of along them, so that they become able to distinguish between convex and concave slopes, and between valley bottoms and hill tops; thirdly, children develop an ability to see from the contours that the elements which make up the terrain form patterns which constitute landform types. Boardman (1982) has shown, in a study of 336 children aged from 11 years to 14 years, that stages two and three above are not fully grasped until the middle years of secondary schooling and await other geographical skills, such as an appreciation of landscapes. However, Bale (1987) points out that relief elements are frequently represented in children's picture maps and plasticine models, and although their representations lack accuracy, primary-aged children are certainly familiar with notions of high–low, up–down, steep–gentle. He suggests that whilst the teaching of contour lines is best left out of the primary curriculum, the concept of relative relief can be incorporated into maps in other ways. For example, selected points can be marked with a plus (+) or a minus (−) to signify relative height or simple layer colouring can be used to designate land of varying height. However, although educational texts, like Bale's, report on the success of these methods, I know of no formal experiments assessing how children respond to different forms of relief symbolization.

Learning about maps

The traditional view of children's mapping capabilities, based largely on Piagetian expectations, is set out by Boardman (1983) (see Table 12.2). This guide, which has proved a valuable learning framework, suggests that mapping is best introduced after the age of 7 years, when children reach the projective stage of spatial development. According to Downs *et al.* (1988), at this age children should have a better grasp of *context*, an ability to recognize systematic interrelationships between components of a map; an understanding of *iconicity*, an appreciation that map components are analogues which are to be interpreted symbolically not literally; and some sense of *convention*, a realization that the graphic form of map components is arbitrary and thus neither inflexible nor inevitable. Boardman's contribution to map work is discussed in more detail in Chapter 12.

Not all share these views. Yet, despite a growing interest in map work in the primary curriculum (Mills, 1981; 1987), few studies have attempted to assess and compare alternative ways of introducing young children to mapping tasks. However, two studies are interesting in this respect. In an early experiment, Muir and Blaut (1969) compared the mapping skills of a group of 5- and 6-year-old children who had been introduced to map work by means of aerial photographs with another, similar aged, group who had been taught without these stimuli. In later mapping tests the former group outperformed the other. Blaut (1987a) has since argued that aerial photographs are key devices for 'connecting the child's natural mapping to school education in all macro-environmental subjects' (p. 32). Blaut believes that mapping skills can be taught at school-entering age. This can be done by working with 'black-and-white aerial photographs, tracing from these photographs, and then generalising or abstracting from iconic forms to map-signs' (p. 31). Another procedure involves the use of paper laid on the floor as a simulation of the surface of the world and toys placed on the paper as 'signs' for salient features like houses and cars. Blaut's ideas are based firmly on the premise that mapping is a natural skill, innately determined and akin to language development and so available to the very young. We will develop the educational implications of this perspective later in Part Four.

In another study, Atkins (1981) taught a group of 4- and 5-year-old children how to use maps, globes and compass directions. These children were then compared to another group, who had not received the same training, across a series of mapping tasks. The trained group were not only better in mapping skills immediately after the course, but also in tests a year later. The significance of these two studies is that they challenge the conventional wisdom of the classroom by demonstrating that it is possible to teach young children simple mapping strategies at ages well before those traditionally associated with map work.

Summary

A growing body of evidence suggests that children as young as 3-years-old are capable of performing rudimentary mapping tasks, especially those which rely upon iconic stimuli. To Blaut (1991) mapping behaviour in young children

appears to reflect a normal and early development of the ability and desire to use the imagination to construct a picture of very large places, making great creative use of fragmentary perceptual information which is integrated into the whole using a map-like (eye-in-the-sky looking down on the world) set of transformations: figurative rotation to an overhead perspective, reduction of scale, and interpretation of semantic meanings, some of this in exploratory behavior within the macroenvironment (the bits and edges of it which are accessible), some of it in behavior with models (toys) and other representations, some of it in speech, song, gesture, dance, and games. (p. 67)

The nativist underpinnings of Blaut's ideas directly confront the conventional wisdom of the classroom, whose roots are firmly set within the Piagetian tradition. If the true potential of children as environmental mappers is to be realized there seems to be a strong case to build map work into pre-school activities and the early school curriculum. These ideas are discussed further in Chapter 12.

9

The importance of sex-related factors to children's environmental competence

This chapter gives special consideration to the importance of sex-related factors to children's spatial and environmental skills. Many studies have drawn attention to the better performance of boys compared to girls across a broad range of spatial tasks. In this chapter we will discuss the nature of the issue, look at the timing and development of sex-contrasts, and review competing explanations for these differences.

The nature of sex-related variations in spatial and environmental skills

Both Harris (1978 and 1981) and Newcombe (1982) provide comprehensive reviews of studies which show that boys consistently perform better than girls on certain small-scale, laboratory tests designed to assess spatial ability. Sex differences of this kind have been highlighted in tasks involving the judgement of shapes, how they fit together, and the ability to rotate and manipulate form (Bergan *et al.*, 1971; Connor and Serbin, 1977; Connor *et al.*, 1978; Vandenberg and Kuse, 1979).

Others have demonstrated that these sex-related differences extend to how boys and girls are able to comprehend large-scale environments. For example, Siegel and Schadler (1977) have shown that when children aged between 4.5 and 6 years were asked to place model furniture in the correct position within a scaled reproduction of their classroom, boys were far more accurate than girls. I asked (Matthews 1987a), 166 children aged 6–11 years to draw a map of their home area, using three different stimulus response techniques: free-recall sketching and the interpretation of either a large-scale plan or a vertical aerial photograph. Strong, significant sex differences were found, both in relation to the quantitative accretion of environmental knowledge and in the qualitative manner that children were able to externalize about place. By the age of 11 years boys were able to draw maps broader in conception and more detailed in content than similar aged girls, and in terms of mapping ability and mapping accuracy a higher proportion of boys managed to reproduce the environment in a spatially coherent way. These sex differences are seen to persist, at least, into early adulthood. Working with college freshmen, Herman *et al.* (1979) found that after three weeks of residency on a campus, men were able to recall and to recognize from photographs many more buildings than women. Bettis (1974) has also shown that these sorts of sex differences are replicated in simple map-reading exercises. He tested 1,700 fifth grade children on skills such as the interpretation of map distances, the direction of river flow, knowledge of place names, etc., and out of the forty-nine questions boys outperformed girls on forty-two of these. Investigations of self-reported ratings of spatial competence confirm that women frequently admit difficulties in giving directions and following routes. For example, Thompson *et al.* (1980) asked college students 'How good is your sense of direction?' Men's self-assessments were significantly higher than women's. Furthermore, Kozlowski and Bryant (1977) have shown that self-ratings of this kind and performance are significantly related.

However, Cohen (1981) argues that some caution needs to be shown with respect to generalizations about male superiority in spatial skills, as sex-related differences on spatial tasks are not entirely independent of the nature of the diagnostic exercise. He found that boys tended to perform better only when the complexity of the task increased. On the basis of such findings Harris (1979; 1981) proposes that boys outperform girls on spatial tasks involving both *spatial orientation*, defined as 'the perception of position and configuration of objects in space, with the observer as a reference point', and *spatial visualization*, defined as the 'comprehension of imaginary movements of objects in three-dimensional space' (p. 88) with the observer removed from the stimulus. We will now examine at what age these sex differences in spatial skills first appear and whether they increase or decrease with age.

The timing of sex-related differences

According to Maccoby and Jacklin's (1974) influential review, sex-related variations in spatial skill become most profound with the coming of puberty and the onset of adolescence. They focused on studies which had tested children for both *visual, non analytic* and *visual, analytic spatial ability* and concluded that male advantages did not appear until the age of 13 or 14 years. However, Newcombe (1982) points out that this review was far from complete and that a number of studies by this time had suggested an earlier onset for male superiority. For example, Keogh (1971) had demonstrated that 8- and 9-year-old boys were more capable than girls in copying designs by walking, and several other studies (Witkin *et al.*, 1967; Wapner, 1968; Bergan *et al.*, 1971; Witkin *et al.*, 1971; Keogh and Ryan, 1971) had pointed to boys, as young as 7-years-old, excelling in a variety of spatial tasks.

Since this time a growing number of studies have revealed significant sex-related differences prior to adolescence. With respect to large-scale environments, both Siegel and Schadler (1977) and Herman and Siegel (1978) have shown that boys, whether in kindergarten, second grade or fifth grade, were likely to be more accurate than girls in constructing models of their classroom. In another study, Hart (1979) encouraged the 4–10-year-old children of 'Inavale' to construct models of their locality in order to assess their ability to represent the spatial relations of the large-scale environment beyond their homes. He found that the boys' 'maps' were significantly better organized as a whole and only a few girls managed to produce clusters of elements which were coordinated either in a positional or metric sense. I found (Matthews, 1984c; 1986c; 1987a), working in suburban Coventry that contrasts among my sample first became evident around the age of 8 years, from which time boys drew maps larger in area and more detailed in content than their girl counterparts.

However, Newcombe (1982) points out that the nature of the task has an important effect on performance. In studies of spatial representation not demanding reproduction and recall, sex-related differences are not consistently found in children younger than 13 years of age (Cohen et al., 1979; Allen et al., 1979; Cohen and Weatherford, 1980). I also found (Matthews 1987a; 1988) that male advantage was significantly affected by both the method of stimulus presentation and the nature of the environment to be recalled. For example, boys recalled their home area most vividly when prompted by an iconic stimulus, all children preferred free sketching to describe their route to school, and no sex differences of any consistent kind were found for the results derived by map interpretation. Morrison (1974) and Phillips and Noyes (1982) reported similar findings in their studies of adults' map-use abilities. As Fairweather (1976) comments, the male advantage appears most pronounced in tasks involving transformations of visual stimuli. Equally, when I asked my sample to draw maps of their journey-to-school, employing the stimulus techniques described above, statistical testing confirmed strong similarities between the performances of boys and girls throughout the age-span, with neither group recalling as much environmental detail as on their home area maps. This suggested to me that the way children encounter environments is crucial to their imagery. The habitual routine of a journey from home to school, which is shared by both boys and girls, provides a more passive imprint of the environment than that derived through free play within a neighbourhood.

The development of sex-related differences

Newcombe (1982) and Linn and Petersen (1985) draw attention to a large number of studies which suggest that small sex-related differences in spatial ability present in childhood increase somewhat in size with age. For example, both Droege (1967) and Flanagan et al. (1964) reported increases in the size of sex differences in spatial perception from the first to the last year of high school. Wilson et al. (1975) found that differences between male and female scores on a variety of mental rotation tests widened from the age of 14 years through to the late twenties. Bennett *et al.* (1974) and McGee (1979) both observed that boys excelled on spatial visualization and spatial orientation exercises and that their advantage increased with age. More recently, I noted that differences in the environmental capabilities of boys and girls, which opened up at the age of 8 years, were more profound by the age of 11 years (Matthews, 1986c; 1987a). From their review, Linn and Peterson (1985) go on to suggest that once sex differences of this kind become evident, especially those related to spatial perception and mental rotation, so they are likely to persist across the life span.

However, not all researchers arrive at these conclusions. For example, Porteus (1965) and Vandenberg and Kuse (1979) have found that sex differences on spatial tests remain relatively stable in adolescence and early adulthood. Whilst Nash (1979) argues that 'sex-related differences, emergent during adolescence' are 'age bound and ephemeral' rather than 'the beginning of lifelong, sex-defined differentiation' (p. 290). In summary, findings on the development of sex-related differences are very mixed and there is no consistent evidence to support growing differentials which continue into adulthood.

Explanations of sex-related differences in spatial and environmental skills

Three broad competing explanations can be recognized: genetic and hormonal, experiential and interactional. We will now examine these in turn.

Genetic and hormonal explanations

In general, these contend that differences in the organization of the brain of men and women, coupled with sex-differentiated effects of hormonal activity, are the root cause of sex differences in spatial ability. According to McGlone (1980) there is now a body of evidence which supports the notion that the male brain is more lateralized than that of the female. As a result of which, the right hemisphere of the male brain is given over more exclusively to visuo-spatial functions and the left hemisphere to oral and verbal functions, and this contrasts with the more bilateral organization of the female brain. McGuinness (1974; 1976a; 1976b) further contests that differential hormonal activity heightens male sensitivity to visual stimuli, so accentuating their cerebral advantage. Taking a wide amount of research into account, Harris (1981) proposes that a 'neurological program' for male spatial superiority would go as follows:

> Fetal testicular hormones act on an initially sexually undifferentiated nervous system so as to bring about sensitisation to visual input (presumably through brain

stem influence), earlier right-cerebral hemisphere development, and ultimately greater lateral separation of function with consequent enhancement of right-hemisphere functional efficiency. Thalamic and hippocampal differences may also be involved. (p. 111)

However, these views are by no means universally shared. Bryden (1979) and others (Willis *et al.*, 1979; Birkett, 1980), for example, take issue both with the notion of differential lateralization and its supposed effects on spatial ability. They show the evidence that McGlone reviewed was characterized more by a lack of striking sex differences and those that were found could be the product of how subjects approached their respective tasks, rather than genetic pre-disposition. In addition, critics like Harris (1981) and Kinsbourne and Hiscock (1978) point out that lateral specialization has always been behaviourally inferred from behavioural asymmetries rather than measured directly by neuroanatomical and neurophysiological indicators.

Experiential explanations

Proponents of this school of thought argue that different life experiences are sufficient to explain sex differences in spatial ability. Keating (1976), for example, suggests that sex-related differences in spatial ability arise because boys are often given greater encouragement to develop such ability through their toy and play activities. Parental influences are very important in this context. In a systematic count of the contents of the bedrooms of 1–6-year-old children, Rheingold and Cook (1975) found that boys had significantly more vehicles, sports equipment, toy animals, machines and educational materials, whereas girls had more dolls, dolls' houses and domestic toys. Also, Fagot (1978) observed that parents of 2-year-old children allowed boys to manipulate and explore objects more readily than girls. In this way, certain objects, toys and patterns of behaviour become defined in the child's eyes as *masculine or boyish* and others as *feminine or girlish*. In consequence, it is perhaps not surprising that Sears (1965), in an 'area usage' exercise for the sex-typing of 4-year-olds, noted that boys spent more time in that part of a large nursery school where blocks, wheel toys, and carpenter tools were found, in comparison to girls, who spent more of their time in areas given over to dolls' houses, cooking equipment and dressing-up. Similarly, in his developmental study of children's relation-ship to the physical environment, Hart (1979) found that boys modified the landscape more frequently than girls. For example, in creating settings for their play, boys built physical structures more often than girls. Girls also had houses, forts and so on, but they physically manipulated the environment much less. A number of studies has shown that sex differences in parental attitudes extend to social control beyond the home. Boys are more likely to be allowed to wander further afield from their homes, to explore more areas, to make greater use of space and in general, to spend more time playing outdoors (Coates and

Bussard, 1974; Harper and Sanders, 1975; Hart, 1979; van Vliet, 1983). In summarizing the findings of various studies on the early environmental experiences of children, Saegart and Hart (1978) note that girls appear to be more constrained, both in terms of their movements and in the nature of their manipulation of the environment. They suggest that whilst girls are being prepared for the home, boys are out practising their environmental skills.

The different amounts of self-directed spatial exploration and opportunities for free manipulation of the environment that seem to characterize girls and boys as they get older quite probably have serious consequences for the development of certain cognitive abilities. Among the first to suggest such a relationship were Munroe and Munroe (1971) in their Kenyan studies. They found that spatial ability was positively related to the distance which young children travelled from their home base, a finding which was replicated by Nerlove *et al.* (1971). In both cases it was found that Logoli boys, between the ages of 3 years and 7 years, who travelled further from their home on average than age-matched Logoli girls, were more skilful at certain tests requiring the capacity to perform a set of behaviours ordered sequentially in space, such as the spatial task of copying block patterns.

More recently, others have suggested that this sort of relationship extends to how children are able to cognize large-scale space. For example, Hart (1979) in his New England field studies found a positive relationship between accuracy and the extent of children's sketch maps and the limit of their home range, with boys outperforming girls in these exercises. I found (Matthews 1986c; 1987a; 1988), working in suburban Coventry, a positive relationship between home range behaviour and both information on place (mean number of elements per map) and awareness of place (the spatial spread of children's information surface) (see Figure 9.1). In either case boys were found to be the most confident and capable mappers, although, in general, those children who roamed furthest from their homes, regardless of sex, were the most skilled at environmental recall and representation. What is especially interesting about this study is that I found that the differences between the performances of boys and girls opened up at the time when boys were given greater sanction in their play activities. Up until the age of 8 years any differences between the responses of the sexes were small, but from this time onwards, boys revealed a broader appreciation of environmental artefacts, with their home area maps containing up to twice the amount of detail drawn by girls of the same age. These differences extended to the qualitative aspects of mapping as well. Boys showed a greater ability to represent space in a more sophisticated and integrated manner and at an earlier age than girls. For example, when describing their journey to school and home area some 7- and 8-year-old boys were able to employ planimetric drawing, a skill not grasped until much later by girls. By the age of 9 years none of the boys drew simple pictorial maps, whereas some 11-year-old girls continued to represent space in this way. Also, boys were found to be much more aware of spatial properties and of the relationship between

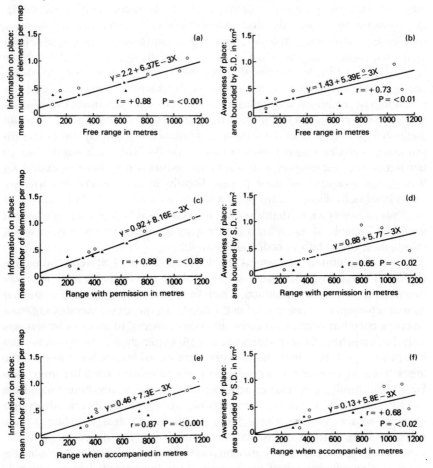

Figure 9.1   The relationship between home range and environmental cognition.
Boys: ○, girls: ▲

environmental elements than girls. From a young age, whether describing a familiar route or their neighbourhood, boys managed to reveal a grasp of place relatedness, many conveying an Euclidean sense of place. Most girls found such skills tantalizingly elusive, and the majority continued to represent space only in the most rudimentary of terms.

In order to examine further the effects of gender-related differences in home range behaviour on the acquisition of spatial and environmental skills, I set up a project with a group of Coventry schoolchildren aged between 8 years and 11 years (Matthews, 1987c). Prior testing had established that the boys' home range was greater than that for the girls. A number of other pre-conditions were considered important to the research design. First, if significant gender-related differences in spatial competencies exist these should be evident regardless of the environmental context (Acredolo *et al.*, 1975; Anooshian and Young, 1981). In consequence, it was decided to test children's understanding of place relationships after a controlled exposure to an unfamiliar environment. Secondly, a common problem when studying young children is to find a suitable medium with which to examine their spatial knowledge of large-scale places. Ideally, experimental testing of spatial representation should employ tasks which minimize performance demands. In this context McNamara (McNamara *et al.*, 1984; McNamara, 1986) has argued that 'priming' offers a useful methodology to overcome the difficulties produced by retrieval and inferential processes acting on spatial representations. Like McNamara, it was decided to familiarize the respondents with places located on a map prior to examining their spatial awareness of these places. Thirdly, in order to examine whether sex-related skills diverge at any point it was recognized that the tasks needed to be of varying complexity. In this respect it was decided to design a project which would be capable of assessing whether gender influences the way in which information is mentally encoded and stored.

Especially useful in this respect are the observations of Stevens and Coupe (1978). They distinguish two competing theories of storage and retrieval, defining the poles of a continuum, which focus on the structure and content of mental representations of space. On the one hand, hierarchic theories suggest a complex encoding system, whereby different 'clusters' of an environment are stored in branches of a graph theoretic tree. Accordingly, mental representation is organized such that, first, increasingly more spatial knowledge is given at the lower levels of a hierarchy; secondly, near places prime each other more than far places; thirdly, inter-cluster accuracy is high; and finally, boundaries have no effect on spatial organization. In contrast, non-hierarchic theories describe a simpler storage system, where there is no hierarchical structure to the representation. Instead environments are mentally represented as networks. Consequently, everything is represented at the same level; retrieval encourages topological transformation of space; inter-cluster accuracy is low; and boundaries accentuate mental distortions of space.

With these ideas in mind, I divided my sample to form two groups (A and B), matched in terms of an equal girl-boy ratio and with sex-range experiences that conformed to the overall trend. The children were informed that the aim of the exercise was to construct a map of an unfamiliar area which they were to visit. The two groups were 'primed' about their task in different ways, with children in Group B undertaking a slightly more complex exercise.

Group A. A specially prepared map at a scale of 1:2,500 was presented to each child. The instructor informed the children about the map symbols and what area the map represented. The children were then taken to the study area and told that they could use the map to help find their way during the visit. On arrival the children were escorted by the instructor on 'a standard walking route', which lasted about an hour and covered an area of 0.3 km^2, during the course of which local environmental features were pointed out.

Table 9.1 Sex differences in spatial skills

	Group A	Group B
Information on place	x	x
Type of information	/	/
Spatial orientation	x	/
Spatial accuracy	x	/
Topological distortion	/	/

Notes:
/ significant difference (X^2, $p = <0.05$)
x no significant difference

Source: Matthews (1987c)

Group B. These children were prepared in exactly the same way, but on this occasion the visit to the unfamiliar area was interrupted by a short break of 30 minutes. On arrival only half of the 'standard walking route' was followed. After the interlude the remainder of the route was completed. Children's attention was drawn to exactly the same environmental features as Group A, but they were only provided with that part of the map which pertained to the area they would see. By disrupting the visit in this way the intention was to create a 'mental boundary', thus adding complexity to the cognitive task of spatial organization.

All children handed in their maps on return to the school and were then asked to draw a map of the *whole* area they had visited. The results showed that the nature of the exercise and the research design had a considerable bearing upon latent sex differences (see Table 9.1). When asked to map an unfamiliar area to which all had prior 'priming', girls and boys performed similarly on tests of *information on place, spatial orientation and spatial accuracy*. Differences were found only in terms of *type of information*, with boys giving greater emphasis to routeways and *topological accuracy*, with girls showing a greater inclination to distort their maps in a stylized manner. Such evidence appears consistent with the notion that sex differences in cognitive mapping are the product of environmental experiences, in that when contact with a place is controlled boys and girls perform in a broadly similar manner. However, when the exercise was complicated, in this case by an interruption, boys performed much better than girls in all but one of the spatial assessments. On this occasion boys and girls remembered the same number of details about the environment, but girls were unable to arrange these elements in a spatially coherent manner. These results suggested to me that 'priming' has the effect of reducing disjunction between the spatial capabilities of boys and girls only on simpler tasks. When the task is complicated, the advantages which boys have gained through their more extensive movements through space become readily apparent.

Also, from the results a tentative case for gender-related contrasts in retrieval strategies can be made. In general, the maps of most children showed a combination of hierarchic and non-hierarchic procedures, to a greater or lesser extent. In these cases intra-cluster accuracy was high, but only some inter-cluster relationships were correctly portrayed. However, with age and expanding environmental experience an increasing proportion of boys were able to draw complex maps, showing an understanding of both intra- and inter-cluster relationships. In these instances the maps generally showed good positional appreciation and less tendency towards topological schematization, skills which are consistent with the principal claims of hierarchic theories. Accordingly, some of the older boys in Group B managed to convey an Euclidean grasp of space regardless of the 'mental boundary' imposed by a disrupted visit. In contrast, most girls were only able to demonstrate an awareness of intra-cluster organization and a significant proportion produced highly stylized representations of space. Few girls drew maps of high accuracy, none in Group B, suggesting that their views of space reflected simpler non-hierarchical perspectives. The spatial distortions that resulted in many girls' maps with the imposition of a 'mental boundary' further supports this assertion. It would seem that boys' greater environmental experience equips them with more complex encoding systems, which they can call upon to help solve locational problems of varying complexity. Girls, on the other hand, are impaired by their more constrained environmental behaviour. This is not to say that these competing theoretical perspectives are developmentally sequential. Many of the oldest children, regardless of their home range behaviour and sex, represented space using 'combined' or non-hierarchical structures. However, repeated transactions with a broad range of places appear to offer a means by which children's views of the environment and their accompanying spatial competencies can be heightened.

If sex-related differences in range behaviour are the basis of variations in the recall of large-scale environments, they ought to be associated with *within* sex differences as well. Several studies bear this out. For example, Witkin *et al.* (1962) interviewed middle-class mothers of 10-year-old children who had performed well or poorly on different tests of spatial ability. Those who excelled in these tasks were seen to come from families where independence-granting was greatest, such that fewer restrictions were imposed on them in terms of where they played and what they played with. I also noted (Matthews, 1987a; 1988), that those girls who roam as freely as their age-matched counterparts do as well as boys on all tests of environmental recall and organization. Clayton and Woodyard (1981) nicely summarize these ideas by observing that spatial knowledge and understanding should be viewed as 'evolving from an autobiography of experiences that happen to take place in space'.

However, Harris (1981) is not entirely convinced that all sex differences in spatial ability are rooted in childhood experiences. He points out that if this were the case then instruction and practice should dissipate any environmental disadvantage. He cites several studies which have shown that girls continue to do less well than boys on a range of small-scale spatial exercises, despite specific training (Thomas *et al.*, 1973; Mitchelmore, 1974).

Interactional explanations

These explanations suggest that sex differences in environmental ability are an outcome of the interplay of genetic and social factors. For example, McGuinness (1976a; 1976b; McGuinness and Pribram, 1979) argues that small initial differences between the sexes in visual and auditory sensitivity encourage different self-selecting behavioural responses which give rise to sex-related differences in spatial ability. Thus, whilst girls' early lead in language development disposes them towards one direction, the different sensitivities of boys takes them along a different path: 'While girls are becoming increasingly skilful in expressive language skills, boys are still focused on things and on spatio-perceptual activities' (Harris, 1981, p. 113). Once along this 'spatial' course, even though they catch up with girls in terms of language development, boys are encouraged to maintain their early environmental skills by toys and other objects provided for them.

Another possibility is that sex differences in androgen levels encourage different types of behaviour which become reinforced by socially mediated factors. For example, Maccoby and Jacklin (1979) have shown that a high level of androgen is significantly related to high-energy, rough-and-tumble play in early childhood. Although there is no conclusive evidence to suggest that androgens work directly on the brain to stimulate visuo-spatial ability, they seem to encourage those sorts of activities which lead to the manipulation of and movement through the environment. In addition, parents appear less likely to restrict the range behaviour of those children whose 'masculinity' engenders a view that they are able to look after themselves.

Newcombe (1982) suggests a third interactional viewpoint which relates boy's later pubertal maturation to the activities they engage in, the personalities they develop and their spatial competence. Waber (1976; 1977a; 1977b) has shown that boys reach puberty about two years later than girls on average. Whilst Waber postulates that later maturation, in itself, generates greater hemispheric specialization in the brain, so giving rise to higher levels of spatial ability, others disagree with her interpretation. Both Harris (1981) and Newcombe (1982) draw attention to the social environments of late maturers and suggest that boys continue to devote their energies to play and exploration at an age when girls are settling down to more passive activities and interests.

Summary

Whether tested in the laboratory or in the large-scale environment, a consensus suggests that boys perform better than girls on many tests of spatial reasoning. However, the reasons for these differences, their timing and their developmental significance are disputed. Understanding is confounded by a lack of agreement over how to define spatial ability and how best to measure it. There seems to be some centring on the skills of *spatial orientation* and *spatial visualization*, but until researchers from different backgrounds are clear about what they are assessing and which methods enable true environmental potential to be unravelled, explanation is likely to depend upon the competing claims of rival research traditions. In this section we have given most attention to the importance of environmental experience as a determining factor. In many Western societies and elsewhere (see Chapter 2), girls' environmental behaviour tends to be restrained by the social mores of their parents, teachers and peers. Thus, not only is environmental exploration and freedom denied to them, but also their confidence and ability to cope with environmental matters are likely to be undermined. Saegert and Hart (1978) make a useful analogy between the environmental experiences of the sexes and the roles of driver and passenger in a car. Whilst the driver, like boys, is allowed decision-making, experimentation and self-directed learning of the environment, the passenger, like girls, can only suggest and observe. Whatever the explanation for these sex-related variations in environmental competence, there are a number of educational consequences. The ability to organize, arrange and recognize spatial elements and properties of landscapes is an attribute advantageous to the intending geographer, whereas the ability to handle and rotate shapes has a bearing on mathematics, geometry and graphic subjects in general. The educational significance of these points will be considered in more detail in Part Four, but clearly what action should be taken to compensate for these differences in spatial ability depends upon whether genetic, experiential or interactional models are preferred.

10

An empirical evaluation of the development of environmental cognition

In Chapter 4 we examined a range of competing theoretical propositions on the ability of young children to make sense of their everyday world and their knowledge of space and place. This chapter reviews empirical evidence concerning how children come to understand and represent large-scale environments, as well as providing an opportunity to evaluate the rival claims of the Piagetian (constructivist), nativist and empiricist schools of thought.

Piaget revisited

In this section we will review some of the evidence for and against Piaget's developmental sequence of spatial representation. Attention will focus on children's ability to comprehend large-scale space. Central to the Piagetian tradition is the notion that young children are capable only of *egocentric* spatial representation and thought. Egocentrism, itself, is further defined by two states. In the first, the infant or *sensorimotor* child (0–2 years) gradually progresses from an egocentric confusion of self and the environment – whereby objects and events are located solely in relation to the body, with no objective awareness of body position, or changes thereof, in large-scale space – to an objective or *allocentric* frame of reference which is based on an understanding of the relative relationships of objects and events. In this context, Bruner (1966) talks of *enacted* representation, which in its achieved form (at about 18 months) sees the child capable of viewing different routes in perceived space (Piaget, 1937), of recognizing modifications in the relative position of objects (Shemyakin, 1962) and of simple tasks of orientation (Acredolo, 1976). The second state normally extends between 2 years and 7 years, and corresponds to the *pre-operational* stage of development. At the outset children are seen to be incapable of decentring their own actions and points of view from other possible viewpoints. They imitate internally actions in and on space and as such their cognitive views of the world are egocentric (self-centred) and iconic. With age, preconceptual notions are replaced by intuitive representations as children begin to effectuate their first complete transformations of space, but at the same time they figuratively overdo it. As such, 7-year-old children's views on space are defined largely by topological structures, rather than by projective and Euclidean representations, which develop later. Children's ability to decentre gradually heightens with the onset of the *concrete operational stage*, but their true grasp of the hierarchical nature of reality is not fully attained until the *stage of formal operations*, when the pre-adolescent begins to elaborate complex rules and relationships.

In summary, three important developmental assertions relating to children's spatial abilities are set out by Piaget:

1. That infants (0–18/24 months) are capable only of egocentric frames of reference.
2. That young children (2–7 years) are unable to decentre their own actions and viewpoints from other possible perspectives.
3. That children younger than 7 years of age are incapable of representing space in other than topological terms.

We will examine each of these in turn.

Egocentrism and infancy

Both Presson and Somerville (1985) and Acredolo (1985) offer extensive reviews of children's spatial representations in infancy. Much of this work refers to children's grasp of small-scale space and so falls outside the scope of this study. However, a number of observations are worthy of consideration. Studies which have confirmed Piaget's early developmental sequence have largely been based on searching and visual fixation experiments. Typical scenarios involve an infant being conditioned to locate an object (Bremner and Bryant, 1977) or an event (Acredolo, 1978) to their left or right in a landmark-free, laboratory setting. After training, the infant is rotated by 180^0 and if the infant continues to respond in relation to his or her own body rather than incorporating information about the change of body position, egocentricity is said to exist. Initial laboratory-based experiments of this kind (Bremner and Bryant, 1977; Acredolo, 1978; Rieser, 1979) suggested that infants aged 6–16 months were only able to respond egocentrically, so confirming what Piaget had contended.

However, more recent work casts doubt upon Piaget's assertions. In this context, Cohen and Cohen (1985) draw attention to the importance of methodology when testing the very young. They point out that by using altered methodologies a growing number of studies have demonstrated that infants are able to respond in non-egocentric ways at ages much younger than Piaget anticipated. Factors found to be important in modifying the infant's style of responding include: *familiarity*, Acredolo (1979) found that 9-month-old infants who were tested in the familiar surroundings of their home as opposed to the rather stressful setting of a laboratory, showed greater tendencies to make objective rather than egocentric searches; *a familiarization period prior to testing*, Acredolo (1982) found that out of a group of nineteen 9-month-old children who were given a 15-minute 'get acquainted' period prior to testing in order to maximize their feelings of security, only three subjects chose egocentrically, a significant departure from the 76 per cent found in the same environment without the extended pre-task familiarization period; *cues available*, Acredolo (1979) found that when a target window was clearly marked with very salient cues, children at both 9 and 11 months were able to turn correctly to locate an object despite body rotation, which suggested to her that infants of these ages were able to give landmark information priority over egocentric information (see also Bremner, 1978; Acredolo and Evans, 1980); *the extent of body rotation*, studies providing the strongest evidence of egocentric errors have used 180° trials, in contrast to when smaller rotations have been used (Rieser, 1979; McKenzie *et al.*, 1984) there has been less tendency to make mistakes of this kind. Presson and Somerville (1985) argue that it is unsatisfactory to use data from 180° trials to advance an argument about general spatial competence, since rotations of this magnitude represent a special case, in that 'they may lead to changes in left–right relations that may be especially difficult as a result of symmetries in the nervous system' (p. 14); and *the mother's movement in space*, Presson and Ihrig (1982) have demonstrated that in many of the initial experiments in which children were supposedly tested in landmark-free settings, both the experimenter and the mother were in effect landmarks – however, they were unreliable landmarks in that they moved around the table, so encouraging the infant, deprived of other reference points, to make egocentric errors.

Evidence of this kind has led Presson and Somerville (1985) to suggest that

> there are no compelling or theoretical or empirical grounds for retaining the notion of an egocentric system of coding in infancy. Infants' stored representations of spatial knowledge can be regarded as objective throughout, since there are at least some task conditions in which their responses reflect objective knowledge. (p. 22)

Young children and egocentricity

Piaget (Piaget and Inhelder, 1967) used perspective-taking tasks to argue that children aged up to 7 or 8 years or even older were incapable of decentring their views on space. His classic perspective-taking experiment involved the child being seated at one vantage point and being asked to predict how an array of objects would appear to a viewer in some other position. In most cases Piaget was able to demonstrate that children tended to act as if the viewer would see the same arrangement as themselves, that is from their current position. This error Piaget called egocentric, and it provided evidence that children of this age span seldom understood that left/right and before/behind were relative to the viewing position. Many studies have replicated this basic egocentric error in other perspective-taking exercises (Flavell *et al.*, 1968; Laurendeau and Pinard, 1970; Fishbein *et al.*, 1972; Kurdek, 1978).

However, Presson and Somerville (1985) contend that perspective-taking tasks of this kind are imperfect measures of children's understanding of spatial relationships. They point out that there are two major ways in which spatial information can be used, which they label as *primary* and *secondary* uses. Primary uses of spatial information include practical orientation and action in relation to aspects of space. Secondary uses of spatial information include symbolic representation which, on the one hand, enables individuals to think about spatial information to which they have no direct access, and on the other, involves skills such as the drawing and reading of maps and mental rotation. Presson and Somerville argue that young children may well have considerable spatial knowledge, which they can draw upon in a primary way as they move around the environment, but that when asked to translate their understanding symbolically, they lack the secondary skills and expertise to depict space in a coherent manner. Piaget is ambiguous about such a distinction and in consequence Presson and Somerville suggest that his observations on children's spatial ability are flawed. Accordingly, performance on the standard perspective-taking task is not a direct index of children's primary spatial knowledge, instead it does little more than show that children of this age range find symbolic representation difficult, simply because they do not have mastery of secondary spatial skills. When asked to select a photograph of how the entire array might look to the viewer, this task demands considerable symbolic understanding about what a photograph can convey about an array. Children who choose an egocentric response 'may know the relation of the array to the viewer implicitly, but they are unable to represent this information symbolically' (p. 19).

Empirical support for this distinction between spatial knowledge and its symbolic representation comes from a number of studies. For example, Huttenlocher and Presson (1979) and Presson (1980) have shown that by simplifying the task, so that children are not asked to think symbolically about the whole array but about parts of it, egocentricity largely disappears. Others (Kurdek, 1978; Houssiadas and Brown, 1980), too, have shown that performance cannot be divorced from the nature of the test material, especially the kinds of stimulus provided and the types of response required. Spencer *et al.* (1980) have shown that by presenting pre-school children with tasks which involve recognition rather than performance, 'one can demonstrate that young children have considerable ability to view and interpret the world from a far from egocentric perspective' (p. 57). Furthermore, in relation to the difference between primary and secondary spatial information, we have seen in Chapter 7 many examples of how very young children are capable of successfully performing navigational and search tasks which involve activity in space, at ages long before those anticipated by Piaget (e.g. Bluestein and Acredolo, 1979; Presson, 1982; Blades and Spencer, 1986 and 1987a; 1987b).

Conceptual and methodological criticisms of this kind suggest to Presson and Somerville (1985) that Piaget's thoughts on spatial representation beyond infancy were too narrowly conceived. Instead, they propose an alternative view based upon 'changes in the nature of children's developing *uses* of spatial information, rather than changes in the form of stored representations' (p. 1). In order to advance this reconceptualization, studies of children's search behaviour are especially needed.

Spatial representation in young children

Piaget was among the first to report data on children's ability to represent space in maps and models. In an early experiment (Piaget and Inhelder, 1956) he asked children to represent a model village in drawings, from a vertical and an oblique viewpoint, and in models, at the same and at a reduced scale. In another experiment (Piaget *et al.*, 1948), he requested children to map their route from school to home and to model their locality in a sandbox. These experiments were instrumental in shaping Piaget's claims that young children possess only topological concepts of space. According to Piaget, their approach depends on bringing together objects in pairs at the geographical scale, but they lack the skills to locate metrically and projectively each element according to a comprehensive frame of reference. Even at the beginning of the concrete operational stage, in the model village situation, children can do little more than attempt to locate each object according to the whole site, though their efforts are flawed by an inability to gauge distance, to reduce scale, and to appreciate the consequences of rotation. Not until the later part of the concrete operations stage, at about 11 years of age, are children thought capable of Euclidean understanding. From thereon, children develop an ability to represent a layout in a completely formal manner, calling on conventions and symbols.

Considerable empirical evidence has confirmed Piaget's developmental sequence of how children model different large-scale settings (Laurendeau and Pinard, 1970; Mark, 1972; Thornberg, 1973). Towler (Towler and Nelson, 1968; Towler, 1970) also discovered a similar pattern of progression, but with a two-year delay in comparison to Piaget's observations.

However, an accumulating body of empirical work questions the generality of Piaget's concept of stage. Recent research has shown that children's performances are not solely dependent on age and that in some contexts very young children can be shown to have Euclidean knowledge. Spencer and Darvizeh (1981a) suggest that previous studies may have underestimated children's absolute competencies because they have relied too heavily on laboratory-based, small-scale tests which are not only divorced from the everyday environmental experiences of children but are also often obfuscated by complex verbal instruction or unusual behaviour.

By comparison, a number of studies (Biel and Torell, 1977; Biel, 1979; 1982) have suggested that young children are capable of showing quite advanced spatial knowledge when tested in an environment which is familiar and commonplace, such as the home area, and when the research procedure is simple and readily understood. For example, Conning and Byrne (1984) tested a group of children aged between 3 years 5 months and 4 years 7 months in two familiar large-scale environments, the ground floor of their own house and the area around their home in which they frequently went on walks with their parents, and one novel environment, a simple outdoor route. The study focused on the ability of these children to make direction estimates.

Although direction estimates provide only one measure of spatial knowledge they have formed the basis of a number of studies (Hardwick et al., 1976; Piché, 1977; Anooshian and Young, 1981) and have the advantage of overcoming the execution problems of verbal, modelling and drawing tasks. Every effort was made to ensure that the task was comprehensible to the pre-school subjects and the equipment used would not be too formidable. As a result the mounted 'sighting tubes' and 'telescopes' of previous studies (Hardwick et al., 1976; Anooshian and Young, 1981) were abandoned for a wooden arrow. In each setting children were asked to point to out-of-sight targets using the wooden arrow and an experimenter checked the bearing using a compass. If the subjects responded by pointing along the path they had just walked, this was taken to be indicative of topological understanding. In contrast, pointing the crow-flight direction to an object implied knowledge about the distance between locations and their relative bearing and, if reasonably accurate, this was taken to be representative of Euclidean understanding. Conning and Byrne found that some children showed consistent Euclidean knowledge in all settings. Sixteen out of twenty-four children had accurate bearing knowledge within their own homes and seven of those had integrated and accurate knowledge of the position of locations within their home neighbourhood. Of the others, some seemed to understand the notion of projective space in that they avoided path responses. Euclidean knowledge was found least in the novel environment, even after some familiarization. This finding that the type of knowledge expressed is dependent on the nature of the environment (both size and place) and the level of familiarity is consistent with a view which suggests that 'development does not take place in stages across all domains of knowledge, but that a child's ability is unevenly distributed across tasks' (Conning and Byrne, 1984, p. 173).

From the results of another set of experiments (Landau et al., 1981; Landau et al., 1984; Landau and Spelke, 1985) Landau and her colleagues argue that the facets of 'a spatial knowledge system' may well be intact quite early on in life. In studies with 'Kelli', a congenitally blind child, during the age range of 34–60 months, they found that once she had travelled along routes with particular landmarks she was able to make Euclidean judgements by finding new paths and detours around these objects. Spatial inferences of this kind point to an ability to make logical decisions based upon an understanding of the geometrical components of an environment. However, Landau points out that children's early environmental competence is often suppressed by motor bias and the need to learn that certain objects and not others make good landmarks.

Summary

The Piagetian expectations that environmental cognition during infancy is characterized by a set progression from an egocentric to an allocentric frame of reference, and that young children are incapable of demonstrating an understanding of configurational knowledge, can no longer be accepted without qualification. Considerable evidence suggests that young children have developed much environmental competence, and at ages long before Piaget and his followers anticipate. By using altered methodologies, frequently set in large-scale environments which are familiar to the child and whose task demands are not too high, an accumulating body of empirical studies have shown that young children do not view the world as egocentrically as Piaget contends. Indeed, rather than regarding egocentricity and allocentricity as developmentally sequential, 'we may need to see them as reflecting different spatial skills for engaging the environment' (Heft and Wohlwill, 1987, p. 183). As Neisser (1976) argues, very young children and even babies demonstrate by their everyday actions that they possess 'orienting schema', cognitive maps of those parts of the environment through which they move. The problem facing those interested in studying children's understanding of place and space is to devise suitable methodologies which enable children's environmental competencies to be uncovered.

Nativism

Perhaps the strongest claim for young children possessing relatively complex environmental cognitions comes from the work of nativists. Unlike Piagetians, they suggest the innate existence of a spatial knowledge system, which opens up independently of the modality of experience. Workers like Blaut and his colleagues (Blaut, 1987a; 1991; Blaut et al., 1970; Blaut and Stea, 1971; 1974) argue that young children are natural macroenvironmental mappers, whose spatial abilities have simply been underestimated, largely as children lack the expressive skills to demonstrate their environmental knowledge and partly because researchers have misjudged children's incipient capabilities by adopting adultocentric forms of testing and assessment. Blaut believes that as with language acquisition, children have 'a competence-at-birth' to deploy protomapping skills and to display primitive locative abilities (see Chapter 4). He sees a close relationship between children's natural ability to learn a language and the competence required to order the macroenvironment. Indeed, in the child's language-learning and language-using activities

> there is a double mapping or structuring involving first the well-formedness of sound combinations and second the correspondence of sound combinations to non-linguistic reality. Perhaps the child's use, first, of gestures and sounds, then of material sign vehicles to represent the macroenvironment, is the same process. (Blaut, 1991, p. 63)

Here Blaut is suggesting that there is no difference between a *spatial* process, such as environmental mapping, and a *temporal* process, oral–aural language; he sees both as *spatio-temporal*.

What evidence is there to support the nativist assertion that primitive cognitive mapping is a phylogenetic ability, 'inherited by human infants as it is by birds, fishes . . . and rats'? Blaut cites the results of a number of studies which show that young children, aged 3–6 years, can do creditable mapping, make things that look very much like maps, and use these maps in 'simulated place-problem-solving (make-believe navigation)', without prior instruction.

First, in an early study (Blaut *et al.*, 1970) Blaut found that children aged 5–6 years, from three different cultures (United States, Puerto Rico, St Vincent), were not only capable of recognizing vertical black and white photographs as pictures of large-scale environments but could also identify on them 'macro-features of landscape-gestalts', like roads, settlements, woods, street corners, etc. Furthermore, this ability was present among children who had never seen the surface of the landscape from an overhead vantage, and some had seen no television nor had significant exposure to photographs from any aerial perspective, as sometimes found in magazines. Secondly, in a follow-up study (unpublished, cited in Blaut, 1991) Blaut tested the ability of twenty 4-year-olds to navigate a route with toy cars on a large-scale aerial photograph played with on the floor, a task which the majority of the study group accomplished 'realistically'. He also found that 5- and 6-year-olds could trace maps from vertical air photographs and use these maps to solve simulated navigational problems, even in the absence of the initial iconic stimulus. Thirdly, in several further studies, all with a focus on children's toy play and macroenvironmental play (Blaut and Stea, 1971 and 1974), Blaut was able to demonstrate that 3-year-olds could construct simple models of the environment, and that this ability grew more sophisticated in children aged 4 and 5 years.

In summary, what Blaut's work has revealed is that very young children, at and beneath the age of school entrance, possess a range of protomapping abilities which allow them to represent macroenvironments in 'language-like sign behaviour' incorporating three basic skills:

1. A *semantic* skill of using material sign-vehicles to represent landscape features and complexes of features.

2. A *syntactic* skill of rotating macroenvironments to an overhead vertical perspective.
3. A further *syntactic* skill of scale-reduction (Blaut, 1991).

However, Blaut acknowledges that protomapping skills are only mapping skills in a limited sense, in that 3-year-olds are not cartographers. Yet children of this age can already make, read and use very simple maps and these skills appear as cultural universals. That young children are natural mappers and that young children everywhere have incipient spatial abilities, are difficult propositions to establish.

A growing number of studies provide corroborative support for Blaut's assertions. For example, we have seen in Chapter 8 many instances of young children's competencies with mapping tasks: Bluestein and Acredolo (1979) revealed that 3- to 5-year-olds could carry out simple location and map-reading exercises; Walker (1980), McGee, (1982) and Matthews (1985a) showed that children aged 5 years and over could interpret aerial photographs and use maps for interpretative purposes; and Blades and Spencer (1987a; 1987b; 1987c) observed that 4- to 6-year-olds could solve environmental maze problems using a map, as well as engaging in relatively sophisticated mapping behaviour, such as employing alpha-numeric grids to determine location. In one experiment, Spencer *et al.* (1980) studied the reactions of 3–5-year-old children to six vertical aerial photographs and a set of oblique sketches, presented as perceptual maps. Every child managed to identify at least six elements and some mentioned as many as twenty-five features. There was a close correlation between children's performances with the photographs and with the maps.

Additional, indirect, support comes from the work of Siegel and Schadler's (1977) study of cognitive mapping by kindergarten children, Conning and Byrne's (1984) study of pre-school children's spatial competence, and Landau and Spelke's (1985) studies of map use by blind and sighted 4-year-olds. In a further experiment with 'Kelli', a congenitally blind child with no previous map-use experience, Landau (1986) describes how she was able to use a two-symbol map to guide her locomotion in space and how she could do so under conditions where the map and space were aligned in front of her (canonical condition), and under various other transformations: sideways, front–behind and vertical rotations. In these conditions there was no straightforward spatial relationship between Kelli's position in space and her represented position on the map; therefore, relatively complex spatial judgements were called for, including mental alignments of the map with external space. Control data from sighted children confirmed that, by 4 years of age, they too could interpret and use these maps with confidence. Landau suggests these results show that 'a core of the knowledge' required to use maps is already well established in both blind and sighted children during early childhood. Also, map-use ability appears to be 'a natural function of the spatial knowlege system required to support other kinds of spatial inferences seen in young children' (p. 220) and which arises independently of any specific experience of map-reading.

Despite all of this evidence of early mapping abilities, we still know very little about the manifestation of these sorts of skills in children younger than 3 years of age. None the less, recent work with neonates (Antell and Caron, 1985) suggests that from a very early age children have the ability to discriminate differences in spatial relationships between two simple geometric forms, such as a cross and a square, whilst McComas and Field (1984) claim the early presence of an ability to establish spatial coordinates for positioning things outside of the body. With subjects of this age considerable ingenuity is needed to gain insights into their true capability, but even then speculation remains as to whether revealed skills are innate or the product of extremely early learning processes.

The proposition that mapping behaviour is a cultural universal is grounded in theoretical conceptions of the functions of human mapping. Blaut suggests that maps 'have basic cultural functions involving the communication, recording, and heuristics of geographic information for long-term deposit or immediate use in practice, play or ritual' (Blaut, 1991, p. 64). Blaut supports his assertions by referring to empirical studies which have shown that mapping behaviour can be found among ancient peoples (Mellaert, 1967; Varanka, 1987); non-Western peoples (Spink and Moodie, 1972; Munn, 1973; Blakemore, 1981); children everywhere (see Blaut above). However, Blaut acknowledges that the search for evidence as to whether maps and mapping are indeed present in all cultures has barely just begun, although it seems likely to him that 'the evidence will accumulate rapidly when we begin looking for it' (p. 66).

Recent work by Matthews and Airey (1990) in rural Kenya provides some support for Blaut's claims. We looked at the mapping skills of 7–13-year-olds in Kanyakine, a Kimeru-speaking region of central Kenya. This area was chosen as it provided an opportunity to examine how children in 'impoverished societies' were able to construe their everyday world. An initial check confirmed that the region had not been mapped at a scale less than 1:50,000 and that there were no maps of the local villages. Furthermore, when tested, the youngest children had not been taught any map work in school, nor did they have access to any maps. None of the children had television in their households and there was a paucity of printed matter, such as magazines and books. Despite material deprivation of this kind and their lack of contact with formal maps, we found that all of the 7-year-olds sampled (n = 20) were able to attempt a drawn map of their route from home to school, and most managed to demonstrate more than just a minimalist wobbly line linking the two places. Table 10.1 shows the range of data drawn by this age group. Clearly, not only is the concept of route-drawing already instilled by the age of 7 years, but also, without any formal training or prompting, the majority of children showed an ability to conceive of space as viewed from 'an-eye-in-the-sky'. In another cross-cultural study, Spencer and Darvizeh (1983) looked at the environmental skills of a group of twenty Iranian children, aged 3–5 years. Like studies of Western children

Table 10.1 Information on children's route-maps: 7-year-old Kanyakine children, Kenya (n=20)

	Nodes	Districts	Paths	Landmarks	Mean total
Mean number of elements/maps	3.4	0.9	3.6	2.9	10.8
	Functional		Natural		
Nature of elements (per cent)	86		14		
	Pictorial		Pictorial-plan		
Grades of map (per cent)	46		54		

Source: Matthews and Airey (1990)

which have shown that the very young possess unexpected environmental capabilities, they found that their sample were able to carry out successfully a range of mapping tasks, including the tracing of complex novel and familiar routes and verbal descriptions of their home area.

Summary

The work of Blaut and his colleagues challenge Piaget's notions that young children have limited spatial cognitions. Piaget's theory of cognitive development largely relates to children's thoughts about abstract space, especially geometric relations. In contrast, Blaut and Stea have shown that young children's mapping abilities emerge naturally, independent of training, and

> involve a . . . powerful ability to abstract in a spatiotemporal (not simply spatial) sense, an ability which involves mapping (rotation, reduction, sign-interpretation) as a means of communication and working (or playing) with the large environment, something much closer to language than it is to Piagetian spatial cognition.
> (Blaut, 1987a, p. 31)

This suggestion that mapping emerges from the same root process as language is given additional credence by the observation that the physical skill of making, interpreting and using maps is roughly coterminous with the development of linguistic production, that is, at 3–5 years of age. Moreover, new findings on the universality of mapping, especially in the very young, suggests to Blaut that 'there is reason now to avoid the assumption that a young child thinks and acts egocentrically in the . . . sense of being unaware of a macroenvironmental reality apart from and outside of itself' (p. 31). Rather, children seem to have, at all times, a degree of awareness of both the macroenvironment in a global, unspecific sense and of a boundary between self and the macroenvironment.

Empiricism

In contrast to the nativist school of thought, environmental learning theorists assume that knowledge of the environment is a function of accumulated and organized perceptual experiences representing interactions between the organism and the environment. Thus, from the perception of successive information over time, a more generalized and context-independent knowledge structure emerges that is capable of sustaining a wide range of spatial behaviours (Kuipers, 1982). According to Appleyard (1973) there are three types of knowledge that result from environmental learning:

1. *Operational knowledge* – concerned with features that are critical to the functioning of the environment (e.g. location of shops, schools).
2. *Responsive knowledge* – how people react to features like landmarks.
3. *Inferential knowledge* – an ability to generalize and to make inferences that extend beyond what is actually known.

Of these, responsive knowledge is environment-dependent, but operational and inferential knowledge are person-dominant, in that they are products of information derived from personal experience. In this regard empiricism highlights the relationship between movement, exploration and the development of spatial understanding and draws attention to developmental psychology's early lack of attention to ecological contingencies.

In Chapter 6 we have reviewed a variety of studies which have shown that activity-in-space considerably affects and enhances children's views on place and space (Cohen and Cohen, 1985). However, whether environmental understanding is solely a function of transactional behaviour is difficult to determine and evidence remains largely equivocal. For example, Acredolo (1978) has demonstrated that 16-month-old infants are better able to maintain orientation than 6- or 11-month-old infants. In addition, she found that change in orientation ability was greatest between the two older ages. These differences were explained in terms of the greater locomotor independence of the older group. As children begin to walk so they add new dimensions to their experience, and it may be that this activity is an important component in the development of orientation. Berthenthal *et al.* (1984), like Acredolo, link the change-over from egocentric to allocentric frames of reference in infants to the onset of self-mobility. They have shown that with greater mobility and independence of movement young children are more likely to respond in objective ways in tests of spatial orientation. In a further study on the relationship of walking and orientation in space, Heth and Cornell (1980) compared the wayfinding ability of newly walking 1-year-olds with 3-year-olds in a two-choice maze. On initial testing, 3-year-olds were more accomplished in incorporating feedback following an error and were better able to use information gained from viewing or walking the reversal of the route. However, after observing their mother walk the route, many 1-year-olds were able to learn the route as rapidly as their elders and their ability to incorporate feedback from error trials was greatly improved. This suggested to Heth and Cornell that with environmental experience infants become increasingly competent in independently abstracting environmental information, such as landmarks, for wayfinding.

Not all agree about the importance of locomotor independence to the acquisition of early spatial skills. For example, McComas and Field (1984) question the effect of self-mobility as a determining factor. In their trials they found there was no significant difference between the performance of an 'inexperienced' group (two weeks crawling) and an 'experienced' group (eight weeks crawling) on the standard Acredolo orientation test. They also contest Acredolo *et al.*'s (1984) assertion that movement encourages enhanced attention to changes in visual perspective. McComas and Field point out that the pre-locomotor infant already has gained considerable expertise in the coordination of perspectives simply through the experiences that result from developing head, hand and trunk movements. Also, Bower (1966) has shown that 6-week-old infants display size and shape constancy and that both are the result of parallax, that is, seeing one object moving in front of another, whilst Acredolo (1983) has suggested that infants' developing ability from birth to track objects visually is a formative environmental strategy. Taken together, what these results suggest is that spatial understanding and incipient environmental skills may well be formulated very early on in life. Bremner and Bryant (1985) point out that much greater attention needs to be given to the kind of transformations of the world that come about as soon as infants are able to sit up and control their head movements: 'we may need to distinguish between position relative to the body, position relative to the head, and position in the external world.' Indeed, Bremner (1978) argues that developing locomotion merely accelerates spatial understanding, rather than acting as the initial trigger. Once the infant competently achieves self-mobility he/she is more able to recognize anomalies with an egocentric perspective and this hastens the onset of an allocentric reference system.

Blaut and Stea (1969; 1971; 1974; Blaut; 1987a; 1991) acknowledge that place-learning becomes a more crucial problem once children become fully mobile, able and free to move inside and outside their dwelling. Up until this time young children's 'global maps' are diffuse and indistinct, but full mobility sharpens children's views of the macroenvironment, not only enabling them to ponder locational problems, but also providing them with opportunities for their solution. When direct locomotion to distant points becomes difficult, children adopt inferential solutions of which 'mapping becomes a favoured way' (Blaut, 1991, p. 13). This sort of ability is itself related to children's toy play. Blaut and Stea build upon Erikson's (1977) observation that young children's toy play is, among other things, experimentation with reality, primarily having to do with social interaction, but also with the manipulation and testing of material things. For them, all forms of play on the ground or floor with material things that serve as substitutes for real-world objects, have a special function with regard to macroenvironmental learning. 'The act of reducing reality in scale, observing it from an overhead perspective, and infusing it with small objects which, to the child, are signs representing larger objects . . . is, in a literal sense, model-thinking' (Blaut, 1991, p. 11). They point out that the macroenvironment to a child of 2 or 3 years is often remote and inaccessible in a proximal sense. Moreover, most of its parts are seen at a distance and from an oblique perspective. Children cannot achieve and seldom have the opportunity to see space from a vertical vantage. For all of these reasons, Blaut and Stea believe that children's toy play on the floor or ground with any object substituting for a real-world object, has the specific function of creating a map-like model of the world which enables children to experiment with and learn about places, at ages before they are mobile enough to see them from various coordinated perspectives. Playing with miniature landscapes in this way familiarizes children with important mapping processes, including *rotation* of perspective, *reduction* in scale and *abstraction* to iconic signs, which supplement direct locomotion through landscapes. Strategies of this sort help explain the precocious ability of 3–5-year-olds to read and interpret aerial photographs. However, Blaut speculates as to whether the source of such mapping tendencies is a product of an innate place-structuring mechanism or primarily an early learning (enculturation) process based upon experience and a social support system.

Environmental experience continues to be of importance to children's development of spatial understanding even when full locomotor independence has been achieved. Children gain much of their environmental information from interaction with their surroundings. Many studies report on the effect of different environmental circumstance upon children's general environmental competencies (see Chapter 6). For example, I have demonstrated, working with 6- to 11-year-olds in suburban Coventry (Matthews, 1986c; 1987a), the close relationship between home range and children's ability to recount their everyday environments. Those children who roamed furthest from their homes and were given greatest environmental freedom performed significantly better on a range of spatial tests compared to children with limited range experiences. Similar findings have been reported by Hart (1979) in New England and by Munroe and Munroe (1971) and Nerlove et al. (1971) in Kenya. Others (Cohen and Weatherford, 1981; Herman et al., 1982; Cornell and Hay, 1984) have shown how active as opposed to passive environmental encounters affect environmental performance. Person-related variables may also contribute to environmental interaction and hence, an understanding of place and space. Hazen (1982) has shown that very young children often fall into two groups: those who appear naturally inquisitive (*active explorers*) and those who interact more passively with their surroundings (*passive explorers*). In her studies, Hazen found that the former group had a heightened awareness of place and spatial relationships. Maurer and Baxter (1972) and Orleans (1973) have shown how the different experiences of children from different social class and ethnic backgrounds affect the type of environmental knowledge stored. While Cohen and Cohen (1982) and Butterworth (1977) report that when children invest an environmental activity with a particular purpose or theme, their environmental recall is improved. These ideas are in accord with Anooshian and Siegel's (1985) suggestion that, as with non-spatial thought, we ought to give more attention to the social and emotional import of the events encountered in the development of children's spatial thought.

Another important part of empiricist reasoning is that as geographical environments seldom can be perceived from a single vantage point their comprehension inevitably depends upon an ability to piece together disparate pieces of information gained from travel and environmental experience over time. In order to do this effectively individuals will need to generalize and to make inferences which go beyond the information given. A number of studies have shown that very young children, often as young as 3-years-old are capable of making inferences of this kind (Mohr et al., 1975) although environmental experience seems to affect performance. For example, when Herman et al. (1985) tested the ability of 3- and 5-year-olds to point to the location of target places within their nursery school, which they could not see from their vantage position, 5-year-olds were more accurate, especially in discerning the bearing of those places which were not connected by a straight-line walking path. These differences are not explained by length of attendance at the school as Herman et al. pair-matched their age-sample by this factor. Instead it is suggested that the wider environmental experience of 5-year-olds in general leads to more efficient storage strategies for spatial inferences. This seems even more likely given that boys, with their greater freedom to explore their immediate home base, consistently outperformed their age-matched girl counterparts.

Summary

Empirical evidence of this kind suggests that children, like adults, gain much of their environmental information through close contact with their everyday surroundings. Downs and Stea (1977) have conceptualized some of the major spatial behavioural experiences that are formative to children's understanding of the environment (see Figure 10.1).

However, whilst movement, locomotor independence and spatial exploration appear important to the development of spatial thought, experiences of this kind need not be the source of environmental reasoning. Critics (Pick et al., 1976; Pick, 1976) point out that explanations based solely upon environmental transactions are unlikely to account for the wide range of skills and abilities of children of different ages, and hence, are too simplistic. Instead, it is better to view experiential factors as a contributory influence rather as a determining effect upon children's cognitive structures. When Hart and Moore (1973) reconceptualized Piaget's ideas on children's cognitive development, they

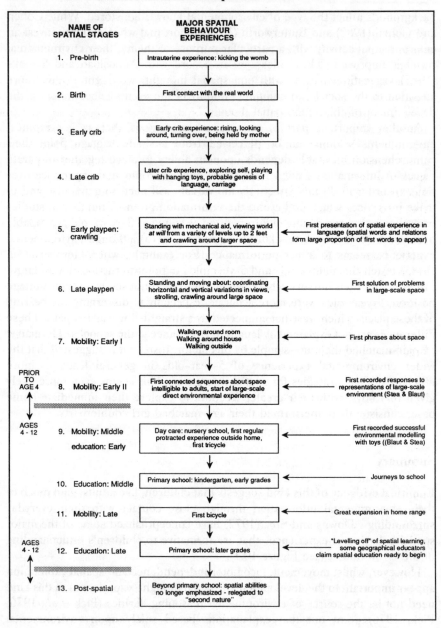

NAME OF SPATIAL STAGES	MAJOR SPATIAL BEHAVIOUR EXPERIENCES	
1. Pre-birth	Intrauterine experience: kicking the womb	
2. Birth	First contact with the real world	
3. Early crib	Early crib experience: rising, looking around, turning over, being held by mother	
4. Late crib	Later crib experience, exploring self, playing with hanging toys, probable genesis of language, carriage	
5. Early playpen: crawling	Standing with mechanical aid, viewing world *at will* from a variety of levels up to 2 feet and crawling around larger space	First presentation of spatial experience in language (spatial words and relations form large proportion of first words to appear)
6. Late playpen	Standing and moving about: coordinating horizontal and vertical variations in views, strolling, crawling around large space	First solution of problems in large-scale space
7. Mobility: Early I	Walking around room Walking around house Walking outside	First phrases about space
8. Mobility: Early II	First connected sequences about space intelligible to adults, start of large-scale direct environmental experience	First recorded responses to representations of large-scale environment (Stea & Blaut)
9. Mobility: Middle education: Early	Day care: nursery school, first regular protracted experience outside home, first tricycle	First recorded successful environmental modelling with toys ((Blaut & Stea)
10. Education: Middle	Primary school: kindergarten, early grades	Journeys to school
11. Mobility: Late	First bicycle	Great expansion in home range
12. Education: Late	Primary school: later grades	"Levelling off" of spatial learning, some geographical educators claim spatial education ready to begin
13. Post-spatial	Beyond primary school: spatial abilities no longer emphasized - relegated to "second nature"	

PRIOR TO AGE 4

AGES 4 - 12

AGES 4 - 12

Figure 10.1   The experiential basis of children's cognitive mapping skills (Based on: Downs and Stea, 1977)

attempted to recognize the role of environmental transactions to the onto-genesis of macroenvironmental understanding. Moore (1976) later extended these ideas by proposing a transactional-constructivist approach to environmental knowing. The essence of this perspective is that whilst transactions are crucial to children's understanding of large-scale space, spatial information still needs to be registered in relation to some particular reference system if it is to have any meaning. Different reference systems seem apposite at different times. Spencer *et al.* (1989) note that many researchers have speculated on whether children first achieve an integrated image of body layout, then extend this frame of reference to their immediate world, and from this proceed even further outwards to consider spatial relationships between objects. Pick and Lockman (1981), whilst espousing the developmental importance of different frames of reference, suggest that a sequence of this sort need not be the case. They point out that individuals need not achieve mastery of the first frame of reference before working on the next, and some individuals may continue to refine each of these well into adult life. Once these different frames of reference have been established, individuals are able to call upon a *multiplicity* of reference systems when attempting to make sense of spatial relationships. Liben (1981) suggests that in this way environmental knowing is seen to be an outcome of active construction and the interplay of various experiential circumstances, whereby children construe the cognitive structures used to organize their spatial experiences.

Summary

The evidence above lends support to Blaut's (1987b) observation that considerable debate still surrounds 'how, why and what age or stage . . . children attain cognitive mapping ability and a parallel ability to solve locational problems, that is to navigate or traverse a space when a destination is not perceptible from the point of origin' (p. 301). However, there appears to be burgeoning support for the view that both developmental and environmental psychology, where influenced by the work of Piaget and Werner, have underestimated the environmental skills and potential of young children (Spencer and Darvizeh, 1981a). By assuming that children are simply 'primitive' adults, 'incapable of abstract thought, of rationality, of fully adult behavior, of fully developed spatial cognition' (Blaut, 1987b, p. 302), many early developmental studies failed to test for such capabilities or often failed to notice them. More recently, empirical work has shown that by using appropriate methodologies, especially those which focus on young children's real-life behaviour, in familiar, large-scale settings, children have levels of environmental competence which cannot be explained by theories which depend soley on prescribed stages of cognitive development.

Yet, no one theory seems to be able to account for the diversity and range of children's environmental ability. Blaut (1987b) highlights a number of gaps in the present state of the art.

First, in order to find out whether cognitive mapping ability, which includes solving navigational problems and problems of learning about spaces which cannot be perceived all at once, appears at the developmental level where macroenvironmental transactions are first encountered, more work needs to be carried out with children at an age when they first begin to move purposefully about their everyday surroundings. To date, insufficient attention has been given to children younger than 3 years of age, by which time children are at an advanced stage of geographical wisdom.

Secondly, there is a need to find out whether cognitive mapping is homologous to language. 'Do cognitive mapping operations correspond to the mapping operations which are involved in the use of grammar in any language?' (p. 301). Chomsky (1988) has suggested that basal grammar, principally the sentence-proposition, seems to be a cultural universal, and the underlying competence may be present at birth. Mapping is a language of space and certainly appears to be a cultural universal. It, too, follows syntactical rules which regulate order and symbolization. Does this mean that mapping competence is truly innate?

Thirdly, to ensure that empirical studies do not continue to underestimate children's environmental competencies, research design needs to be more sensitive to variables which may interfere with performance, such as, culture, class, gender, age, and variables of physical and psychological ability or handicap. This is not to suggest that research design has been deliberately unfair in the past, but that some experiments have unwittingly employed methodologies which favour 'the performance of some taxa and inhibit the performance of others'.

Finally, theoretical developments depend on not confusing place-learning with other learning processes such as how children learn about small and manipulable objects, about the social environment, about space in the abstract. Instead, Blaut suggests that place-learning in childhood is sharply different from other early learning processes in three respects:

1. Places cannot be seen as a whole from any one earthbound vantage point.
2. They cannot be explored adequately, if at all, by the very young.
3. Place-learning has specific importance for the individual, an importance perhaps grounded in phylogenetic evolution.

11

Children's feelings and attitudes towards their everyday environments

Children's environmental imagery reflects not only their understanding of spatial relationships and locational characteristics, but also their feelings and attitudes to the world about them. Some places may be remembered because they serve a particular purpose, for example, for navigation or orientation, while others may be highly imageable because they evoke emotional responses, whether positive or negative, in the child. In this chapter we will review those studies which have attempted to uncover children's affective images of the environment. First, children's disposition towards various environmental elements is presented; secondly, children's environmental attitudes and preferences are explored in the context of real-world settings; thirdly, how children perceive environmental *affordances* is discussed; and lastly children's sense of place is examined.

Children's environmental sensitivity

Environmental preference: an innate or a learned response?

Several authors have demonstrated that children express different landscape preferences to adults (Miller and Rutz, 1980; Balling and Falk, 1982). According to Kaplan (Kaplan, 1972; 1973; 1976; Kaplan, *et al.*, 1972) these differences are innate and a product of evolution. Appleton (1978), too, has argued that a preference for a particular type of landscape may also be part of mankind's biological heritage. Arguments of this kind are based upon a view which sees humans as a knowledge-dependent species, whose initial survival depended on an ability to process environmental information rapidly and to seek out habitats which maximized the advantage of bipedalism. In consequence, it is reasonable to assume that natural selection worked to keep our ancestors in certain types of environment, in particular open savannahs. It is also intuitively plausible that, over a period of generations, these early hominids came to respond selectively to savannah settings as places where they felt relatively safe and where food was available, and subconsciously they began to prefer these sorts of environment. Although subsequent species development has demanded that humans cope with virtually all kinds of geographical environment, Kaplan expects that an innate preference for open, grassland landscapes is still an integral part of human nature.

In order to test this assertion, Balling and Falk (1982) compared the reactions of children and adults to a series of slides representing five contrasting types of biomes: tropical rain forest, desert, savannah, temperate deciduous forest and coniferous forest. Respondents were asked to score these environments, both as places to live and to visit, on a six-point scale ranging from extremely desirable to extremely undesirable. The results showed that overall savannah and open forest scenes were the most preferred, while the thick forest, jungle and desert slides were clearly disliked. However, there was a marked variation of preferences with age. The strongest preference for savannah was found among the two youngest age groups, third- and fifth-grade children. However, by mid-adolescence the mean preferences for savannah, deciduous forest and coniferous forest were indistinguishable.

Balling and Falk (1982) interpret these results as providing limited support for Kaplan's assertions. They point out that if there is some innate predeliction for savannah-type environments it is most likely to be expressed in early childhood. The decline in preference for this type of biome that occurs with age is simply a product of experience and cultural expectation. Very simply, humans learn to like other types of setting, especially those which they are most familiar. However, Balling and Falk recognize that their work looks at *visual preferences* only, and is not meant to offer an insight into human adaptive tolerance or adaptive range.

Lyons (1983) takes issue with such functionalist-evolutionary explanations. Rather, she believes that landscape preferences are socially constructed and are strongly influenced by the social experiences of age, gender and place of residence. She points out that it is extremely difficult to isolate biologically heritable preferences. For example, Cavalli-Sforza and Feldman (1981) document many ways in which cultural transmission operates on the phenotype through the action of siblings, parents, teachers, institutions, the mass media and society in general, often resulting in patterns very similar to those that result from genetic transmission. To show that preferences are not culturally determined requires that similar patterns be found in non-Western societies and to date, very little work of this kind has been carried out. Also, she casts doubt upon how Balling and Falk interpret their results. Among the slides classed as representative of savannah landscapes were scenes depicting savannah-like parks and play spaces, where children spend a lot of their leisure time, and not just open grasslands. For there to be a truly genetic influence, preferences for East African savannah landscapes need to be expressed consistently and discretely in early childhood.

Lyons (1983) went on to replicate Balling and Falk's study with 281 respondents aged from 8 to 67 years, but she drew her sample from residents of

Table 11.1 Landscape preferences: summary of results

Attribute	Finding
Age	Young children show significantly higher preferences than do other age groups. Elders show significantly lower preferences
Gender	Males and females over all ages and residences show similar preferences
Residence	The 'home' biome is most preferred
Age and gender	Differences in male and female preferences open up at grade 9
Age and residence	Differences between urban and rural preferences open up at grade 9
Residence and gender	Differences between rural males and females. Differences between urban males and females. Subjects of the same sex and different residence show no significant difference in landscape preference

Source: Lyons (1983)

different types of biome, temperate deciduous forest, desert and northern coniferous forest, and from urban and rural locations. The results are summarized in Table 11.1. What these findings suggest is that landscape preference is strongly affected by contextual factors, with subjects of different ages having varying amounts of knowledge or experience. Buttressing such an interpretation is a constructivist assumption that children learn from their environmental encounters. Lyons points out that both direct and indirect sources of environmental information will shape children's views on place. However, like Kellert (1978) and Zube *et al.* (1974), she found that landscape exposure as a child was a salient factor in adult imagery.

Psychometric analysis

A number of studies have shown that children's reactions to the environment depend, in part, on their personality and individual preferences. In his studies with adults, McKechnie (1977) developed a classification, the *environmental response inventory* (ERI), which differentiated between ranges of environmental behaviour according to measures based on design, recreational and leisure, and locational preferences. What McKechnie was able to show was that individuals have different predispositions to differing types of environment, which encourages varying reactions and responses to the components of place. Bunting and Cousins (1985) have extended these ideas to look at children's beliefs and values about the environment. Working with 1,100 children stratified by grade (4, 6, 8 and 10), they developed a *children's environmental response inventory* (CERI) based on eight dimensions which encapsulate children's place reactions:

Pastoralism, a positive response to natural environments.
Urbanism, an attraction to built environments.

Environmental adaptation, a belief that people have the right to use technology in order to manage nature.

Stimulus seeking, an enjoyment of environmental adventure.

Environmental trust, a sense of confidence in all environmental settings.

Antiquarianism, an attraction towards historical and traditional environments.

Privacy, a positive appreciation of solitude.

Mechanical orientation, an affinity to mechanical structures and the enjoyment of manual activity.

What psychometric analysis, of the kind provided by ERI and CERI, suggests is that individual differences in cognitive imagery and environmental competence cannot be entirely explained by factors like levels of development or environmental experience, but may instead be due to deep-seated, personality traits. The relationship between personality and landscape preferences has been further explored by Abello and Bernaldez (1986) and Abello *et al.* (1986). They examined individual responses to various natural settings and found that individuals often reacted to an environment in different ways. Whether a place was seen as 'exciting' or 'alarming', or 'stimulating' or 'deterring' depended on a personal capacity for accepting risk or challenge.

A number of studies have attempted to examine what facets of an environment particularly attract or repel children. Both Zube (1984) and Bernaldez *et al.* (1984) report on the importance of water as a scenic component for children's preferences. Together with Bernaldez *et al.* (1987a), they also note that children under 15 years tend to prefer less naturalistic, less complex landscapes than adults. In another exercise, Bernaldez *et al.* (1987b) examined the reactions of 483 children aged 11 and 16 years to fifty paired sets of landscape photographs. Multivariate analysis of the children's responses revealed three independent preference dimensions:

1. Clear, illuminated scenes rich in detail vs. darker, shadowed scenes, with less detail definition.
2. Diverse, contrasted and varied scenes vs. more monotonous landscapes.
3. Bland, smooth surfaces vs. harsh, rough, rasping surfaces.

Age was seen to have a significant effect. The younger children showed less preference for shadowed scenes (first dimension) and for harsh scenes (third dimension); no significant difference was noted for the second dimension. Bernaldez *et al.* (1987b) suggest that these variations arose because young children find some environments more intimidating and alarming than others; accordingly, feelings of 'risk' and 'uncertainty' encourage negative reactions. Fear and insecurity have also been identified by Appleton (1978) as very important ingredients in landscape aesthetics. Children's changing attitudes with age partly reflect a growing sense of control and challenge, so whilst harsh environments are seen as 'aggressive' and disturbing at the age of 11 years, by

the age of 16 years they are seen as stimulating and exciting. Bernaldez *et al.*
(1987b) liken the reasons for this changeover from rejection to attraction to
Baldwin and Baldwin's (1981) observations on the behaviour of non-human
primates. In this case, maturing males increasingly accept environmental
challenge and tend to explore increasingly risky environments, leaving the
young and females in safer environs. Indeed, Bernaldez and Parra (1979) have
noted that sex has some influence on landscape preference. Male students have
been shown to prefer wild, spontaneous, disordered landscapes, while female
students are attracted by more organized, humanized places.

Children's environmental attitudes to their everyday worlds

Children's feelings about places have been explored in a variety of ways. Taken
together, what emerges from these disparate studies is that children, from an
early age, have a strong affective sense of nature. For example, Hart (1979)
examined children's 'favourite places' in a New England township by means of
a questionnaire survey and by following children on a series of child-led 'place
expeditions'. Hart categorized the results into four main types:

1. *Land-use*, places valued because of the uses children put them to in their
   play.
2. *Social*, places valued because some individual lives or works there or because
   some particular social event occurs there, such as cubs or brownies.
3. *Commercial*, places valued because of what can be bought or otherwise
   obtained there.
4. *Aesthetic*, places valued because of what they look or feel like (Hart, 1979,
   p. 160).

However, Hart points out that children selected very different types of places
when interviewed compared to when leading an investigator to their favourite
haunts. In particular, children identified many more small places valued for
their special purposes on the 'place expeditions' than during the interviews. He
also observed that place preferences varied with age. Relatively more of the
younger children (kindergarten to third grade) described 'commercial' or
'social' (people's homes) places, whereas the older children (fourth to sixth
grade) stressed those places which were valued because of their 'land-use' and,
in some cases, 'aesthetic' qualities. Although parental sanctions regulated
children's environmental transactions, most children rated local water elements, such as rivers, lakes, brooks and frog ponds, very highly. In addition,
woods and trees provided exciting opportunities to play climbing and hiding
games. Interestingly, more girls than boys expressed a preference for places
inside their homes, perhaps a reflection of their more limited environmental
range.

Table 11.2 Favourite-place types

Place type	Mean representation rate
Home sites	1.19
Open space	1.12
Vegetation	.91
Natural ground surfaces	.84
Pathways and associated surfaces	.75
Sports facilities	.39
Non-residential buildings	.33
Macro landscape features	.33
Fences	.28
People	.27

Note:
Mean representation rate is the number of mentions
in a given category divided by the number of
drawings (n = 96)

Source: Moore (1986)

Moore (1986) investigated children's favourite places by asking them to draw where they went after school or on weekends, around their homes and neighbourhoods. He carried out his survey in three contrasting types of urban setting: a 'big city', a 'new city' and an 'old city'. Assuming that children's drawings represent individually significant and memorable experiences, only two features, lawns (71 per cent), and playgrounds and schoolyards (65 per cent), were consistently represented on more than half of the drawings. In total, fifty-two sorts of places were recorded. Moore went on to categorize this element set into a number of different types of favourite place (see Table 11.2). What the results convey is children's close affinity to the natural world. A picture of habitual range emerges, with day-to-day leisure time oriented around children's homes and nearby open spaces, streets and parks, and trees, wherever they could be found. Moore suggests that the high ranking of 'fences' reflects their positive function as an enclosing element, affording privacy and a sense of security, and not their negative purpose of restricting access.

These results are also of interest for what elements are missing. Those environmental features most recorded can be explained in terms of their nearness, intrinsic attractiveness and cultural or social significance. For the less popular items, Moore suggests that a number of factors combine to limit their attractiveness. For example, considering the 'normal' attraction of children to water, the low rate of mention of acquatic elements was simply a reflection of a lack of water-play opportunities close to home. Similarly, the low incidence of 'animals' was an outcome of the ephemeral nature of child–wildlife relationships in urban settings. Very simply, 'animals are not place specific' (Moore, 1986, p. 15) and children are constantly on the move. Drawings of local shops were surprisingly low. Moore speculates that a reason for this was that children associated local shops with running errands and domestic chores and not with play. The low incidence of 'child-made places', like forts, clubhouses, hiding places and secret places, was also surprising, especially as these are the very kind of sites that adults portray as ideal childhood environments. Moore suggests that these sorts of experience are difficult for children to recall, for as with wildlife, they also bear aspects of impermanence.

A number of studies note that children frequently invent names to describe their favourite places. For example, I have described how children in suburban Coventry labelled the 'Moth-hawk tree' on their maps (Matthews, 1984a), whereas others referred to such local features as the 'Dump', the 'Compound', 'Charlie's field', and the 'Black alley'. Moore (1986) reports that two local ponds in Mill Hill had been given special names by the local children, 'Queenie' and 'Number-one newting pond', whereas an abandoned marl hole was known colloquially as 'Brickers'. Moore coins the term *toponymy* to describe this practice. For him, it indicates 'a degree of proprietorship that can only happen when adult culture does not dominate the scene too heavily' (p. 225). Names such as these are also highly resistant to change, as if they represent a kind of environmental permanency which is important to children's place-learning. Moore (1986) describes how some six years earlier he had photo-graphed a site in Mill Hill known as the 'Roller-coaster place', because local children used it for racing go-karts, on return to the same place the name and local use still continued even though the site had been cleared and its topography completely remoulded by bulldozers.

Not all places are remembered because of their positive imagery. Hart (1979) investigated children's sense of *dangerous and scary places*. Abandoned buildings, woods, snakes and 'bear's places' were frequently and vividly recalled, as were attics, cellars, garages and bedrooms at night. Consensual place fears of this kind resemble the archetypal scary places of children's literature. Hart suggests 'they are probably passed on to us as part of place mythology, but all share some common features which are understandably fear-provoking: they are all uninhabited and dark, offering unlimited opportunities for imagination' (Hart, 1979, p. 334).

A comparison of the results of Hart (1979) and Moore (1986) suggests that children's varying transactions with place are instrumental in shaping their affective images of space. Some environmental information, however, will be the result of indirect experience. For example, Hart investigated children's 'desired' environments beyond their home area. The results were extremely patchy and mostly products of word-of-mouth communication from adults. Children who had heard their parents talk enthusiastically of a place were likely to show the same fondness for that location. Other sources of information were television commercials, picture books and travel posters. Occasionally, children generalized from their own indirect experiences, such that a good meal at a Chinese restaurant led to a positive image of China.

Ward (1977), drawing upon a range of studies on children's urban behaviour, offers a classification of children's reactions to place. First, there are the *antiquarians*, who cherish an environment precisely because of its associations with continuity and familiarity; secondly, there are the *explorers*, who positively enjoy and savour the challenge and uncertainty of moving and roaming in a newly discovered environment; and thirdly, there are the *neophiliacs*, for whom newness, neatness and tidiness represent the best qualities of life. What Ward's classification suggests is that young children are keenly aware of the landscape that surrounds them and through their actions and behaviour places become imbued with symbolic and cultural significance.

The affordances of places

In Chapter 4 we reviewed Gibson's (1950; 1958; 1966; 1979) theoretical ideas on functional ecology. According to Gibson (1979), environments and their elements are experienced not only as configurational settings, but also as places which *afford* different kinds of opportunities. Different places will have different levels of functional significance for the child, who, in turn, assesses the *affordances* of places through the stimulus information which they impart. Consequently, for an environmental element to have an affordance, its functional meaning must be directly perceivable. The functional salience of an environmental feature depends, in part, on how the receiver interprets perceptual information. In this regard, children and adults will often assess the affordance of an environment in different ways.

Barker and Wright's (1955) ecological study, *Midwest and its children*, illustrates how children perceive the functional significance of places. They discuss how certain aspects of an environment exert a 'coercive influence' on perception and activity. For example, when Midwest children see an open level area, free from obstruction, they often remember these settings not for their designative purpose (that is, the Courthouse lawn, the football field, the school gymnasium), but as potential sites for vigorous activity, such as 'running and romping'. 'Open spaces seduce children. The behavior settings of the Midwest are loaded with these perceived, seductive characteristics' (Barker and Wright, 1955, p. 55). In their review of children's environmental cognition, Heft and Wohlwill (1987) draw attention to the early work of Martha Muchow (Muchow and Muchow, 1935). In her observations on children playing around a canal basin in Hamburg, she notes how the fences separating the area from the street formed focal points of activity. Although intended as boundary markers, these fences were perceived as features 'to be climbed and to be perched on by the children, and similarly, the embankments were for sliding, running and climbing' (Heft and Wohlwill, 1987, p. 193).

Other examples of children perceiving environmental elements as affordances are noted by several studies. Hart (1979) discusses how places are remembered not for what they are but for what they afford the child. Hence, when children talk about areas within their home town they frequently use descriptors to distinguish between 'dangerous' and 'scary' places. In our Kenyan study (Matthews and Airey, 1990), we observe how children use the school compound as 'a safe haven', where they can relax and mix with their peers without reproach from their parents. Also, how the surrounding 'bush country' is perceived as dangerous and potentially threatening, even though there was little evidence to support such a view. In one village, an especially prominent tree was regarded as 'a testing ground' for acceptance into a local boys' gang. In order to gain entry, boys had to demonstrate their agility and lack of fear by climbing up to its highest branches. Many children represented this tree on their sketch maps. Lukashok and Lynch (1956) point out that among the most common recollections of adults about their childhood are references to play opportunities afforded by the environment: places where, as children, they could hide, jump, climb and swing.

Heft and Wohlwill (1987) speculate that if landscapes are remembered in terms of their affordances, contextual and functional knowledge may well precede configurational knowledge. Also, in time, the perception of affordances may lead to an understanding of configuration. For example, the configuration of a road or path may become known, simply because it leads to a particular child-centred goal, such as sweet shop or a school. They suggest that Gibson's work deserves closer attention in these respects:

> If investigators would begin to examine environmental knowledge in terms of the affordances of places, they might discover not only that such knowledge is basic to children's understanding about their environment, but also that children are more knowledgeable about the environment than has yet been revealed. (p. 193)

A sense of place

A sense of place describes a particular kind of relationship between individuals and localities. For individuals different places are imbued with different meanings. Relph (1976) suggests that the meaning of a place comes neither from its whereabouts, nor from the trivial functions it serves, nor from the community that occupies it, nor from superficial and mundane experiences. Rather a sense of place is an *affective bond* that develops between people and locations over time. Tuan (1974) borrows Auden's word, *topophilia*, to describe this affective relationship. Walmsley and Lewis (1984) note that although the notion of topophilia covers aesthetic, tactile and emotional responses, the most prominent sentiment is a *sense of belonging* or a place-rootedness. A sense of place relates to varying spatial scales. Psychoanalysts, such as Searles (1959) and Jung (1969) have recognized the strong affinity to home locales and environmental belongingness that develops in early and middle childhood. Sanchez-Robles (1980) has shown how individuals develop 'ties' to items of furniture, to their home, to particular buildings, to their neighbourhood, to their city and to their nation.

How children develop a sense of place has interested a number of researchers. To some extent children's ability to ascribe meaning to places depends on their ability to conceptualize space. Piché (1981) has shown that 5-year-old children are unable to differentiate between proximate space and distant space and so conceptions of 'here' and 'elsewhere' are imperfect and incomplete. At this age the home is the sole source of symbolic attachment. As children grow older, so their conception of places beyond the home improves. Piaget and Weil (1951) suggest, however, that not until the age of 11 years is the notion of 'country' fully grasped, but once this is achieved children quickly develop an affective relation to the 'terra patria' and begin to judge foreigners. Jahoda (1963) also notes that children's understanding of distant places develops with age. He interviewed a group of Glaswegian children, aged 6 to 11 years. Their verbal answers were sorted into four categories: (i) no conception of Glasgow as a unit; (ii) conception of Glasgow, but not as part of Scotland; (iii) conception of Glasgow as part of Scotland, but not of Britain; and (iv) correct conception. Although by the age of 11 years most children were able to understand the position of Glasgow within a broad place hierarchy, some 12 per cent were still unable to conceive of Glasgow as a unitary whole.

More recently, Daggs (1986) examined the emergence of the concept of a geographical hierarchy in a developmental framework with children in grades 1 to 3. Children's sense of place was examined in three ways. First, children were questioned to assess their familiarity with the basic order of a set of geographical units. For example, children were asked: 'Are the people in town (X) in Pennsylvania? Can a person leave the United States and remain in Pennsylvania?' Secondly, children completed a graphical test, whereby a page contained a circle which was identified as a geographical unit, such as a state. Children were then asked to draw a second circle on the page to represent another unit, such as a town or a country. In a third test, children's sense of relational space was further explored with reference to a large-scale physical model of a park. After identifying the basic components of the model (playground, tent, pond, sandbox, etc.), children were asked: 'If you were in the sandbox would you be in the park?' or 'Can you be in the tent and the playground at the same time?' Daggs found a statistically significant difference in performance between grades 1 and 2 and grades 1 and 3 on the verbal test and between grades 1 and 3 on the graphic test. In each case performance improved with age. She found that whilst performance was reasonably high for grade-2 children, nevertheless, some children had not mastered the idea of a geographical hierarchy. All three grades performed well on the model exercise, perhaps a reflection of the concrete nature of the model or because children were more familiar with the geographical elements used in the exercise.

Gould and White (1968) have revealed how, by the time children are ready to leave school they have developed strong local attachments to their home area.

They sampled school-leavers in twenty-three widely dispersed schools in Britain. Students were asked to rank each county according to its perceived level of residential desirability. Although a national consensus was found which highlighted the whole of the south coast, each school produced a dome of high desirability centred on its local area. A similar result was found when Gould (1966) carried out a survey among undergraduates in the United States. On this occasion, although the west coast was the most favoured region and most students consistently assessed Alabama and its neighbouring southern states to be residentially unattractive, Alabaman students still scored their locality highly. Gould and White (1986) repeated the survey in Tanzania, Ghana and China and in each case an extremely strong and persistent local effect was found.

In a further study, Gould and Ola (1970) were interested to see whether attachment to places changed with age. They looked at the place preferences of children and adults in Nigeria, West Africa. Their survey was carried out in Oyo, which was just north of Ibadan, and at the edge of the core region of the country. At the age of 13 years there was a strong local effect, with very little preference expressed for elsewhere. By the age of 15 years other nearby large places were now considered attractive, but were still not as highly regarded as the immediate home place. By the age of 23 years the principal towns and cities of Nigeria now competed with the home region, but rarely exceeded it, in terms of desirability. Their conclusion was that attachment to the home region appears resistant to changing circumstance, although location in invisible information space and individuals' growing receptivity to different communication sources, exert a powerful effect on place preference.

At a different spatial scale, Hess and Torney (1967) investigated children's sense of belonging to their homeland. Their main concern was the political socialization of children into the system of the United States. They uncovered a three-stage process in the development of the concept of a nation: in the first stage the focuses of attachment are national symbols, such as the flag and the Statue of Liberty; in the second stage, the concept of nation is understood, including abstract qualities and ideological context; and in the third stage the country is seen as part of a larger organized system of countries. Gottman (1952) believes that this sort of process, whereby children become imbued with a common cherished heritage, is a cultural universal. He suggests that in this way an *iconography* or a mental partitioning of the world becomes set and that these territories of the mind are more stable and less flexible than political boundaries.

Summary

Children have a strong affective sense of the world around them. Their views on place and space are coloured by emotions and feelings, which give rise to powerful environmental pulls and pushes. Hart (1979) points out that as adults we have difficulty in empathizing with the attitudes of childhood. We have mostly forgotten our own childhood fears and excitements, and often no longer recognize the fascination that small, local places can offer. Moore (1986) notes that children are highly discriminatory about their use of local resources. Through their environmental transactions they create a complex 'woven metaphor' of personal playtraces. 'These are no ordinary weavings ... they vibrate with life as new threads weave in while others dwindle away ... hues shimmer and change ... in lockstep with the playtrace patterns' (p. 38). Environmental transactions, such as these, enable children to perceive the environment, a process which Gibson suggests is instrumental to place-learning. Indeed, the affordance of environmental features may be the first step towards environmental knowing. However, children's views on place are not shaped by direct experiences alone. Knowledge of distant places is largely culturally determined. In this respect, children model themselves on the values of their surrounding adult world. Perhaps, too, some of these place fears and attractions reach back thousands of years into the depths of pre-history.

Part 4

Children's environmental needs

In this Part we examine some of the practical implications of contemporary research on children's environmental capability. Two issues are discussed. Chapter 12 looks at how recent work on young children's environmental skills and competencies challenges many of the educational assumptions of established practices. There is now a growing body of opinion which suggests that mapping skills can be taught from the age of school entrance and graphicacy should be given as much prominence within the early school curriculum as numeracy, literacy and articulacy. Chapter 13 highlights a number of planning issues. By studying children's images of place and space adults are offered peepholes into the private geographies of childhood. Such information offers planners an invaluable opportunity to design environments which not only accommodate children, but also are responsive to their varying needs.

12

Educational issues: Geography and graphicacy

Different theoretical viewpoints lead to different expectations about the environmental competencies of young children. Uncritical acceptance of Piagetian, age-dependent state theory, supported by laboratory and small-scale tests – mostly divorced from children's daily experiences – has meant that educational practice has been dominated by a theoretical perspective which argues that children younger than 7 years are incapable not only of rational mapping behaviour, but also of any true understanding of place. Indeed, in a recent paper on geographical education Downs *et al.* (1988) offer a stout defence of Piagetian theory, which they see as a particularly productive theoretical structure for curricula development in geography. Three advantages are listed. First, it is inclusive, in that it is a general theory of cognitive development which spans a wide range of ages and domains. Secondly, it encourages curricula whose objective is to match simultaneously children's existing schemata and also which move beyond children's current understanding. 'This active approach to learning allows the child to assimilate material while at the same time leading the child to modify existing schemata to accommodate the discrepant material' (p. 684). Thirdly, its emphasis on representation, space and logic are ideas which are especially valuable for the comprehension and production of maps.

There is now a burgeoning body of opinion which refutes such Piagetian strictures. Convincing evidence suggests that young children's capacity to structure and organize environmental information may well have been under-estimated. Although young children may use their body as a central reference point, this does not imply that they are locked into an egocentric frame of reference and hence incapable of understanding Euclidean relationships until much later years, nor does it suggest that a Piagetian staged system of development is inevitable. Also, children probably have more ability to represent and use their cognitive representations of space than is conventionally acknowledged. What children appear to lack is a conscious awareness of which strategy is most appropriate, as well as the expressive skill to make investigators aware of their true abilities. When guided by adults children as young as 3-years-old are able to perform geographical tasks with considerable acumen.

Indeed, by using altered methodologies, related to their world of experience, very young children have been shown to possess a range of mapping and spatial modelling skills, often demonstrating a level of environmental competence more advanced than credited by the Piagetian tradition. In this chapter we will examine the traditional wisdom of the classroom with respect to mapping skills and the place of geography, examine current curricula developments in geography and map work, and review studies which suggest that mapping behaviour and a sense of place should be given a much earlier prominence in the school curriculum. In order to provide a reasonable scope for this chapter, attention focuses upon recent educational developments in the early phase of primary education in England and Wales. (For an appreciation of recent developments in the American school curriculum see Downs *et al.* 1988.)

The traditional view: Geography and mapping skills

Geography is the study of places. Among their interests, geographers seek to understand what places are like, where they are and why they are as they are (Catling, 1987). The study of geography, therefore, provides an ideal opportunity to introduce children to the world around them, as well as to develop mapping and spatial reasoning skills. For a long time, however, advice to teachers was conservative and largely wedded to Piagetian values. Accordingly, geography was given little prominence in the belief that most mapping tasks were beyond the capability of the very young and that the egocentricity of the young child led inevitably to a *domo-centric* view of the world. For example, as recently as the mid-1970s, Long (1974), in his *Handbook for geography teachers*, was suggesting that 6- and 7-year-olds should only draw around the base of objects in order to get some idea of a plan. Not until the age of 9 years were children considered able to grasp the purpose and meaning of a map. This sort of advice followed on from earlier statements by Prior (1959) and Satterly (1964), both of whom argued that maps were inappropriate media for primary school children. A Department of Education and Science survey (HMI, 1978) of primary education in England at this time noted that 'many schools made no use of maps, atlases and globes' (para 5.136) and the making of maps and plans was given little attention. Even where work centred on the neighbourhood of the school, maps of the locality were introduced relatively infrequently. In a review of map work in schools, Catling (1979a) noted that there was a general attitude that whilst infants should be active, juniors were expected to work in *passive* situations. Thus, when 7–11-year-old children were given maps, little effort was made to help them. He argued that it was no surprise, therefore, that children of this age range should find map exercises unattractive and often difficult. As late as 1982, Graves, in the *New UNESCO source book for geography teaching*, was still espousing caution about primary school map work.

Although educational practice was stoutly grounded on Piagetian principles, conventional classroom wisdom about children's geographical skills was largely a function of anecdotal evidence, and there was seldom any attempt to evaluate the efficacy of rival teaching programmes. Commenting upon the state of geographical education in the primary school curriculum at this time, Catling (1979b) observed that the subject was largely taught in an 'unstructured' and 'fragmented' manner.

Not all educationalists agreed with the decision to insulate primary-aged children from place, space and map work. Two geographers, Balchin and Coleman (1965) argued that *graphicacy*, the skill of communicating about places by means of plans, maps, diagrams and graphs, should be viewed as 'the fourth ace' in the educational pack, alongside literacy, numeracy and oracy. They pointed out there was no good reason why graphicacy should not be taught from the time of school entrance, rather than being left to the age of 7 or 8 years. 'After all ... graphical talent is ... more spontaneous than writing or numbers, and there is no need to leave it unchannelled' (*TES*, 5 November 1965). Indeed, the HM Inspectorate survey (1978, para. 5.14) noted that four-fifths of all classes already made some use of graphical and other diagrammatic forms of presentation in mathematics. Despite these sentiments and observations, map work in particular and geography in general, remained 'cinderella' subjects in the primary curriculum. For example, two contemporary surveys revealed that 71 per cent of primary school teachers never used large-scale maps of any sort (Cracknell, 1976), whilst only 6 per cent featured the term 'geography' (Bassey, 1978).

Developing children's environmental skills: Recent curricula changes in geography and map work

There is now plenty of evidence to suggest that young children are capable of a wide range of environmental skills, including rudimentary mapping behaviour and an incipient understanding of places. These sorts of findings, when taken together with the criticisms of map work in primary education noted above, and closer central government interest in the curriculum in general (for example, see communications between the Minister of State for Education and the Geographical Association in Bailey and Binns, 1987 and DES, 1982; 1983; 1985; HMI, 1986), have brought about a radical reappraisal of the teaching of geography and graphicacy within the primary school.

The last ten years or so has seen considerable enthusiasm for the development of geography in the primary curriculum. Encouragement has been forthcoming from a number of sources, including the Department of Education and Science and the Geographical Association. In *Geography from 5 to 16* (HMI, 1986) a series of useful objectives are set out for the early primary (see Table 12.1) and late primary phases. It can be seen that considerable emphasis is given to the study of the local environment and the development of basic

Table 12.1 Objectives for geography in the early primary phase

---

The curriculum for the early years should provide pupils with learning experiences of a geographical nature that will enable them to:

1. Extend their awareness of their surroundings
2. Identify and explore features of the local environment
3. Distinguish between the variety of ways in which land is used and the variety of purposes for which buildings are constructed
4. Recognize and investigate changes taking place in the local area
5. Gain some understanding of the different contributions which a variety of individuals and services make to the life of the local community
6. Relate different types of human activity to specific places within the local area
7. Develop an awareness of cultural and ethnic diversity within our society, whilst recognizing the similar activities, interests and aspirations of different people
8. Extend their vocabulary and develop concepts which enable them to describe the relative position and spatial attributes of features within their environment
9. Understand some of the ways in which the local environment affects people's lives
10. Develop an awareness of seasonal changes of weather and of the effects which weather conditions have on the growth of plants, on the lives of animals, and on their own and other people's activities
11. Begin to develop an interest in people and places beyond their own immediate experience
12. Observe accurately and develop simple skills of enquiry
13. Extend and refine their vocabulary and develop language skills
14. Develop mathematical concepts and number skills
15. Develop their competence to communicate in a variety of forms, including pictures, drawings and simple diagrams and maps

---

Source: HMI (1986)

mapping skills.

A powerful polemic on the distinctive contribution of geography to children's education is made in the Geographical Association's publication, *A case for geography* (Bailey and Binns, 1987). Among the contributors, Catling (1987) gives particular attention to the criteria for a geographical content in the primary classroom. For Catling, 'the child *is* a geographer'. He contends that 'no child, in reality, comes to school who is not already a geographer' (1987, p. 19). Catling arrives at this conclusion not through extensive empirical testings but from a constructivist conviction. He argues that, from birth, children show a fascination with the world around them. Through their environmental experiences, whether direct or indirect, they develop a sense of locational awareness and 'construct strategies for explaining to themselves where they and other features are in their environment, and how these elements relate to each other' (p. 19). As young children become aware of distant places so 'they evolve mental schemes to relate these places to themselves' (p. 19). Accordingly, environmental competence is a life-long process, intricately bound in with exploration and information processing.

From this basis, Catling proposes that the starting point of any primary school curriculum should be the child's world of experience. By this token, geography is the ideal subject through which to develop children's sense of place. He suggests a series of sixteen questions which can form the basis of subject work planning, or provide a means for assessing current curricular practice, only some of which are reproduced below. For example, Catling asks (1987, pp. 19–20), in what way and to what extent does the primary school geography curriculum:

1. Recognize, explore and extend each child's cognitive map so that it becomes a more effective tool for making sense of the world around?
2. Value, examine and enhance children's territorial understanding, and help build an appreciation of territorial relationships in the wider world?
3. Build upon and extend children's interactions with places, through first-hand experience and by examining and learning about such people-and-environment interactions through secondary sources?
4. Examine people's experiences of place, so that children consider what it would be like to be a person living in that place?
5. Harness children's fascination for and curiosity about place?
6. Deepen and extend children's understanding of the nature of places: of their main features, the processes at work, their current state, their development, the changes that are taking place?
7. Enable children to examine their own attitudes to and about places?
8. Foster children's capacities to imagine places (real and imaginary)?
9. Develop children's understanding of maps?

Whilst Catling acknowledges that many primary schools may already display 'good practice' in relation to these principles, criteria such as these would particularly alert non-specialist geography teachers to some of the exciting ideas and ways in which geography could be applied in the classroom.

An initial difficulty which many teachers faced when attempting to revise their syllabuses in the light of new developments was a lack of suitable classroom material. There is now a growing range of primary geography texts (for example, Bale, 1987; Blyth, 1984; Catling *et al.*, 1981–2; Fisher and Hicks, 1985; Mays, 1985; Mills, 1987; Scoffham, 1981) and journals (such as *Primary Geographer, Teaching Geography*) which suggest ways to enhance children's place knowledge and heighten their environmental skills. Given that pupils' range of place knowledge and place experience varies spatially, temporally and socially (Pearce, 1987), there appears to be a consensus that a good geographical education depends not only on rich and lively resources and classroom activities, but also on specific place-based work, 'including studies in the school environment itself, in the immediate locality, and further afield' (Pearce, 1987, p. 35). Awareness of and understanding about the environment as a 'real place' can only be achieved through direct contact. In consequence, field work is now regarded 'as intrinsic to the learning and teaching of geography as clinical practice is to medicine' (p. 35).

Considerable efforts have also been made to remedy the deficiencies noted in the HMI (1978) report with regard to map work in primary schools. Whilst it was generally accepted that primary schools had clear guidelines on the

Table 12.2 Mapping tasks for primary school children

5–7 years	9–11 years
By the age of 7 children should normally be able to: 1. Follow directions using left, right, forwards, in a circle, etc. 2. Describe the relative locations of objects using before, behind, in front of, etc. 3. Sort objects by relative size and draw round them 4. Sort objects by their shape, such as squares, circles, etc., and draw round them 5. Draw round life size objects, such as coins, toys, etc., to show their shapes in plan form 6. Draw routes between objects drawn, such as a path of an imaginary crawling insect 7. Draw symbols to illustrate picture maps or imaginary maps 8. Measure spaces between objects using hands or feet *7–9 years* By the age of 9 children should be able to: 9. Plot the cardinal directions NESW 10. Use a compass to find NESW in the school playground 11. Draw a plan at a very large-scale, such as a desk top with objects on it 12. Measure from a large-scale plan, such as a teacher-prepared plan of the classroom 13. Insert in their approximate positions on the plan objects in the room, such as blackboard, tables 14. Record around the plan features seen from the room, such as playground, trees 15. Draw free-hand a map showing a simple route, such as the journey to school 16. Make a simple model of part of the neighbourhood, such as a row of shops 17. Give locations in grid squares, such as A1, B3, etc., as on an A to Z map 18. Measure straight line distances between two points on an A to Z road map 19. Draw some conventional symbols on an imaginary map and add a key 20. Identify different countries shown on atlas maps	By the age of 11 children should normally be able to: 21. Plot the sixteen points of a compass 22. State bearings in degrees: 45, 90, 135, etc. 23. Indicate directions in the neighbourhood 24. Align a map of the school and neighbourhood by means of a compass and buildings 25. Find directions and bearings using a compass 26. Orientate a large-scale map (1:1,250 or 1:2,500) using buildings as reference points, e.g. church 27. Relate position on the ground to location on a large-scale map 28. Use grid lines to locate points 29. Give four figure grid references using eastings and northings 30. Draw a plan of the classroom and/or school 31. Identify and name rooms on a teacher-prepared plan of the school 32. Make measurements on large-scale maps of the local area (1:1,250 or 1:2,500 or 1:10,000) 33. Measure the straight line distance between two fixed points on maps of progressively smaller scales 34. Measure the winding distance along roads between two fixed points on maps of progressively smaller scales 35. Compare symbols for the same feature on maps of progressively smaller scales 36. Realize that the degree of generalization on maps increases with decreasing scale 37. Appreciate that some symbols on smaller maps are disproportionate to the size of the objects they represent 38. Identify features on a low-level oblique aerial photograph of the local area 39. Make a scale model of part of the local area showing roads and buildings 40. Give locations on atlas maps using latitude and longitude

Source: Boardman (1983)

development of literacy and numeracy skills, because of the importance of English and mathematics in the early curriculum no such framework was available for mapping. Boardman (1983; 1985) responded to this need by providing a valuable list of graphical skills considered appropriate for pupils of different age groups (see Table 12.2). His ideas broadly correspond to those further suggested by the Geographical Association in their handbook, *Geographical work in primary and middle schools* (Mills, 1981; 1987). Boardman's mapping scheme is based on four basic concepts which he contends children must grasp in order to understand and use maps: *direction, location, scale* and *symbolism*. He also emphasizes the importance of involving children in practical activities when learning the map skills relating to these concepts. Boardman's intention was to encourage teachers to try techniques earlier on in the primary curriculum and to foster innovative map use and map interpretation work throughout the school. He points out that the skills listed for each age range are tentative and that the scheme is not intended to be applied rigorously to all children in all circumstances. 'Some children will master the various skills at earlier ages than those suggested: slow learning children will not attain them until much later' (Boardman, 1985, p. 129).

The sequence of teaching and learning which Boardman advocates is, however, based on a Piagetian interpretation of spatial understanding which postulates that children advance through three stages of conceptual thought. During infancy, conceptions of space are purely *topological*; during the early junior school years, children's spatial concepts are *projective* in nature; only towards the end of their primary school years are children able to see space with *Euclidean* clarity. Accordingly, mapping tasks which relate to the real world are best approached after the age of 7 years, when children are moving beyond an egocentric frame of reference. Although no rival scheme has been proposed in any detail, the work of others (see Chapter 8) suggests that Boardman's schema may underestimate the true environmental potential of the very young. Apart from its own intrinsic value, map work can also lead on to a range of interesting topic work about the local environment. Indeed, the report *Geography from 5 to 16* (HMI, 1986) recognizes that the majority of primary-age children will encounter geography through topic work. Keen advocates of this approach are Coleman and Catling (1982). They have shown how land-use maps not only assist in map-reading skills, but also provide a rich store of information which can be used in projects from the primary class through to the upper school.

Some of the most exciting developments in the teaching of primary geography in the last decade have come about through the use of 'new technology'. Microcomputer packages are now commonly used to introduce children to map work. An early example is *Introducing map skills* (Cambridge University Press, 1983), which enables children to practise grid references, scales, compass directions and bearings, and culminates in a 'game' which tests children's understanding of distance and direction. Even more impressive is the BBC's *Domesday project*, available on interactive videodiscs. The Domesday package consists of two discs, termed *local* and *national*. The local disc consists of some 150,000 screen pages of text, over 80,000 pictures of places and landscapes and 24,000 Ordnance Survey maps at six different scales. Data for this disc were collected by over 15,500 schools and community groups, each responsible for a 4×3 km block. In contrast, the national disc is a very wide database offering information on *culture, economy, society and environment*. In all, there are some 9,000 sets of data and 40,000 photographs on the national disc. In summary, the criticisms made by the HM Inspectorate (1978) about map work and geography in primary education no longer seem justified. Graphicacy is now an accepted part of the primary curriculum, and children are increasingly encouraged to take a full and active interest in their localities. Indeed, the Geographical Association's logo, 'Geography is going places' aptly summarizes the achievements and approaches of the 1980s.

Environmental education

At the same time as the Geographical Association was campaigning on behalf of geography, the Town and Country Planning Association was attempting to raise the profile of environmental education in primary schools. A central aim was to involve children in issues relevant to their locality, so that they would develop a keener sense of place and become more able to participate in shaping their own environments. Impetus was given to their ambition by the Department of Environment's report (1979) which suggested that 'environmental education in schools ... be given a much higher priority than at present ... its standing should be on par with other subjects.' Journals such as the *Bulletin of Environmental Education* and *Childhood Environments Quarterly* have been especially valuable in this context, as both attempt to provide teachers and interested organizations with lively and regular updates about schemes and projects which seek to enhance children's awareness of their environment.

Since 1987 the *Annual Review of Environmental Education* has offered a timely overview of recent achievements and developments. The publication of *Environmental education from 5 to 16* (HMI, 1989) confirmed the new status of environmental studies within the primary curriculum. Beyond the school, there is now a vast network of organizations, professionals and campaigning groups, all attempting to foster a closer interaction between children and their outdoor surroundings. The report of the Earthkids Project (1990) is especially useful in this respect in that it provides a comprehensive listing of books, resource packs, resource centres and sources of funding relevant to environmental education.

The national curriculum

Geography's position in schools has now been consolidated by its identification as a *foundation subject* in the national curriculum. The focus of the geography curriculum is on three profile components and five attainment targets (see Figure 12.1), which are to be developed within four key stages (KSI 5–7 years; KSII 7–11 years; KSIII 11-14 years; KSIV 14–16 years) and ten attainment levels. This is not the place to examine the credence of such an approach. What

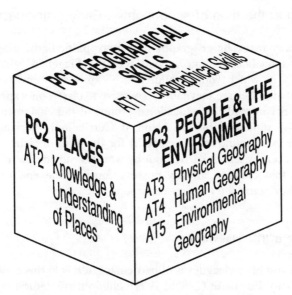

Figure 12.1   Profile components (PC) and attainment targets (AT) in geography in
the national curriculum

is of interest, however, is the emphasis that KSI gives to the study of locality and
mapping skills. For example, the Statutory Orders specify that much of pupils'
learning should be based on direct experience, practical activities and exploration of the local area. They should also be given opportunities to use
information technology (IT). Included among the geographical skills are
recommendations that children should: learn to use pictorial maps and to
extract information; be helped to add information to pictorial maps; draw their
own representations of actual or imaginary places; draw around objects to make
a plan; and follow a route on a map of the local area.

This commitment to 'a sense of place', environmental understanding, IT,
and graphicacy has been warmly welcomed. However, critics point out that by
attempting to include all specific content to be taught in the attainment targets,
the programmes of study display an unnecessary rigidity. Many fear that an
inevitable outcome is that teaching strategies will become content-led and that
children will not be allowed time to consolidate their experiences. More
specifically, criticism can be levelled at the conservative nature of the geographical skills which young children are expected to attain. For example, not until
the age of 7 years and above are children thought capable of: using letter and
number coordinates to locate features on a map; identifying features on aerial
photographs; locating features on a large-scale map; and making a map of a
short route. These are all skills within the grasp of children as young as 3 and 4
years (see Chapter 8). The Piagetian tradition is alive and well and living in
primary education.

Mapping at the time of school entry: Early graphicacy

Despite the headway made by geography and more particularly, graphicacy within the primary school curriculum, we have seen that Piagetian expectations still shape the way in which young children are exposed to environmental issues. Educational attitudes are inevitably responsive to classroom experiences and the lack of criticism made by educational groups of the attainment levels (geographical skills) stipulated by the National Curriculum Working Party suggests that there is a groundswell of support for the kind of skills outlined above. However, recent research carried out by workers outside the Piagetian tradition suggests that children already possess considerable environmental aptitudes before they reach the primary classroom.

Natural mapping in the classroom

The work of Blaut and his colleagues is of particular interest in this regard (see Chapters 4, 8 and 10). For Blaut (1987a; 1991), children are natural mappers. Mapping behaviour is seen to be a normal activity, akin to language behaviour, and equally as basic. From this theoretical stance, he proposes a number of advances that can be made in early education.

Map skills. Children can be taught map skills at school-entering age provided that natural mapping is incorporated into the process. This can be done by working with large, vertical, black-and-white aerial photographs. Children should be encouraged to trace from these and then generalize or abstract from iconic forms to map signs. Another procedure he suggests involves the spreading of large sheets of paper on the floor to simulate a surface. Children could then place toys, cut-outs and shapes, on this surface to represent landscape elements.

Maps for young children. Natural mapping in young children employs a downward, eye-in-the-sky perspective on the landscape. Map design for young children can be adapted to suit this pattern. For example, maps can be laid out on the floor and children encouraged to look down on them and play on them. Blaut points out that these maps need not be of simple design, as, contrary to some structural views (Petchenik, 1987), children gain most from and relate most enthusiastically to complicated maps (Muir and Blaut, 1969; Muir, 1985).

Macroenvironmental experiences. Children can be taught most effectively about large-scale environments and maps in situations of direct experience. The ideal strategy involves movement through the landscape, especially free exploratory behaviour. Blaut also favours the use of 'moving classrooms', such as the views offered from train and bus windows. More speculatively, he suggests the use of airplanes as 'flying classrooms' to generate a 'giant's eye view' of the world.

Teaching reading and writing as mapping. A central part of Blaut's treatise is that mapping has common roots with writing. Natural mapping in very young children is described as a form of sign behaviour, using material media and a clear syntax. Writing is likened to mapping in that it is 'a material, spatio-temporal, representation with meaningful signs and rules for the syntactic placement of symbols (in both up-down and left-right coordinates)' (1987a, p. 32). All of this suggests that there is a strong natural link between mapping and reading and writing, which could be tapped to teach children language skills through the use of maps. Although still at an exploratory stage, Blaut proposes that one sort of exercise could involve the use of 'flat tokens' inscribed with simple words and pictures. For example, a noun like *'house'* would have a drawing and a picture, whilst a verb like *'go'* would have a word and action cartoon. These discs could then be linked together into phrases and sentences, to give both a semi-iconic and written display.

According to Blaut (1987a) the practical outcome of these suggestions is that if children are taught in ways that develop their own natural mapping behaviour they will significantly improve their learning of such skills. It follows that if geography and other macroenvironmental subjects can be introduced in the same way, children's incipient understanding of places will be greatly enhanced.

Early geographical education: An evaluation

Spencer *et al.* (1989) raise a fundamental issue about teaching schemes aimed at the very young when they ask, 'Do children in such programmes gain a greater environmental awareness, greater graphicacy, and better locational skills than comparable children not in such programmes?' (p. 251). There is some evidence that they do. Recall Muir and Blaut's (1969) finding that 5- and 6-year-old children, who had been introduced to mapwork by means of aerial photographs, consistently outperformed a similar age group who had not encountered these stimuli, in later tests of mapping skills. Also, Atkins' (1981) observation that 4- and 5-year-old children who had been taught simple graphical skills not only performed better than an untutored group on tests of mapping ability immediately after the course, but they continued to do so a year later. Further support for the value of early environmental training is provided by Spencer *et al.* (1984). They were concerned with evaluating environmental education programmes in nursery and primary schools. In one project, a group of 3- and 4-year-old children attending a morning nursery class learned about spatial relationships within a house and investigated the three-dimensional structure of a house. Performances of this group were compared against a control group of similar aged children attending the school during the afternoon, but who did not receive any instruction. The children took part in a series of pre- and post-project assessments. The results showed that whilst the performance of the control and experimental groups were broadly similar in the pre-test stage, and the competence and knowledge of the control group had changed little by the subsequent post-test, children who took part in the programme performed considerably better in the later assessment.

In another project 7- and 8-year-old children were tested on their ability to draw maps of their route from school to the village centre and of their classroom, before and after instruction. Initially, children were found to have very little idea about map making; most of their maps consisted of linked pictures and few demonstrated any discernible structure. In contrast, the final maps were much more organized and accurate and consisted of many more place elements. Egocentricity was also reduced. This can be demonstrated by the following observation. As part of the instruction stage, children collaborated with the experimenters in building a scale model of their classroom. At first, when children were asked where they were in relation to the model most tended to see themselves outside of it. By the end of the teaching period, all but a few children were able to place a representation of themselves within the scaled classroom. Clearly, in both projects, those children who had taken part in the teaching programme had significantly benefited from their experience.

Geography and gender

Teaching programmes aimed at encouraging early environmental skills may also go a long way towards offsetting those gender-related differences in spatial competencies which often develop during middle childhood. In Chapter 9 we reviewed a broad range of studies which noted that from about the age of 8 years onwards, boys' greater environmental range encourages a heightened awareness of large-scale space. Boys are more likely than girls to excel in tests of mapping ability and map accuracy and many achieve a Euclidean grasp of space well before their female counterparts. I argue (Matthews, 1987a; 1989a; 1989b), that sex differences of this kind provide some understanding as to why geography remains an essentially male-dominated discipline in secondary and higher education. By the time young girls complete their primary education many show less environmental capability than boys. The ability to organize, arrange and recognize properties of landscapes are attributes advantageous to intending geographers, whilst emphasis upon map work and mapping skills during early secondary schooling may perpetuate the advantages enjoyed by boys. As a result girls may be less inclined to succeed in geography and given a choice will presumably take up other disciplines in which they achieve greater satisfaction. Lee (1985) has shown that fewer girls than boys enter GCSE examinations in geography and correspondingly there are less girl entrants for A level and degree courses. Although in the decade since 1970 females have begun to move into other male subject strongholds like physics and chemistry, in comparison, female growth rates in geography have remained low. Similar observations have been made by Roder (1977) and Maddux (1982) in their commentaries on American geography courses.

At present there seems a general lack of appreciation of the needs of young girls in relation to fundamental aspects of geographical study. Recognition that sex-stereotyping in early childhood has a significant bearing on spatial expertise is a necessary first step towards making geography a more attractive subject for all. A new emphasis within the early phase of primary education on environmentally based studies and a greater focus upon developing early mapping skills would undoubtedly help girls overcome the disadvantages which accrue from their more restricted home ranges. Indeed, Matthews (1987a; 1987c) and Webley (1981) have shown that those girls who share the same environmental experience as boys do equally as well on tests of spatial competence. However, not all agree with this line of reasoning. McGee (1979), for example, found that training was unlikely to reduce disjunction between male–female performance on some tests of spatial ability, as boys continued to do better on mental rotation tasks.

Summary

Today, the geographical content of early primary education is unlikely to be criticized for the weaknesses highlighted by HM Inspectorate in the late 1970s. The national curriculum has secured the place of geography as a foundation subject within the primary school. However, whether the geography attainment targets and their associated levels sufficiently acknowledge the incipient geographical skills of the very young is a matter of much conjecture. Contrary to Piagetian expectations, which seem to be implicitly recognized by the programmes of study of ATI (geographical skills), there is now ample evidence to suggest that a sense of place has already emerged by the time children have arrived at infant school. Environmental learning starts as soon as the child begins to move about, and children arrive at school with their own personal geographies. Geographical work in the primary phase has much scope and potential, especially if, as Bale (1987) suggests, teaching strategies are built upon these extra-mural experiences of children. In the past, attempts to build balanced curricula have meant that insufficient attention has been given to the 'vernacular' geography of the very young (Stradling et al., 1984). As a result, most primary courses have provided children with very different geographical experiences to those they are used to. The rooting of geographical work in the locality, which is now part of the national curriculum, is a welcomed development, but there is little indication that the new programmes of study will build upon the geography of what is already known.

An integral part of geographical competence is mapping behaviour and graphicacy. The work of Blaut and others suggests that children, as young as 3- and 4-year-olds, engage and use protomapping skills of map syntax and map signing long before they are able to read and write. If, indeed, natural mapping has 'strong homologous roots with reading and writing' (Blaut, 1991, p. 58), there is case for using mapping-based exercises to develop the skills of literacy during the early primary phase. Also, if children of nursery school age can use maps, locate objects on a map by simple alpha-numeric grids, interpret aerial photographs, provide relatively detailed accounts of familiar routes in complex, real-world settings and offer descriptions of their home area using a variety of media, amongst other mapping skills, it is disappointing to see new educational initiatives continuing to recommend that these sorts of tasks should not be set for children younger than 7 years of age. This is especially so, given the disparity between the environmental experiences of boys and girls, and its affect on spatial skills, which opens up at about this age. Until there are further attempts to monitor and evaluate the effectiveness of different teaching and learning strategies, the anecdotal wisdom of the classroom is likely to prevail.

13

Planning issues: Environments for children

When the Dutch masters painted children, they portrayed them as small adults, their activities and behaviour were unmistakably adult-like, only their size distinguished them. The temptation to view children in these terms lingers on, especially in relation to environmental planning. Even today, despite a burgeoning body of research on child development, which highlights the singular needs of children, most large-scale environments are designed to reflect only adult values and usages. Children are seemingly invisible on the landscape. At best, they are provided with some sort of token playground, but otherwise they must fit in to the alien environments of the adult world. In this chapter we will examine the conventional response towards planning environments for children, distinguish the environmental needs of children and suggest ways in which children can become part of the environmental planning process.

Environments for children: The conventional approach

Outdoor play is an important contributory factor to children's environmental experience. Whatever the reasons for play, 'its environmental implications are many. It affords sensory pleasure . . . , improves certain skills . . . and encourages creativity' (Ittelson *et al.*, 1974). In addition, it brings children into contact with the world beyond the home and is an essential part of children's developing transactions with place. The conventional approach towards providing play opportunities for children in most residential settings has almost always meant the provision of playgrounds. However, there is growing doubt about the efficacy of such a solution. Segregated play spaces of this kind appear to be a poor reflection of most children's needs.

Playground design and provision

There appears to be a general agreement, in both educational and environmental planning fields, that the *traditional* playground provides an unrewarding

221

environment for children's outdoor activities. Frost and Klein (1979) describe the traditional playground as 'a collection of single-function equipment; merry-go-rounds, seesaws, jungle gyms, slides and swings' (p. 46). These environments are essentially static, tubular, safe, predictable, replicable and designed to catch an adult's eye (Brown and Burger, 1984). They offer children little more than a chance to exercise or an opportunity for functional play. Despite their monotonous sterility, traditional playgrounds have often been the only planning response to children's outdoor recreational needs. When Hayward *et al.* (1974) carried out a survey to determine who used traditional playgrounds they found that they were primarily used by younger children, often accompanied by adults. Also, they noted that the separate elements of the traditional playground encouraged discrete sequences of behaviour, rather than a more desirable continuous mode of activity.

Concern about the value of traditional playgrounds as environmental settings for children's play has encouraged the growth of *contemporary* playgrounds. These playgrounds are not easily described by equipment names, instead they have been constructed with 'novel forms, textures, and different heights, in aesthetically pleasing arrangements' (Hayward *et al.*, 1974, p. 134). Rohane (1981) describes contemporary playgrounds as a 'quantum advancement in playground design', because they provide and support developmentally-appropriate activities.

In attempts to enhance the educational value of contemporary playground settings a number of authors have suggested sets of design principles. For example, Rohane (1981) proposes that playgrounds should offer at least four different activity opportunities:

1. *Child-people* settings, such as places for role-playing, manipulative play, physical skills, and creative or constructive play.
2. *Child-biotic* settings, including both cultivated and 'wild' patches.
3. *Child-ambient* settings, areas where children can play with water, slides (gravity), or experiment with other facets of their ambient environment, such as weather labs.
4. *Child-spatial* settings, places where children can experience different components of their spatial environment, such as elevated sites, tunnels, boundaries and pathways.

Moore and Cohen (1978) outline a further set of potential guidelines. For them, the play environment should 'allow for activities to flow and move actively and continuously with multiple branches and alternatives at crossroads and decision points. When a child has come to the end of one activity . . . there should be immediately and obviously a choice of continuing options' (p. 269). Specific suggestions include the provision of both defined and ambiguous play settings, such as playhouses and sand or woodworking areas; spaces designed to enable social interaction; places where children can 'let off steam'; 'retreat and breakaway points'; 'accomplishment points'; 'loose part' places, areas provided with numerous loose, dynamic, interchangeable elements; places for 'plants and critters'; and settings which offer 'a variety of spatial experiences'.

Hill (1978), too, provides a number of design suggestions, some very specific. He advocates that playgrounds should be 1,000 sq. ft to 3,000 sq. ft in size. They should contain multi-purpose play structures and offer protection from the prevailing weather. In order to encourage 'cognitive play', manipulative objects and loose props should be offered. Within the playground there should be room for four major categories of play: *physical, social, creative* and *quiet*. At all times, children should be given the opportunity for continuous play, without breakdown and unnecessary interference.

Although the theoretical virtues of contemporary playgrounds appear clear enough, the evidence that these environments offer more enriching and satisfying play places than more traditional playgrounds has not gone un-challenged. For example, Brown and Burger (1984), in an observational study of pre-school children's free play in six outdoor playgrounds, found that playgrounds with more contemporary designs did not necessarily promote greater amounts of educationally desirable social, language, or motor be-haviours. Rather, there were differences in children's behaviours on various playgrounds, but not strictly according to the extent to which they reflected contemporary designs. The most important design characteristics were zoning, 'encapsulation' and the provision of appropriate play materials. Henninger (1977), too, suggests that traditional and contemporary playgrounds offer different sorts of challenges and so the settings complement each other by stimulating different important play types. In contrast, empirical support for contemporary playground design comes from a number of studies. Van Valkenberg (1978) and Strickland (1979) both found that contemporary play areas were used more often and for longer periods than traditional playgrounds. Also, contemporary playgrounds generally supported more educationally valu-able forms of play, that is, more complex social and cognitive behaviours. In addition, Callecod (1974) and Kruidenier (1978) note that children over-whelmingly favoured the more challenging and complex nature of these settings.

Even though contemporary playgrounds seem to offer considerable scope for imaginative play, Pollowy (1977) is critical of the playground solution, in general, as the only planning response to children's environmental needs. He contends that 'The designs of our environments have not yet accepted children's activities and their play as the *most* necessary function of early life' (p. 320). Indeed, a growing body of opinion (Esbensen, 1980; Moore, 1986) suggests that there is a need for more diverse and flexible planning strategies, which are responsive to children's disparate activities. An implicit part of this argument is that playgrounds, no matter how exciting or creative, isolate children from large-scale society and, in effect, contribute to a process of *childhood ghettoization*. Playgrounds may suit adults in that they contain children in neat, identifiable compounds, but they cannot hope to cater for all of the environmental needs of the developing child. In summary, 'adult' planners need to be much more aware of the complexity and diversity of child–environment relationships so that more satisfying and accommodating places can be created for children.

The invisible child? The environmental needs of children

In 'The Year of the Child' (1979), a conference was held in Toronto which focused on the conditions of children in urban settlements, mainly in the Western world. From the proceedings, a number of papers (Michelson and Michelson, 1980; Hill and Michelson, 1981) make the point that we need to differentiate, absolutely, between the needs, aspirations and behaviour of children and adults. Some major distinctions include the following.

1. Children differ from adults in terms of their behaviour. What goes on during the day of an average child is different in content and 'other concrete manifestations' from that of adults. Play and education form a major part of children's daily experiences.
2. The land uses and facilities which involve children are frequently different from those of adults and even when shared, are largely used for different purposes.
3. The free range of children and the types of environmental setting which they enter is more restricted than that of adults. In some respects, children have much in common with the handicapped, the elderly and other 'minority' groups, in that their behaviour is often constrained by physical ineptitude, limited access to transportation, lack of money and roles which separate them from a larger and more diverse daily round.
4. In the course of their environmental transactions, children commonly encounter threats which often go unnoticed by adults. Many childhood hazards are not dangers in later life.
5. Children are unable to influence economic and political decision-making and management, which typically determine the structure of the environmental system in general, and land-use patterns in particular. Thus, the environments which have the greatest significance for children are decided for them by adults and for reasons which bear little regard for their needs, aspirations and behaviour.
6. Even when the same environment affects both children and adults, their interpretation and meaning of these places are not likely to be the same. Children and adults often differ in how they see, feel about and react to a landscape and their views on environmental planning are unlikely to coincide.

For these reasons, Michelson and Michelson (1980) argue that it is imperative that environmental decision-makers should take up and consider the interests of children when planning places. Fookes (1980) suggests that this is no easy task. When considering the environment as a place for children to grow up in, it is important to remember the year-by-year development of each child. 'How often do we forget, for instance, the differences between the two-year-old and the child of five or six, when we talk about children?' (p. 164). Hence, any particular kind of space typically provided for children, like a playground, is likely to be appropriate for only a limited age range, being too advanced for younger children and too elementary for teenagers. Doxiadis (1974) and others (Hart, 1979; Herman *et al.*, 1987; Matthews, 1989b) have shown that as children get older their perspectives and horizons broaden to include use of increasingly larger territorial units. A 2-year-old, for example, will have begun to have meaningful experiences outside of the home, the life of a 5-year-old will have expanded even more, by the age of 7 or 8 years exploration and play will have extended to include the neighbourhood and by the age of 10 years many children will have some conceptualization and experience of their home locale. Despite children's evolving and developing use of the outdoors, van Vliet (1983) points out that planners and designers 'have not systematically concerned themselves with the functions of streets, shops, clinics, cinemas, buses, offices, and cafes in children's everyday experiences' (p. 578). This is especially so for adolescents, who make extensive use of this 'fourth environment', that area beyond the home, school and playground. Anthony (1985) has shown how shopping malls figure significantly in the daily lives of a group of teenagers. Although adults primarily used these places to make purchases, many of the adolescents interviewed in her survey spent up to five hours at a time simply 'hanging around' these malls with their friends. Anthony suggests that the popularity of such places is that they may well 'serve as an antidote to the regimentation of school and home life'. However, the possibilities for such alternative usage is largely ignored in planning schemes. It would seem that the commercially oriented planning of places is largely aimed at one age group, working adults, and even then inadequately enough.

Childhood city or shared city?

Most studies of children's environmental needs have focused on their behaviour within urban places. However, there appears to be little consensus in terms of how to cater for children's varying needs. Ward (1977) queries, 'Do we want to provide for the child as a special kind of person or as someone who is becoming an adult?' (p. 203). Ward further muses on what sort of city we should aim for. Do we want places where children can expend all their 'comic dignity' on playing in unwanted patches specifically set aside to contain their activities or should we seek a shared city, designed for the well-being of adults and children alike? Ward does not want a childhood city. He points out that despite the ample provision of formal parks and playspaces in many municipal areas, children play anywhere and everywhere. Churchman (1980) observes that playgrounds attract relatively few children beyond the age of 5 years. Children who are old enough to go outside unaccompanied spend large amounts of time on the pavements, streets and other areas of their immediate neighbourhoods. Little (1980) describes how children's days are often filled by 'sweet nothings', those seemingly inconsequential exchanges between children and their environment, like kicking a stone in a street, that offer time for quiet thought and reflection. Little argues that much of the pleasure children get from the environment is coded in personal, symbolic terms that rarely get mentioned to anyone and which certainly cannot be created by unsympathetic and insensitive planning schemes which separate children from the world of experience.

In an attempt to explore urban and suburban children's perceptions of their own environments, Jacobs and Jacobs (1980) interviewed 132 children, aged between 10 years and 17 years, in and around the Montreal area. Their perceptions were compared to a group of adults from the same locality. What they found was that whereas adults emphasized the benefit and necessity of parks and playgrounds, the key to children's satisfaction depended on their opportunity to design and modify the environment according to their perceived needs. Hart (1979) arrives at the same conclusion from his study of young New England children. He suggests that the freedom to make environmental modifications offers children the chance to make themselves 'at home' in a place. Successful environmental planning, therefore, depends on 'convincing planners of the need to think more generally of how to create environments in which children may "find" or create their own settings for play' (p. 349).

Jacobs and Jacobs went on to suggest four further premises for successful planning, with children in mind.

1. *The integration of the child in the city requires community accommodation.* When economic motives dominate planning decisions, children become marginalized. Community welfare depends upon children's ability to integrate into the mainstream.
2. *Play depends upon access, proximity and control around the home.* In the Montreal survey, 67 per cent of the suburban children and 45 per cent of the urban group indicated that they used facilities close to the home (backyard, road, street, driveways and lanes) as primary play spaces. These unofficial play areas enabled children to exert some degree of control over the environment and provided the chance for them to determine the type of play they wanted to participate in.
3. *Perceived opportunities for change are essential.* When children in Montreal were asked what would they like to have in their neighbourhood that was currently unavailable, the majority responded that they did not know. Jacobs and Jacobs suggest that such a response is typical of a group whose customary exclusion from the planning process has left them with a feeling of powerlessness. In effect, children have been denied the opportunity to

control their environment in a manner in keeping with their perceptions.

4. *Mobility is essential to growth and development.* The urban environment offers children diverse opportunities for exploration and play. Spatial restrictions impair environmental awareness and create a discontinuous sense of the larger world. In the Montreal survey some 36 per cent of urban children had not travelled on the metro (subway) within the confines of their city.

In essence, what this survey suggests is that the preconceived values of adults impinge upon children's environmental opportunities and inhibit their transactions with place. Verwer (1980) arrives at similar conclusions through his study of children's behaviour in the Netherlands. He argues that children's playgrounds should be viewed as a last resort. They represent a well-intentioned answer to a situation which is essentially wrong. They signify 'a form of impoverishment' since children should feel safe to go exploring throughout the whole environment in which they live. Freedom of this sort demands a number of requirements to be met.

1. *Safety.* For a safe residential environment, special attention should be given to road safety and water safety. For example, traffic must be subservient to pedestrians and cyclists, and special attention should be given to making water sites free from danger.
2. *Congeniality.* Environments outside the home need to be attractive to children of all ages. For example, intimacy is important for young children. Children under 6 years rarely play more than a 100 metres from their homes, that is, within calling distance. They require small-scale facilities which offer emotional and physical security, such as 'small sand pits, shallow ponds, low walls, and little variation in height'. Because many large physical structures, like high-rise blocks, lack intimacy, special attention should be given to their entrances and immediate surroundings.
3. *Tolerance.* Planning should allow for the mutuality of children's and adults' activities. A residential environment should encourage children's games and prohibitions need to be kept to a minimum. Specific actions might include banning barbed wire, not sowing delicate plants, growing plants to cover bare soil, and making paths visible and logical.
4. *Accessibility.* Environments outside the home should be accessible and free from obstruction, enabling children to move around freely and in safety. In high-rise blocks, special attention needs to be given to that space between indoors and outdoors, where children's movement is too often impeded by steep staircases or lift buttons which are too high and too stiff.
5. *Variation and liveliness.* Residential environments should be designed with their users in mind. Both children and adults have a part to play in making places 'identifiable', 'challenging', 'surprising' and 'fascinating'.
6. *Paths and routes.* Connections between services and homes should be direct, safe, as short as possible, and offer shelter when needed.
7. *Play facilities.* These should be an integral part of the community setting, not

isolated or separated from adult activity spaces.

8. *Involvement.* For the residential environment to function well, local residents should be encouraged to support and maintain their local facilities.

Adaptation to children's rights

According to Moore (1986), 'access and diversity emerge as the most important themes in childhood-environment policy' (p. 234). Following his extensive survey of children's play behaviour in America and England, Moore argues that environmental planning needs to go beyond the narrow vision of playground provision. Children require environments with sufficient diversity that their individual needs can be met and these places need to be accessible to all. All too often, children's outdoor activities are severely constrained. Every child needs access to environmental opportunities which enable that child to express his or her own individuality. Hill and Michelson (1981) have demonstrated the importance of accessibility to how children make use of places. They conducted a survey in Toronto designed to investigate how teenagers link up with particular urban amenities. The results revealed that small variations in distance were of crucial significance. For example, teenagers living closest to public libraries attended most often, whereas those living more than two kilometres away visited the least. In general, they found that access to suitable opportunities had a significant effect on levels of participation over a wide range of activities. Hill and Michelson went on to argue that if a child has poor access to a reasonable number of opportunities for constructive, purposeful activities 'the consequence may be excessive amounts of time spent in passive ways, such as simply hanging around streets or shopping centres or watching television' (p. 215).

Indeed, the right to a stimulating and developmentally appropriate environment and the right to play are part of the UN Declaration of the Rights of the Child (Moore, 1986, p. 51). However, Moore acknowledges that this does not mean children's activities should be segregated from those of adults, but it does call for an understanding by adults of 'the complex ecological relationships and varied contexts of children's lives' (p. 51). These sentiments echo those of Hart (1979), who calls for a truly ecological approach to planning. Key concepts for Hart include 'multi-purpose land uses', 'flexible development' and 'local initiatives', all of which should be set in the context of the developing social ecology of childhood. Moore, too, goes on to suggest a number of policy directions which would enhance the environmental experiences of children and extend their childhood rights.

1. *Making streets liveable.* Streets provide an especially important element in children's daily round. They should be safe, offer opportunities for play and social-mixing, and should not be stressful.

2. *Conservation of special childhood places.* Important childhood resources should be recognized, especially the role of informal spaces.

3. *Roughing-up urban parks and greens and urban wildlife management.* Although parks are popular among children and adults, their highly formalized structure often inhibits play and exploration. By incorporating more diverse, natural landscapes children's opportunity to manipulate the environment to suit their changing needs and imaginations would be extended. Roughing-up would also encourage the development of ecologically diverse habitats, which would enliven and enrich children's environmental transactions. Others, too, share Moore's concern for the importance of integrating aspects of nature within the range of the urban child. For example, both Knight (1980) and Sharonov (1980) stress the significance of exposure to water, natural hiding places, vegetation and other aspects of natural systems to the mental and physical development and well-being of children.

4. *Adventure playgrounds and beyond.* As presently conceived, adventure playgrounds are not attractive to all children and many parents have severe reservations about their safety. Those most likely to attend are outgoing, gregarious children, with parents who positively encourage outdoor adventure. Moore suggests that additional solutions need to be found which offer children the same levels of social and environmental engagement, but which provide improved access and wider appeal.

5. *Community initiatives.* Children's activities should not be 'partitioned off to create childhood ghettoes', but instead every attempt should be made to make children's environmental education an integral part of community life. This calls for new educational initiatives, revised professional roles and flexible local structures. In addition, successful implementation of these suggestions demands that children must be incorporated into the planning process. To be effective, participation in environmental design and management must begin early on in life, so that consultation and collaboration become an accustomed practice.

In summary, a consensus appears to be emerging which suggests that neighbourhoods need to be safe and secure, provide opportunities for exploration and offer children scope for modification. Emphasis, too, should be on the distribution of smaller-scale projects and land uses, located within the fabric of neighbourhoods, rather than on large-scale, specialized facilities. Highly formalized and partitioned environments are unattractive to most children, especially as they spend much of their time in streets and on empty sites, and encourage a division of activities between children and adults, whereas a preferred goal is a shared landscape.

Children as environmental planners

A number of studies (Hill and Friendly, 1980; Jacobs and Jacobs, 1980; Little, 1980) stress that the particular environmental needs of children of different ages are not necessarily specifiable or logical to adults. Children themselves assign and weigh the criteria by which they judge places. Because adults have different outlooks and are pursuing different interests, they are often unable to see, let alone understand, the child's point of view (Michelson and Michelson, 1980). The work of these authors suggests that not only should designers and planners be more sensitive to the varying needs of children of different ages, but also children and their expressed views and perceptions should be incorporated into the planning process.

Jacobs and Jacobs (1980), in their Montreal survey, have shown that some adults can take the point of view of the child more accurately if they have relevant academic training. However, there are good reasons why it is better to have children involved directly. For example, at present children are seldom given the opportunity to exercise any control over their surroundings, and this may hinder the development of respectful attitudes towards the environment. There should be every incentive for helping children to develop such a feeling, for as Churchman (1980) points out, adults frequently accuse children of not respecting property. Also, adults often get angry when they see children playing in places not planned or not 'imagined' for children's use. Yet these forms of spaces, not intended for children, reflect needs and desires which can only be revealed if the views of children are respected in the process of design and management. Alam (1980) argues that, at present, children represent a handicapped and disadvantaged group in relation to environmental design. What is needed is the provision of neighbourhood facilities which enable children to take a full and active part in their locality. Therefore, planning must not only be at a 'human scale', but should be at a small enough scale for use by most children.

However, Verwer (1980) cautions that children may be very conservative in their design suggestions, for in their short lives they may not have had much exposure to a wide range of alternatives. A fundamental dilemma is also raised by Michelson and Michelson (1980). They point out that whilst it may be desirable to incorporate the views of children, how can persons with little or no prior experience in professional or political spheres function positively with others in such realms? Not only this, children may simply lack the ability to express their ideas coherently and sensibly. Nagy and Baird (1978) express similar reservations. They examined the ability of a group of fourth-grade students to plan a model town. What they found was that the ideal landscapes created by these young children did not seem to match their preferences. Clearly, these untrained children found the planning task complex and as such were likely to make errors in terms of the creation of ideal places.

The answer to these problems may be in the initiation of more relevant and thorough environmental education programmes. For example, Jacobs and Jacobs (1980) contend that the development of children's ability to articulate perceived needs should become a formal part of the school curriculum. They propose a programme of environmental learning, commencing in the primary school, where children would be given the responsibility for setting up and restructuring their own environmental arrangements. Such experience need not be confined to model landscapes. At the age of 8 or 9 years, children could be given responsibility for planning real-world settings, such as the school playground and by mid-secondary school level, experiments could extend to the wider school environs. Inclusion of this type of training in the school curriculum would 'set in motion a critical expectation on the part of children that they can exert control over their environment' (p. 137). Verwer (1980), too, favours the development of environmental learning schemes. However, he suggests the use of administrative procedures as educational opportunities for children, that is, children should be given a chance to take part in actual planning initiatives. Verwer believes that the inclusion of children would provide a humanizing factor, their perspectives offering richness and originality to the perspectives of adults. The importance of environmental experience is further stressed by Vogt *et al.* (1980). They describe how, in Norway, children learn to express their environmental concerns through their families personally taking responsibility for neighbourhood maintenance.

An interesting scheme which attempted to tap the imagination of children as urban planners was the 'Children's participation in futures' project or 'Gruppo futuro', which ran during 1978–9. Schools in Napoli, Oxford, Glasgow and Montreal took part in the exercise. The intention was to provide children with opportunities to experiment with as many media as possible in order to 'express, propose, question, and build' (Nicholson and Lorenzo, 1980) alternative environmental futures, with minimal interference by adults. At first, children were found to be inhibited in terms of their convictions, which Nicholson and Lorenzo put down to the prohibitive nature of most schooling. However, as the project developed, the role of the investigators became that of providing 'an initial spark of an idea', with children only too eager to develop and formulate their own plans. What the project revealed was that children were natural environmental experts. Given autonomy, freedom and the confidence to initiate ideas and plans, children provided a view of the world which was different in scale and detail to that of adults. Children's concerns reflected their immediate community, as well as their feelings and intuitions about everyday places. These observations led Nicholson and Lorenzo to propose that children have the capacity and ingenuity to take part in the planning process, and by working alongside adults, better environmental futures would result. De Monchaux (1981) has taken these sorts of ideas further in her book *Planning with children in mind*. Here she presents a model guide on how to involve children through consultation and participation in the planning process. In her work de Monchaux makes the important point that adults frequently use the term 'play' to belittle children's use of space. For her, play means 'all those independent activities that children adopt by choice as an enjoyable and interesting way of behaving, beyond the adult imposed demands of home, family and school' (p. 58). De Monchaux cautions that the only way that special childhood places can be identified and conserved, and not forever tidied up, is through children's genuine involvement in decision-making.

According to Moore (1986), collective, democratic decision-making is not an easy process, especially 'in our spoon-fed, consumer-oriented culture: it is, however, a skill that can be learned at an early age' (p. 251). He, too, proposes that young people need to participate, as equal partners, in making decisions about their own environmental futures, rather than accepting answers from 'experts'. To date, mainstream urban policy-making is still dominated by the prescriptions of elite experts, who specify what *ought* to be done on behalf of their clients. 'Young people, especially, have been so little involved in decision-making that their special needs in the urban environment have hardly ever been considered' (p. 251). By involving children early on in childhood in the politics of place, individuals would learn to 'explore and understand the phenomenal world' that surrounds them.

In summary, the participation of children in the process of environmental design would at least ensure that the environments which are created would be more appropriate to children's disparate activities and interests. At present, planners and decision-makers seldom include persons with either empathy or sympathy towards children and their ongoing needs, let alone children themselves. Yet, we have seen that children's views on place are often very different to those expressed by adults. Michelson and Michelson (1980) argue that a 'pro-child' policy in every nation and culture is needed, which, if instigated, 'would spill over to benefit many other segments of the population' (p. 91). However, universal solutions to child–environment relationships are unlikely. Alam (1980) makes the point that actions taken by and on behalf of children must be consistent with the traditional cultures within which they are set.

Summary

There is a growing recognition of the limitations of playgrounds of all kinds as play settings for children. Although playgrounds may offer freedom and privacy, they remove children from other available play opportunities in the surrounding environment. Studies of playgrounds of all types suggest that they are greatly underused and that from the middle years of childhood children prefer the complexity of the 'real world'. Clearly, play environments extend beyond the planned play spaces provided by adults for children. Many planners and researchers now recognize that prepared settings contribute to but a small part of children's complete play experiences. However, as Ittelson et al. (1974)

suggest 'it would be unfortunate to give an impression that there is sufficient understanding of children's play requirements to posit an ideal play setting' (p. 184). Qualities such as 'diversity', 'accessibility' and 'responsiveness' seem desirable, but these do not specify a design solution. Similarly, whilst the chance to explore and discover new environments in safety seems an undeniable right, the practical problems that this poses are almost unsurmountable.

There are signs that planners are becoming more aware of children's outdoor recreational needs. We have seen that children play everywhere throughout the residential community. Planning for children's play must recognize this phenomenon. Esbensen (1980) draws attention to three national schemes which have attempted to devise guidelines designed to protect children's rights to play. Whilst these guidelines may be far from ideal, they are a step towards a greater *play consciousness.*

Sweden. The Swedish Norms for Buildings (1976) state that children must have equal play opportunities regardless of the density of the residential environment. Builders and developers are required by law to provide a variety of play areas close to new housing, and homeowners must form cooperative associations to manage and maintain these communal spaces. In addition, there are requirements for 'park playgrounds' to be built and operated by the municipality.

Denmark. The Building Norms and Regulations (1977) clearly set out the requirements for children's play spaces. The criteria state that when a project is planned for more than eight families, a portion of open space must be provided for children's play. The planning and development of these areas must include landscape variety, equipment and fencing, accessibility, safety from traffic and shelter.

Canada. The National Housing Act (NHA, 1961) stipulates that in new housing areas with over twenty family units, appropriately located and landscaped play areas should be provided for children. Two recent guidelines, 'Play spaces for preschoolers' (1978) and *Play Opportunities for Grade School Children* (1979) have updated the NHA requirements.

Whatever the planned response to children's play, the opportunities available to children will vary according to such factors as age, sex, socio-economic status and, especially, geographical location. The black inner-city child will have one set of play areas which, in turn, will differ to those of the middle-class child of suburbia, and both will be markedly different to the play settings of the child from a rural environment. Each area provides its own set of opportunities and restrictions. Berg and Medrich (1980) compared the effects of the physical environment on children's play in four contrasting neighbourhood settings. They found that whilst children can be happy and achieve successful development in a variety of habitats, a crucial factor in effecting their quality of life was access to other children of approximately the same age. To some extent the physical make-up of the neighbourhood effected such interaction. In one of their study areas, a low-density, hilly neighbourhood, children reported the problems of planning a cohesive social life. In consequence, play often lacked spontaneity and environmental transactions were frequently contrived and discontinuous. This contrasted with the experiences of children from a high-density, but flatter environment. Here play was freer, less structured and more impulsive. Clearly, the nature of the social and physical environment, beyond the organized settings of the home and playground, will influence children's contact with place.

14

Conclusion

Making sense of place involves both place behaviour and place-learning. On the one hand, children's varying environmental transactions bring them into contact with places of different kinds, which shapes their images of near and distant places; on the other hand, children's varying ability to handle spatial information affects their ability to understand locational concepts, such as large-scale spatial relationships, and to solve locational problems, like wayfinding and navigation. The organization of the book has reflected these dual concerns. To some extent, a mutual dependency ties these macroenvironmental concepts together: place behaviour facilitates place-learning, while place-learning encourages more confident place behaviour. For example, we have seen that those children who roam most widely and freely from their home sites are likely to outperform others, whose environmental range is more restricted, on tests of spatial ability. Conversely, developing spatial competence encourages broader transactions with place, such as enabling children to navigate or traverse space when the destination is not perceptible from the point of origin. In the first instance, this chapter offers a summary of some of the important findings which have advanced our understanding of how children make sense of large-scale environments. Then, discussion focuses on a few promising directions which could be taken.

A number of general conclusions can be made about children's ability to make sense of place. First, there is now plenty of evidence to suggest that young children do not view the world as egocentrically, and hence as inaccurately, as Piagetian developmental theory contends. Although young children may use their bodies as a central reference point, this does not imply that they are inextricably tied to an egocentric frame of reference. By using altered methodologies, frequently set in familiar, large-scale environments, very young children are seemingly capable of using spatial reference systems which reflect an incipient understanding of macrospace. For example, studies with infants (0–2 years) point to an early ability to employ an allocentric frame of reference, which partly depends upon a *global map* of the relative location of objects and events. Also, many 3–5-year-olds, in tasks of spatial representation, are sufficiently competent to demonstrate a grasp of Euclidean spatial relationships.

However young children appear to lack an awareness of which strategies are best suited for solving spatial problems of various kinds. When directed by adults and when operating in everyday environments, rather than the strange and unfamiliar setting of a laboratory, young children perform geographical tasks with considerable expertise.

Secondly, and related to the above, young children display a range of protogeographical skills well before the age of school entry. The macroenvironmental repertoire of many 3–4-year-olds includes route-learning and navigational competence, and an ability to use maps, aerial photographs and models of the environment to engage in interpretation and locating tasks, as well as a capability to employ spatial reference systems and orienting schema. Of particular significance, is that many of these skills appear to emerge naturally and consistently, that is, without any formal training and in cultures of all kinds. As Catling (1987) proposes, the child *is* a geographer.

Thirdly, environmental capability appears to depend on a number of individual differences in environmental experience. For example, mobility and activity-in-space seem to be important enriching factors, positively affecting general spatial competence. Sex differences in cognitive skills appear to be explicable in these terms. Thus, boys' freer movement around their home area, compared to girls' narrower, more restricted activity patterns, provides them with a broader and more accurate conception of large-scale space. Equally, children who encounter space directly and actively, perform better on various tests of spatial ability, when compared to others whose environmental transactions have been largely passive.

Fourthly, children have a strong affective sense of place. From a young age, children develop feelings and emotions about their everyday environments which induce powerful, positive or negative images. The role of affect is not only important in explaining how children learn about place, but also, as children's place reactions are often very different to those expressed by adults, it provides a pointer to what sort of environments children find most satisfying.

The remainder of this chapter will focus on a few promising research directions. First, how very young children come to be accomplished environmental mappers is still not clearly understood. Whether environmental skills are partly innate and phylogenetic in origin, or whether they depend upon a sequential patterning of relations between organism and environment, remains a matter of much conjecture. It may be that mobility and experience simply enable children to ponder increasingly sophisticated macroenvironmental problems. In order to clarify the efficacy of these competing perspectives it is essential that more studies are carried out with children younger than 3-years-old, especially at that time when they begin to move purposefully through their environments. Only then, Blaut (1987b) contends, will we be able to ascertain whether 'cognitive mapping, which seems so peculiarly suited to solving navigational problems and problems of learning about places which cannot be perceived all-at-once, does in fact appear at the developmental level where these macroenvironmental problems are first coped with' (p. 301).

Secondly, there is also a need to find out whether cognitive mapping is homologous to language (Blaut, 1987b). At present, the link between cognitive mapping and language development is still speculative and tenuous. Research at this interface is difficult. For example, there is considerable debate as to whether a language acquisition device, as proposed by Chomsky (1985; 1988), exists in the first place. Equally difficult to confirm is the presence at birth, of a place-structuring mechanism, or mapping acquisition device, comprising pro-tomapping components of projection, scale and sign (Blaut, 1987a; 1991). The search for evidence to support these propositions has only just begun. However, evidence as to whether maps and mapping are, indeed, present in all cultures and whether mapping is older than writing would provide additional, albeit indirect, support for Blaut's theoretical claims.

Thirdly, despite persistent claims for an ecologically valid developmental psychology (Bronfenbrenner, 1979; Garbarino, 1985), few studies have exam-ined children's environmental skills in naturalistic settings. Children's macro-environmental behaviour is not contextless nor lacking in purpose, and by the same token, environments are imbued with values and feelings and are seldom neutral. Because of an emphasis on laboratory-based experiments, which are often placeless and decontextualized, children's true ability to understand and represent large-scale space has generally been underestimated. Given that children's performances appear to be linked to the situational context in which they find themselves, there is a continuing need to study children's cognitive mapping abilities and general environmental competence within their everyday worlds. These observations link to Heft and Wohlwill's (1987) recent plea 'to incorporate the role of affective processes into our models for the analysis of environmental knowledge' (p. 198). Although research has shown that affective processes are likely to condition environmental performance, this relationship remains largely unexplored. Further work along these lines appears a fruitful pursuit, especially given children's highly personalized views about place and space.

Fourthly, these sorts of considerations suggest that for a more complete understanding of children's environmental cognition closer attention needs to be given to the type of environmental information available to the child in any given context. If, as Gibson suggests, environmental features are perceived directly without the intervention of cognitive processes, further studies of perceptual learning are called for, 'to reveal the increasing sensitivity of the developing child to environmental information as a function of experience' (Heft and Wohlwill, 1987, p. 198). In a similar vein, others have recently argued (Landau and Spelke, 1985) that spatial knowledge, itself, undergoes little development during childhood; instead, spatial competence improves because children learn to use environmental information in an increasingly sophisticated manner. Indeed, Heft and Wohlwill (1987) suggest that further progress in our understanding of the developmental processes involved in this realm requires a shift from studying how different age groups respond to environmental problems of different kinds to the study of the 'effects of particular forms of environmental experiences, both short and long term, on the child's environmental learning' (p. 198).

Fifthly, some very specific gaps in our understanding of children's environmental knowledge include the following, all of which deserve further attention.

1. *How children learn about distant places.* Attention needs to focus not only on how children of different ages conceptualize about far-away places, but also on children's general receptivity to different types of media flow.

2. *How scale affects children's comprehension of place.* Reality consists of a nested set of place contexts. Studies need to establish whether children's environmental performances are place-dependent rather than generally applicable, such that higher levels of spatial skill may be achieved at successively lower levels of the place hierarchy.

3. *How social and environmental contexts affect children's place-learning.* For example, do children living in high-rise blocks develop a keener sense of large-scale place relationships and at an earlier age, through their particular transactions with space, than children living in lower-level accommodation? Do these children have a heightened ability to use maps and aerial photographs, both of which partly depend on a cyclopian, eye-in-the-sky, view of the world? What is the effect on spatial competence of belonging to ethnic communities whose restricted spatial range constrain children's place behaviour? Are children's environmental competencies universally shared?

4. *How competent are children to use maps, especially to orientate themselves in geographical space or for wayfinding?* A number of studies claim that very young children can carry out elementary map-reading and map-using skills, but there is a paucity of research on whether children can use maps for navigational purposes in real-world settings.

Lastly, to understand how children make sense of place demands a multi-paradigm structure. We have noted how cognitive, developmental, ecological, environmental and social psychologists have contributed to the debate, as well as researchers from backgrounds in Artificial Intelligence, Geography, Planning and Anthropology. However, although substantive bridges are beginning to be built, which encourage multivariate explorations of children's environmental competencies and a healthy sharing of concepts and techniques, there is still some way to go before a collaborative sense of purpose will be achieved. Of particular concern, especially given my disciplinary background, is the seeming lack of interest by most geographers working in the United Kingdom about the whole issue of children's place behaviour and place-learning. The dearth of this kind of research among British geographers suggests that they are guilty of losing sight of the roots of the subject. This is a pity, especially given geographers' interest in real-world settings as contexts for group behaviour and their concern for cross-cultural studies, two aspects which would undoubtedly strengthen research into children's environmental capabilities and sense of place.

Bibliography

Abello, R.P. and Bernaldez, F.E. (1986) 'Landscape preference and personality'. *Landscape and Urban Planning*, 13, 19–28.

Abello, R.P., Bernaldez, F.E., and Galiano, E.F. (1986) 'Consensus and contrast in landscape preference'. *Environment and Behavior*, 18, 155–78.

Acredolo, L.P. (1976) 'Frames of reference used by children for orientation in unfamiliar spaces'. In Moore, G.T. and Golledge, R.G. (Eds) *Environmental knowing*. Dowden, Hutchinson and Ross: Stroudsburg, Pennsylvania.

Acredolo, L.P. (1977) 'Developmental changes in the ability to coordinate perspectives of large-scale space'. *Developmental Psychology*, 3, 1–8.

Acredolo, L.P. (1978) 'Development of spatial orientation in infancy'. *Developmental Psychology*, 14, 224–34.

Acredolo, L.P. (1979) 'The effect of environment on the 9-month-old infant's choice of spatial reference system'. *Developmental Psychology*, 15, 666–7.

Acredolo, L.P. (1982) 'The familiarity factor in spatial research: what does it breed besides contempt?'. In Cohen, R. (Ed.) *New directions in child development*, 15, *Children's conception of spatial relationships*. Jossey-Bass: San Francisco.

Acredolo, L.P. (1983) 'Spatial orientation in infancy: role of body, landmarks and locomotion'. Paper presented at the 19th Inter-American Congress of Psychology, Quito, Ecuador.

Acredolo, L.P. (1985) 'Coordinating perspectives on infant spatial orientation'. In Wellman, H.M. (Ed.) *Children's searching: the development of search skill and spatial representation*. Lawrence Erlbaum: Hillsdale, New Jersey.

Acredolo, L.P. and Evans, D. (1980) 'Developmental changes in the effects of landmarks on infant spatial behavior'. *Developmental Psychology*, 16, 312–18.

Acredolo, L.P., Adams, A. and Goodwyn, S.W. (1984) 'The role of self-produced movement and visual tracking in infant spatial orientation'. *Journal of Experimental Child Psychology*, 38, 312–27.

Acredolo, L.P., Pick, H.L. and Olsen, M.G. (1975) 'Environmental differentiation and familiarity as determinants of children's memory for spatial location'. *Developmental Psychology*, 11, 495–501.

Aiello, J.F., Gordon, B. and Farrell, T.J. (1974) 'Description of children's outdoor activities in a suburban residential area: preliminary findings'. In Moore, R.C. (Ed.) *Childhood city: man-environment interactions*. EDRA: Milwaukee.

Ainsworth, N., Salter, D. and Whittig, B.A. (1969) 'Attachment and exploratory behavior of one year olds in a strange situation'. In Foss, B.M. (Ed.) *Determinants of infant behavior*. Methuen: London.

Alam, A. (1980) 'Problems and possibilities for the children of Bangladesh'. *Ekistics*, 281, 153–4.

Allen, G.L. (1981) 'A developmental perspective on the effects of "subdividing" macrospatial experience'. *Journal of Experimental Psychology*, 7, 120–32.

Allen, G.L. (1985) 'Strengthening weak links in the study of the development of macrospatial cognition'. In Cohen, R. (Ed.) *The development of spatial cognition*. Lawrence Erlbaum: Hillsdale, New Jersey.

Allen, G.L. (1987) 'Cognitive influences on the acquisition of route knowledge in children and adults'. In Ellen, P. and Thinus-Blanc, C. (Eds) *Cognitive processes and spatial orientation in animal and man*. Martinus Nijhoff: Dordrecht.

Allen, G.L., Kirasic, K.C., Siegel, A.W. and Herman, J.F. (1979) 'Developmental issues in cognitive mapping: the selection and utilization of environmental landmarks'. *Child Development*, 50, 1062–70.

Allen, G.L., Siegel, A.W. and Rosinski, R.R. (1978) 'The role of perceptual context in structuring spatial knowledge'. *Journal of Experimental Psychology: Human Learning and Memory*, 4, 617–30.

Altman, I. (1975) *The environment and social behavior*. Brooks, Cole: Belmont, California.

Anderson, J. and Tindall, M. (1972) 'The concept of home range: new data for the study of territorial behavior'. In Mitchell, W.J. (Ed.) *Environmental design: research and practice*. University of California: Los Angeles.

Anderson, J.W. (1972) 'Attachment behaviour of out of doors'. In Blurton Jones, N. (Ed.) *Ethological studies of child behaviour*. Cambridge University Press: Cambridge.

Anooshian, L.J. and Siegel, A.W. (1985) 'Children's knowledge of directional relationships within their neighborhood'. Unpublished manuscript, cited in Spencer, C., Blades, M. and Morsley, K. *The child in the physical environment*. Wiley: Chichester.

Anooshian, L.J. and Wilson, K.L. (1977) 'Distance distortions in memory for spatial locations'. *Child Development*, 48, 1704–7.

Anooshian, L.J. and Young, D. (1981) 'Developmental changes in cognitive maps of a familiar neighborhood'. *Child Development*, 52, 341–8.

Antell, S.E.G. and Caron, A.J. (1985) 'Neonatal perception of spatial relationships'. *Infant Behavior and Development*, 8, 15–23.

Anthony, K.H. (1985) 'The shopping mall: a teenage hangout'. *Adolescence*, 20, 307–12.

Appleton, J. (1978) *The experience of landscape*. Wiley: Chichester.

Appleyard, D. (1969a) 'City designers and the pluralistic city'. In Rodwin, L. (Ed.) *Urban growth and regional development*. MIT Press: Cambridge, Massachusetts.

Appleyard, D. (1969b) 'Why buildings are known: a predictive tool for architects and planners'. *Environment and Behavior*, 1, 131–56.

Appleyard, D. (1970) 'Styles and methods of structuring a city'. *Environment and Behavior*, 2, 100–18.

Appleyard, D. (1973) 'Notes on urban perception and knowledge'. In Downs, R.M. and Stea, D. (Eds) *Image and environment*. Aldine: Chicago.

Appleyard, D. (1976) *Planning a pluralistic city*. MIT Press: Cambridge, Massachusetts.

Appleyard, D., Lynch, K. and Meyer, J.R. (1967) 'The view from the road'. In Lowenthal, D. (Ed.) *Environmental perception and behavior*. University of Chicago: Chicago.

Ardrey, R. (1966) *The territorial imperative*. Artheneum: New York.

Arnaud, S.H. (1974) 'Some functions of play in the education process'. *Child Education*,

51, 72–8.

Atkins, C.L. (1981) 'Introducing basic map and globe concepts to young children'. *Journal of Geography*, **80**, 228–33.

Axia, G. and Nicoloni, C. (1985) 'Children's representation of Venice'. Paper presented at the 16th EDRA Conference, New York.

Baboolal, E. (1981) 'Black residential segregation in south London'. In Jackson, P. and Smith, S. (Eds) *Social interaction and ethnic segregation*. Academic Press: London.

Bailey, P.J. and Binns, J.A. (1987) *A case for geography*. Geographical Association: Sheffield.

Baird, J.C. (1979) 'Studies of the cognitive representation of spatial relations'. *Journal of Experimental Psychology*, **108**, 90–1.

Baird, J.C., Wagner, M. and Noma, E. (1982) 'Impossible cognitive spaces'. *Geographical Analysis*, **14**, 204–16.

Baker, R.R. (1980) 'Goal orientation by blindfolded humans after long-distance displacement: possible involvement of a magnetic sense'. *Science*, **210**, 555–7.

Baker, R.R. (1981) *Human navigation and the sixth sense*. Simon and Schuster: New York.

Balchin, W. and Coleman, A. (1965) 'Graphicacy should be the fourth ace in the pack'. *The Times Educational Supplement*. 5 November. Reprinted in Bale, J., Graves, N. and Walford, R. (Eds) (1974) *Perspectives in geographical education*. Oliver and Boyd: Edinburgh.

Baldwin, J.D. and Baldwin, J.I. (1981) *Beyond sociobiology*. Elsevier: New York.

Bale, J. (1987) *Geography in the primary school*. Routledge: London.

Balling, J.D. and Falk, J.H. (1982) 'Development of visual preference for natural environments'. *Environment and Behavior*, **14**, 5–28.

Banz, G. (1970) *Elements of urban form*. McGraw-Hill: New York.

Barbichon, G. (1975) 'Espace villageois, espace urbain dans l'imagerie enfantine'. *Revue Française de Sociologie*, **16**, 539–60.

Bar-Gal, Y. (1984) 'There are no butterflies there: an inter-cultural experiment in landscape perception'. In Haubrich, H. (Ed.) *Perception of people and places through media*. Freiburg: Germany.

Barker, D. (1979) 'Comments on the spatial world of the child'. In Michelson, W., Levine, S. and Michelson, E. (Eds) *The child in the city*. University of Toronto Press: Toronto.

Barker, R.G. and Schoggen, P. (1973) *Quality of community life: methods of measuring environment and behavior applied to an American and an English town*. Jossey-Bass: San Francisco.

Barker, R.G. and Wright, H.F. (1955) *Midwest and its children*. Row, Peterson and Company: New York.

Bartz, B.S. (1970) 'Maps in the classroom'. *Journal of Geography*, **69**, 18–24.

Bassey, M. (1978) *Nine hundred primary school teachers*. NFER: Oxford.

BBC (1988) *Annual review of BBC broadcasting research*. BBC: London.

Beck R.J. and Wood, D. (1976a) 'Comparative development analysis of individual and aggregated cognitive maps of London'. In Moore, G.T. and Golledge, R.G. (Eds) *Environmental knowing*. Dowden, Hutchinson and Ross: Stroudsburg, Pennsylvania.

Beck, R.J. and Wood, D. (1976b) 'Cognitive transformation of information from urban geographic fields to mental maps'. *Environment and Behavior*, **8**, 199–238.

Becker, F.D. (1976) 'Children's play in multi-family housing'. *Environment and Behavior*, **8**, 545–74.

Bennett, G.K., Seashore, H.G. and Wesman, A.B. (1974) *Manual for the differential aptitude tests: form S and T.* Psychological Association: New York.

Berg, M. and Medrich, E.A. (1980) 'Children in four neighborhoods: the physical environment and its effect on play patterns'. *Environment and Behavior*, 12, 320–48.

Bergan, A., McManis, D.L. and Melchert, P.A. (1971) 'Effects of social interaction and token reinforcement on WISC Block Design performance'. *Perceptual and Motor Skills*, 32, 871–80.

Bernaldez, F.G. and Parra, F. (1979) 'Dimensions of landscape preference from pairwise comparisons'. Paper presented at the National Conference on Applied Techniques for Analysis of the Visual Resources, Nevada.

Bernaldez, F.G., Benayan, J. and De Lucio, J.V. (1987a) 'Changes in environmental attitudes as revealed by activity preferences and landscape tests'. *The Environmentalist*, 7, 21–30.

Bernaldez, F.G., Gallardo, D. and Abello, R.P. (1987b) 'Children's landscape preferences: from rejection to attraction'. *Journal of Environmental Psychology*, 7, 169–76.

Bernaldez, F.G., Ruiz, J.P. and Ruiz, M. (1984) 'Landscape perception and appraisal: ethics, aesthetics and utility'. Paper presented at the 8th International Conference on Environment and Human Action, Berlin.

Bernard, J. (1939) 'The neighborhood behavior of school kids in relation to age and socio-economic status'. *American Sociological Review*, 4, 652–62.

Berry, J. (1968) 'Temne and Eskimo perceptual skills'. In Lee, R.B. and de Vore, I. (Eds) *Man the hunter.* Aldine: Chicago.

Berthenthal, B.I., Campos, J.J. and Barrett, K.C. (1984) 'Self-produced locomotion: an organizer of emotional, cognitive and social development in infancy'. In Emde, R. and Harmon, R. (Eds) *Continuities and discontinuities in development.* Plenum: New York.

Bettis, N.C. (1974) 'An assessment of the geographic knowledge and understanding of fifth-grade students in Michigan'. Doctoral Dissertation, Michigan State University.

Biel, A. (1979) 'Accuracy and stability in children's representations of their home environment'. *Göteburg Psychological Reports*, 9, No. 2, University of Göteburg: Sweden.

Biel, A. (1982) 'Children's spatial representation of their neighbourhood: a step towards a general spatial competence'. *Journal of Environmental Psychology*, 2, 193–200.

Biel, A. and Torell, G. (1977) 'The mapped environment: cognitive aspect of children's drawings'. *Göteburg Psychological Reports*, 7, No. 7, University of Göteburg: Sweden.

Birkett, P. (1980) 'Predicting spatial ability from hemispheric "non-verbal" lateralisation: sex, handedness and task differences implicate encoding strategy effects'. *Acta Psychologica*, 46, 1–14.

Bishop, J. and Foulsham, J. (1973) 'Children's images of Harwich'. *Working Paper*, 3, Architectural Psychology Research Unit, Kingston Polytechnic.

Bishop, R.L. and Peterson, G.L. (1971) *A synthesis of environmental design recommendations from visual preferences of children.* Department of Civil Engineering: Northwestern University.

Bjorklid, P. (1982) *Children's outdoor environment.* Stockholm Institute of Education: Stockholm.

Blades, M. and Spencer, C. (1986) 'Map use in the environment and educating children to use maps'. *Environmental Education and Information*, 5, 187–204.

Blades, M. and Spencer, C. (1987a) 'Map use by young children'. *Geography*, 71, 47–52.

Blades, M. and Spencer, C. (1987b) 'Young children's strategies when using maps with landmarks'. *Journal of Environmental Psychology*, 7, 201–18.

Blades, M. and Spencer, C. (1987c) 'Young children's recognition of environmental features from aerial photographs and maps'. *Environmental Education and Information*, 6, 189–98.

Blair, G.L. (1976) 'Street hassles'. *Peace News*, 19, 32–4.

Blakemore, M. (1981) 'From way finding to map-making: the spatial information fields of aboriginal peoples'. *Progress in Human Geography*, 5, 1–24.

Blaut, J.M. (1987a) 'Notes toward a theory of mapping behavior'. *Children's Environmental Quarterly*, 4, 27–34.

Blaut, J.M. (1987b) 'Place perception in perspective'. *Journal of Environmental Psychology*, 7, 297–305.

Blaut, J.M. (1991) 'Natural mapping'. *Transactions of the Institute of British Geographers, New Series*, 16, 55–74.

Blaut, J.M. and Stea, D. (1969) 'Place learning'. *Place Perception Report*, 4, Graduate School of Geography, Clark University, Worcester, Massachusetts.

Blaut, J.M. and Stea, D. (1971) 'Studies of geographic learning'. *Annals of the Association of American Geographers*, 61, 387–93.

Blaut, J.M. and Stea, D. (1974) 'Mapping at the age of three'. *Journal of Geography*, 73, 5–9.

Blaut, J.M., McCleary, G.S. and Blaut, A.S. (1970) 'Environmental mapping in young children'. *Environment and Behavior*, 2, 335–49.

Bluestein, N. and Acredolo, L.P. (1979) 'Developmental changes in map reading skills'. *Child Development*, 50, 691–7.

Blyth, J. (1984) *Place and time with children five to nine*. Croom Helm: London.

Boal, F.W. (1969) 'Territoriality on the Shankill–Falls divide, Belfast'. *Irish Geography*, 6, 30–50.

Boal, F.W. (1970) 'Social space in the Belfast urban area'. In Stephens, N. and Glasscock, N. (Eds) *Irish Geographical Studies*. The Queen's University: Belfast.

Boal, F.W. (1971) 'Territoriality and class: a study of two residential areas in Belfast'. *Irish Geographer*, 6, 229–48.

Boal, F.W. (1976) 'Ethnic residential segregation'. In Herbert, D.T. and Johnston, R. (Eds) *Social areas in cities*. Wiley: Chichester.

Boardman, D. (1982) 'Graphicacy through landscape models'. *Studies in Design, Education, Craft and Technology*, 14, 103–8.

Boardman, D. (1983) *Graphicacy and geography*. Croom Helm: London.

Boardman, D. (1985) 'Spatial concept development and primary school map work'. In Boardman, D. (Ed.) *New directions in geographical education*. Falmer Press: London.

Bogen, J.E., de Zure, R., TenHouten, W.D. and Marsh, J.F. (1972) 'The other side of the brain'. *Bulletin of the Los Angeles Neurological Society*, 37, 49–61.

Booth, A. and Johnson, D. (1975) 'The effect of crowding on child health and development'. *American Behavioral Scientist*, 18, 736–49.

Bower, T.G.R. (1966) 'The visual world of infants'. *Scientific American*, 215, 80–92.

Bower, T.G.R., Broughton, J.M. and Moore, M.K. (1971) 'Infant responses to approaching objects: an indicator of response to distal variables'. *Perception and Psychophysics*, 9, 193–6.

Bowlby, J. (1953) *Child care and the growth of love*. Pelican: Baltimore.

Bowlby, J. (1969) *Attachment and loss*. Basic Books: New York.

Bremner, J.G. (1978) 'Spatial errors made by infants: inadequate spatial cues or evidence of egocentrism?'. *British Journal of Psychology*, **69**, 77–84.

Bremner, J.G. and Bryant, P.E. (1977) 'Place versus response as the basis of spatial errors made by young infants'. *Journal of Experimental Child Psychology*, **23**, 162–71.

Bremner, J.G. and Bryant, P.E. (1985) 'Active movement and development of spatial abilities in infancy'. In Wellman, H.M. (Ed.) *Children's searching: the development of search skill and spatial representation*, Lawrence Erlbaum: Hillsdale, New Jersey.

Brewer, W.F. and Treyens, J.C. (1981) 'Role of schemata in memory for places'. *Cognitive Psychology*, **13**, 207–30.

Briggs, R. (1973) 'On the relationship between cognitive and objective distance'. In Preisser, W.F.E. (Ed.) *Environmental design research*. Dowden, Hutchinson and Ross: Stroudsburg, Pennsylvania.

Bronfenbrenner, U. (1961) 'The mirror image in Soviet–American relations'. *Journal of Social Issues*, **17**, 45–6.

Bronfenbrenner, U. (1967) 'Socialization and social class through time and space'. In Roberts, J.I. (Ed.) *School children in the urban slum*. Free Press: New York.

Bronfenbrenner, U. (1977) 'The ecology of human development in retrospect and prospect'. In McGurk, H. (Ed.) *Ecological factors in human development*. North-Holland: New York.

Bronfenbrenner, U. (1979) *The ecology of human development*. Harvard University Press: Massachusetts.

Bronzaft, A.L., Dobrow, S.B. and O'Hanlon, T.J. (1976) 'The cognitive maps of adolescents: confusion about inter-town distances'. *Professional Geographer*, **33**, 315–25.

Brown, A.L. (1976) 'The construction of temporal succession by preoperational children'. In Pick, A. D. (Ed.) *Minnesota Symposium on Child Psychology*, **10**, University of Minnesota: Minneapolis.

Brown, J.G. and Burger, C. (1984) 'Playground designs and preschool children's behaviors'. *Environment and Behavior*, **16**, 599–626.

Bruner, J.S. (1966) 'On cognitive growth'. In Bruner, J.S., Olver, R.R. and Greenfields, P.M. (Eds) *Studies in cognitive growth*. Wiley: New York.

Bruner, J.S. (1986) *Actual minds, possible worlds*. Harvard University Press, Massachusetts.

Bruner, J.S. and Connolly, K. (1974) 'Competence: the growth of the person'. In Connolly, K. and Bruner, J.S. (Eds) *The growth of competence*. Academic Press: London.

Bruner, J.S. and Sherwood, V. (1981) 'Thought, language and interaction in infancy'. In Forgas, J.P. (Ed.) *Social cognition*. Academic Press: London.

Bruner, J.S., Jolly, A. and Silva, K. (1976) *Play: its role in development and evolution*. Basic Books: New York.

Brunswik, E. (1956) *Perception and the representative design of psychological experiments*. University of California Press: Los Angeles.

Brunswik, E. (1969) 'The conceptual framework of psychology'. In Neurath, O., Carnap, R. and Morris, C. (Eds) *Foundation of the unity of science: toward an international encyclopaedia of unified science*. University of Chicago Press: Chicago.

Bryden, M.P. (1979) 'Evidence for sex-related differences in cerebral organization'. In Wittig, M.A. and Petersen, A.C. (Eds) *Sex-related differences in cognitive functioning*. Academic Press: New York.

Buchanan, W. and Cantril, H. (1953) *How nations see each other*. University of Illinois

Press: Illinois.

Bunting, T.E. and Cousins, L.R. (1985) 'Environmental dispositions among school-age children'. *Environment and Behavior*, 17, 725–68.

Burgess, J. (1990) 'The production and consumption of environmental meanings in the mass-media: a research agenda for the 1990s'. *Transactions of the Institute of British Geographers, New Series*, 15, 139–61.

Butterworth, G. (Ed.) (1977) *The child's representation of the world*. Plenum: New York.

Byrne, R.W, (1982) 'Geographical knowledge and orientation'. In Ellis, A.W. (Ed.) *Normality and pathology in cognitive functions*. Academic Press: London.

Cadwallader, M.T. (1976) 'Cognitive distance in intraurban space'. In Moore, G.T. and Golledge, R.G. (Eds) *Environmental knowing*. Dowden, Hutchinson and Ross: Stroudsburg, Pennsylvania.

Cadwallader, M.T. (1979) 'Problems in cognitive distance: implications for cognitive mapping'. *Environment and Behavior*, 11, 559–76.

Callecod, R.L. (1974) 'Play preferences of selected grade school children on varying types of playground equipment'. Master's Dissertation, University of Illinois.

Canter, D.V. (1977) *The psychology of place*. Architectural Press: London.

Carr, S. and Schissler, D. (1969) 'The city as a trip: perceptual selection and memory in the view from the road'. *Environment and Behavior*, 1, 7–35.

Carswell, R.J.B. (1971) 'Children's abilities in topographic map reading'. *Cartographica*, 2, 40–5.

Cater, J. and Jones, T.P. (1979) 'Asians in Bradford'. *New Society*, 44, 81–2.

Cater, J. and Jones, T.P. (1989) *Social Geography*. Edward Arnold: London.

Catling, S.J. (1979a) 'Maps and cognitive maps: the young child's perception'. *Geography*, 64, 288–96.

Catling, S.J. (1979b) 'Whither primary geography?'. *Teaching Geography*, 5, 73–6.

Catling, S.J. (1987) 'The child is a geographer: criteria for geographical content in the primary school curriculum'. In Bailey, P.J. and Binns, J.A. (Eds) *A case for geography*. Geographical Association, Sheffield.

Catling, S.J., Firth, T. and Rowbotham, D. (1981–2) *Outset Geography*. Books 1–4. Oliver and Boyd: Edinburgh.

Cavalli-Sforza, L.L. and Feldman, M.W. (1981) *Cultural transmission and evolution*. Princeton University Press: Princeton.

Chase, W.G. and Chi, M.T.H. (1980) 'Cognitive skill: implications for spatial skill in large-scale environments'. In Harvey, J. (Ed.) *Cognition, social behavior and environment*. Lawrence Erlbaum: Hillsdale, New Jersey.

Chomsky, N. (1985) *The logical structure of linguistic theory*. University of Chicago Press: Chicago.

Chomsky, N. (1988) *Language and problems of knowledge: the Managua lectures*. MIT Press: Cambridge, Massachusetts.

Churchman, A. (1980) 'Children in urban environments: the Israeli experience'. *Ekistics*, 281, 105–9.

Clayton, K. and Woodyard, M. (1981) 'The acquisition and utilization of spatial knowledge'. In Harvey, J. (Ed.) *Cognition, social behavior and environment*. Lawrence Erlbaum: Hillsdale, New Jersey.

Coates, G. and Bussard, E. (1974) 'Patterns of children's spatial behavior in a moderate-density housing development'. In Moore, R.C. (Ed.) *Childhood city: man-environment interactions*. EDRA: Milwaukee.

Coates, G. and Sanoff, H. (1972) 'Behavior mapping: the ecology of child behavior in a planned residential setting'. In Mitchell, W.J. (Ed.) *Environmental design: research and practice*. University of California: Los Angeles.

Cobb, E. (1969) 'The ecology of imagination in childhood'. In Shepherd, P. and McKinley, D. (Eds) *The subversive science: essays toward an ecology of man*. Houghton Mifflin: Boston.

Cobb, E. (1977) *The ecology of imagination in childhood*. Columbia University Press: New York.

Cohen, R. (1981) 'The influence of acquisition conditions and task demands in interlocation distance estimates'. Paper presented at the Society for Research in Child Development Conference, Boston.

Cohen, R. (Ed.) (1985) *The development of spatial cognition*. Lawrence Erlbaum: Hillsdale, New Jersey.

Cohen, R. and Weatherford, D.L. (1980) 'Effects of route travelled on the distance estimates of children and adults'. *Journal of Experimental Child Psychology*, 29, 403–12.

Cohen, R. and Weatherford, D.L. (1981) 'The effects of barriers on spatial representations'. *Child Development*, 52, 1087–90.

Cohen, R., Baldwin, L.M. and Sherman, R.C. (1978) 'Cognitive maps of a naturalistic setting'. *Child Development*, 49, 1216–18.

Cohen, R., Weatherford, D.L. and Byrd, D. (1980) 'Distance estimates of children as a function of acquisition and response activities'. *Journal of Experimental Child Psychology*, 30, 464–72.

Cohen, R., Weatherford, D.L., Lomerick, T. and Koeller, K. (1979) 'Development of spatial representations: role of task demands and familiarity with the environment'. *Child Development*, 50, 1257–60.

Cohen, S. and Cohen, R. (1982) 'Distance estimates of children as a function of activity in the environment'. *Child Development*, 53, 834–7.

Cohen, S. and Cohen, R. (1985) 'The role of activity in spatial cognition'. In Wohlwill, J. and van Vliet, W.S. (Eds) *Habitats for children*. Lawrence Erlbaum: Hillsdale, New Jersey.

Cohen, S., Glass, D. and Singer, J.E. (1973) 'Apartment noise, auditory discrimination and reading ability'. *Journal of Experimental Social Psychology*, 9, 407–27.

Cole, M. (1984) 'Society, mind and development'. In Kessel, F.S. and Siegel, A.W. (Eds) *Psychology and society: the child as a cultural invention*. Houston Symposium IV. Praeger: New York.

Coleman, A.M. and Catling, S. (1982) *Patterns on the map: land utilization survey maps as resources for teaching and learning*. Geographical Association: Sheffield.

Conning, A.M. and Byrne, R.W. (1984) 'Pointing to preschool children's spatial competence: a study in natural settings'. *Journal of Environmental Psychology*, 4, 165–75.

Connor, J.M. and Serbin, L.A. (1977) 'Behaviorally based masculine and feminine activity preference scales for preschoolers: correlates with other classroom behaviors and cognitive tests'. *Child Development*, 48, 1411–16.

Connor, J.M., Schackman, M. and Serbin, K.A. (1978) 'Sex-related differences in response to practice on a visual-spatial test and generalization to a related test'. *Child Development*, 49, 24–9.

Cooper Marcus, C. (1974) 'Children's play behavior in a low-rise, inner-city housing development'. In Moore, R.C. (Ed.) *Childhood city: man-environment interactions*.

EDRA: Milwaukee.

Cornell, E.H. and Hay, D.H. (1984) 'Children's acquisition of a route via different media'. *Environment and Behavior*, 16, 627–41.

Cornell, E.H. and Heth, C.D. (1986) 'The spatial organization of hiding and recovery of objects by children'. *Child Development*, 57, 603–15.

Cousins, J.H., Siegel, A.W. and Maxwell, S.E. (1983) 'Way finding and cognitive mapping in large-scale environments: a test of a developmental model'. *Journal of Experimental Child Psychology*, 35, 1–20.

Cracknell, R. (1976) 'Geography in junior schools'. *Geography*, 61, 8–14.

Csikzentmihalyi, M. (1975) *Beyond boredom and anxiety*. Jossey-Bass: San Francisco.

Daggs, D.G. (1986) 'Pyramid of places: children's understanding of geographic hierarchy'. Master's Dissertation, Pennsylvania State University.

Dale, P.F. (1971) 'Children's reactions to maps and aerial photographs'. *Area*, 3, 170–7.

Dart, F.E. and Pradham, P.L. (1967) 'Cross cultural teaching of science'. *Science*, 155, 649–56.

Darvizeh, Z. and Spencer, C. (1984) 'How do young children learn novel routes? The importance of landmarks in the child's retracing of routes through the large-scale environment'. *Environmental Education and Information*, 3, 97–105.

de Monchaux, S. (1981) *Planning with children in mind*. New South Wales Department of Environment and Planning: Sydney.

Dennis, W. (1938) 'Infant development under conditions of restricted practice and of minimum social stimulation'. *Journal of Genetic Psychology*, 53, 154.

Dennis, W. (1940) *The Hopi child*. Wiley: New York.

Department of Education and Science (1982) *Education 5 to 9*. HMSO: London.

Department of Education and Science (1983) *9–13 middle schools*. HMSO: London.

Department of Education and Science (1985) *Education 8 to 12 in combined and middle schools*. HMSO: London.

Department of Environment (1973) *Children and play*. HMSO: London.

Department of Environment (1979) *Environmental education in urban areas*. HMSO: London.

Deutsch, M. (1973) 'The disadvantaged child'. In Harden, J. (Ed.) *Cities and communities and the young*. Routledge and Kegan Paul: London.

Devlin, A.S. (1976) 'The small town cognitive map: adjusting to a new environment'. In Moore, G.T. and Golledge, R.G. (Eds) *Environmental knowing*. Dowden, Hutchinson and Ross: Stroudsburg, Pennsylvania.

Dodwell, P.C. (1966) 'Studies of the visual system'. In Foss, B.M. (Ed.) *New horizons in psychology*. Penguin: Harmondsworth.

Dolhinow, P.J. and Bishop, N. (1970) 'The development of motor skills and social relationships among primates through play'. *Minnesota Symposium on Child Psychology*. University of Minnesota: Minneapolis.

Donaldson, F. (1970) *The child in the city*. University of Washington mimeo.

Douglass, D. (1969) 'Spatial preferences: a multivariate taxonomic and factor analytic approach'. Master's Dissertation, University Park, Pennsylvania.

Downs, R.M. (1985) 'The representation of space: its development in children and in cartography'. In Cohen, R. (Ed.) *The development of spatial cognition*. Lawrence Erlbaum: Hillsdale, New Jersey.

Downs, R.M. and Meyer, J.T. (1978) 'Geography and the mind: an exploration of perceptual geography'. *American Behavioral Scientist*, 22, 59–77.

Downs, R.M. and Siegel, A.W. (1981) 'On mapping researchers mapping children mapping space'. In Liben, L.S., Patterson, A. and Newcombe, N. (Eds) *Spatial representation and behavior across the life span.* Academic Press: New York.

Downs, R.M. and Stea, D. (1977) *Maps in minds.* Harper and Row: New York.

Downs, R.M., Liben, L.S. and Daggs, D.G. (1988) 'On education and geographers: the role of cognitive developmental theory in geographic education'. *Annals of the Association of American Geographers,* **78,** 680–700.

Doxiadis, C.A. (1974) *Anthropolis: city for human development.* Athens Publishing Centre: Greece.

Dresnel, P. (1972) *Open space in housing areas.* National Swedish Institute for Building Research: Stockholm.

Droege, R.C. (1967) 'Sex differences in aptitude maturation during high school. *Journal of Counseling Psychology,* **14,** 407–11.

Earthkids Project (1990) *Earthkids.* National Children's Play and Recreational Unit: London.

Edney, J.J. (1976a) 'Human territories: comment of function properties'. *Environment and Behavior,* **8,** 31–48.

Edney, J.J. (1976b) 'The psychological role of property rights in human behavior'. *Environment and Planning,* **8,** 811–22.

Elliott, H.M. (1979) 'Mental maps and ethnocentrism: geographic characterizations in the past'. *Journal of Geography,* **78,** 250–65.

Elson, R.M. (1964) *Guardians of tradition: American schoolbooks of the nineteenth century.* University of Nebraska Press: Nebraska.

Erikson, E.H. (1950) (2nd ed. 1963) *Childhood and society.* Norton: New York.

Erikson, E.H. (1977) *Toys and reasons.* Norton: New York.

Esbensen, S.B. (1980) 'Legislation and guidelines for children's play spaces in the residential environment'. *Ekistics,* **281,** 123–5.

Evans, G.W. (1980) 'Environmental cognition'. *Psychological Bulletin,* **88,** 259–87.

Evans, G.W., Marrero, D.G. and Butler, P.A. (1981) 'Environmental learning and cognitive mapping'. *Environment and Behavior,* **13,** 83–104.

Fagot, B. (1978) 'The influence of sex of child on parental reactions to toddler children'. *Child Development,* **49,** 459–65.

Fairweather, H. (1976) 'Sex differences in cognition'. *Cognition,* **4,** 231–80.

Fanning, D.M. (1967) 'Families in flats'. *British Medical Journal,* **18,** 302-86.

Farley, J. (1977) 'Effects of residential settings, parental life styles, and demographic characteristics on children's activity patterns'. Doctoral Dissertation, University of Michigan.

Feldman, A. and Acredolo, L.P. (1979) 'The act of active versus passive exploration in memory for spatial location in children'. *Child Development,* **50,** 698–704.

Fishbein, H.D., Lewis, S. and Keiffer, K. (1972) 'Children's understanding of spatial relations: coordination of perspectives'. *Developmental Psychology,* **7,** 21–33.

Fisher, S. and Hicks, D. (1985) *World studies, 8–13.* Oliver and Boyd: Edinburgh.

Flanagan, J.C., Davis, F.B., Dailey, J.T., Shaycroft, M.F., Orr, D.B., Golding, I. and Newman, C.A. (1964) *Project talent: the identification, development and utilization of human talents.* Project Talent Office: University of Pittsburgh.

Flavell, J.H., Botkin, P.T., Fry, C.L., Wright, J.W., and Jarvis, P.E. (1968) *The development of role-taking and communication skills in children.* Wiley: New York.

Fookes, T.W. (1980) 'Children's needs and child–space relationships'.

Ekistics, **281**, 164–7.

Francescato, D. and Mebane, W. (1973) 'How citizens view two great cities: Milan and Rome'. In Downs, R.M. and Stea, D. (Eds) *Image and environment*. Aldine: Chicago.

Frost, J.L. and Klein, B.L. (1979) *Children's play and playgrounds*. Allyn and Bacon: Boston.

Gale, N. Golledge, R.G., Pellegrino, J.W. and Doherty, S. (1990) 'The acquisition and integration of route knowledge in an unfamiliar environment'. *Journal of Environmental Psychology*, **10**, 3–25.

Garbarino, J. (1985) 'Habitats for children: an ecological perspective'. In Wohlwill, J. and van Vliet, W. (Eds) *Habitats for children*. Lawrence Erlbaum: Hillsdale, New Jersey.

Garbarino, J. and Gilliam, G. (1980) *Understanding abusive families*. Lexington Books: Lexington.

Garbarino, J. and Plantz, M. (1980) *Understanding children and urban environments*. ERIC Institute for Urban Education: New York.

Gärling, T. and Böök, A. (1981) 'The spatiotemporal sequencing of everyday activities: how people manage to find the shortest route to travel between places in their hometown'. *Research Monograph*, Department of Psychology, University of Umea, Sweden.

Gärling, T., Böök, A. and Lindberg, E. (1984a) 'Cognitive mapping of large-scale environments: the interrelationship of action plans, acquisition and orientation'. *Environment and Behavior*, **16**, 3–34.

Gärling, T., Böök, A. and Lindberg, E. (1984b) 'Adults' memory representations of the spatial properties of their everyday physical environment'. In Cohen, R. (Ed.) *The development of spatial cognition*. Lawrence Erlbaum: Hillsdale, New Jersey.

Gärling, T., Böök, A., Lindberg, E. and Nilsson, T. (1981) 'Memory for the spatial layout of the everyday physical environment: factors affecting rate of acquisition'. *Journal of Psychology*, **1**, 263–77.

Gauvain, M. and Rogoff, B. (1986) 'The influence of the goal on children's exploration and memory of large-scale space'. *Developmental Psychology*, **22**, 72–7.

Gerber, R.V. (1981a) 'Young children's understanding of the elements of maps'. *Teaching Geography*, **6**, 128–33.

Gerber, R.V. (1981b) 'Competence and performance in cartographic language'. *Cartographic Journal*, **18**, 104–10.

Gesell, A. (Ed.) (1940) *The first five years of life: a guide to the study of the pre-school child*. Harper and Row: New York.

Gesell, A., Ilg, R. and Ames, L. (1946) *The child from five to ten*. Harper and Row: New York.

Gibson, E.J. (1969) *Principles of perceptual learning and development*. Appleton-Century-Crofts, New York.

Gibson, E.J. and Walk, R.D. (1960) 'The visual cliff'. *Scientific American*, **202**, 64–71.

Gibson, J.J. (1950) *The perception of the visual world*. Houghton-Mifflin: Boston.

Gibson, J.J. (1958) 'Visually controlled locomotion and visual orientation in animals'. *British Journal of Psychology*, **49**, 182–94.

Gibson, J.J. (1966) *The senses considered as perceptual systems*. Houghton-Mifflin: Boston.

Gibson, J.J. (1979) *The ecological approach to visual perception*. Houghton-Mifflin: Boston.

Gladwin, T. (1970) *East is a big bird*. Harvard University Press: Cambridge, Massachusetts.

Gold, J. (1980) *An introduction to behavioural geography*. Oxford University Press: Oxford.

Gold, S. (1972) 'Nonuse of neighborhood parks'. *Journal of American Institute of Planners*, 38, 369–78.

Goldberg, S. and Lewis, M. (1969) 'Play behavior in the year old infant: early sex differences'. *Child Development*, 40, 21–31.

Goldfarb, W. (1945) 'Psychological privation in infancy and subsequent adjustment'. *American Journal of Orthopsychiatry*, 15, 247–55.

Golledge, R.G. (1976) 'Methods and methodological issues in environmental cognition research'. In Moore, G.T. and Golledge, R.G. (Eds) *Environmental knowing*. Dowden, Hutchinson and Ross: Stroudsburg, Pennsylvania.

Golledge, R.G. (1978) 'Learning about urban environments'. In Carlstein, T., Parkes, D. and Thrift, N. (Eds) *Timing space and spacing time*. Edward Arnold: London.

Golledge, R.G (1987) 'Environmental cognition'. In Stokols, D. and Altman, I. (Eds) *Handbook of environmental psychology*. Wiley: New York.

Golledge, R.G. and Spector, A.N. (1978) 'Comprehending the urban environment: theory and practice'. *Geographical Analysis*, 10, 401–26.

Golledge, R.G., Briggs, R. and Demko, D. (1969) 'The configuration of distances in intraurban space'. *Proceedings of the Association of American Geographers*, 1, 60–5.

Golledge, R.G., Smith, T.R., Pellegrino, J.W., Doherty, S. and Marshall, S.P. (1985) 'A conceptual model and empirical analysis of children's acquisition of spatial knowledge'. *Journal of Environmental Psychology*, 5, 125–52.

Goodchild, B. (1974) 'Class differences in environmental perception'. *Urban Studies*, 11, 157–69.

Goodey, B. (1971) *Perception of the environment*. Centre for Urban and Regional Studies: University of Birmingham.

Goodey, B., Duffett, A.W., Gold, J.R. and Spencer, D. (1971) 'City scene: an exploration into the image of central Birmingham'. *Research Memorandum*, 10, Centre for Urban and Regional Studies: University of Birmingham.

Goodnow, J. (1977) *Children's drawings*. Fontana: London.

Gottman, J. (1952) 'Political partitioning of our world'. *World Politics*, 4, 512–19.

Gould, P. (1966) 'On mental maps'. *Discussion Paper*, 9, Michigan Inter University Community of Mathematical Geographers.

Gould, P. (1972) 'The black boxes of Jönköping'. In Downs, R.M. and Stea, D. (Eds) *Cognitive mapping: images of spatial environment*. Aldine: Chicago.

Gould, P. and Ola, D. (1970) 'The perception of residential desirability in the western region of Nigeria'. *Environment and Planning*, 2, 73–87.

Gould, P. and White, R. (1968) '*The mental maps of British school leavers*'. Regional Studies, 2, 161–82.

Gould, P. and White, R. (1986) *Mental maps* (2nd ed.) Allen and Unwin: Boston.

Grabow, S. and Salkind, N.J. (1976) 'The hidden structure of children's play in an urban environment'. In Suedfeld, P. and Russell, J.A. (Eds) *The behavioral basis of design*. Dowden, Hutchinson and Ross: Stroudsburg, Pennsylvania.

Graves, N.J. (Ed.) (1982) *New UNESCO source book for geography teaching*. Longman: London.

Griffin, D.R. (1973) 'Topological orientation'. In Downs, R.M. and Stea, D. (Eds) *Image and environment*. Aldine: Chicago.

Groos, K. (1978) 'The value of toy play for practice and self-realization'. In Mueller-Schwarze, D. (Ed.) *Evolution of play behavior: benchmark papers in animal behavior*.

Dowden, Hutchinson and Ross: Stroudsburg, Pennsylvania.

Gump, P. and Adelberg, B. (1978) 'Urbanism from the perspective of ecological psychologists'. *Environment and Behavior*, **10**, 171–9.

Gustke, L.D. and Hodgson, R.W. (1980) 'Rate of travel along an interpretive trail: the effect of an environmental discontinuity'. *Environment and Behavior*, **12**, 53–63.

Hagarty, L. (1975) 'The family at home: a comparison of the time-budgets of families in high rise apartments and detached houses in suburban Metropolitan Toronto'. Doctoral Dissertation, University of Toronto.

Hall, E.T. (1966) *The hidden dimension.* Doubleday: New York.

Hall, S. (1977) 'Culture, media, and "the ideological effect"'. In Curran, J., Gurevitch, M. and Woollacott, J. (Eds) *Mass communication and society.* Edward Arnold: London.

Haney, W.G. and Knowles, E.S. (1978) 'Perception of neighbourhoods by city and suburban residents'. *Human Ecology*, **6**, 201–14.

Hardwick, D.A., McIntyre, C.W. and Pick, H.L. (1976) 'The content and manipulation of cognitive maps in children and adults'. *Monographs of the Society for Research in Child Development*, **41**, No. 3.

Harper, L. and Sanders, K. (1975) 'Pre-school children's use of space: sex differences in outdoor play'. *Developmental Psychology*, **11**, 119–20.

Harris, L.J. (1978) 'Sex differences in spatial ability: possible environmental, genetic, and neurological factors'. In Kinsbourne, M. (Ed.) *Asymmetrical function of the brain.* Cambridge University Press: Cambridge.

Harris, L.J. (1979) 'Variances and anomalies'. *Science*, **206**, 50–2.

Harris, L.J. (1981) 'Sex-related variations in spatial skill'. In Liben, L., Patterson, A.H. and Newcombe, N. (Eds) *Spatial representation and behavior across the life span.* Academic Press: New York.

Hart, R. (1979) *Children's experience of place.* Irvington: New York.

Hart, R. (1981) 'Children's spatial representation of the landscape: lessons and questions from a field study'. In Liben, L., Patterson, A.H. and Newcombe, N. (Eds) *Spatial representation and behavior across the life span.* Academic Press: New York.

Hart, R. and Moore, G.T. (1973) 'The development of spatial cognition: a review'. In Downs, R.M. and Stea, D. (Eds) *Image and environment.* Aldine: Chicago.

Hartup, W.W. and Lempers, J. (1973) 'A problem in life-span development: the interactional analysis of family attachments'. In Baltes, P.B. and Schaie, K.W. (Eds) *Life-span development psychology: personality and socialization.* Academic Press: New York.

Haugen, E. (1957) 'The semantics of Icelandic orientation'. *Word*, **13**, 447–59.

Hayward, D.G., Rothenberg, M. and Beasley, R.R. (1974) 'Children's play and urban playground environments: a comparison of traditional, contemporary and adventure playground types'. *Environment and Behavior*, **6**, 131–68.

Hazen, N.L. (1982) 'Spatial exploration and spatial knowledge: individual and developmental differences in very young children'. *Child Development*, **53**, 826–33.

Heamon, A.J. (1966) 'Visual perception in geography: a study of selected aspects of the development of spatial ability'. Master of Education Dissertation, University of Reading.

Hebb, D.O. (1966) *A textbook of psychology.* Saunders: Philadelphia.

Heft, H. (1983) 'Wayfinding as the perception of information over time'. *Population and Environment*, **6**, 133–50.

Heft, H. (1988) 'The development of Gibson's ecological approach to perception'.

Journal of Environmental Psychology, **8**, 325–34.

Heft, H. and Wohlwill, J.F. (1987) 'Environmental cognition in children'. In Stokols, D. and Altman, I. (Eds) *Handbook of environmental psychology*. Wiley: New York.

Heinemeyer, W.F. (1967) 'The urban core as a centre for attraction'. In Brill, E.J. (Ed.) *Urban core and inner city*. University of Leiden: Netherlands.

Henninger, M.L. (1977) 'Free play behaviors of nursery school children in an outdoor and indoor environment'. Doctoral Dissertation, University of Texas, Austin.

Her Majesty's Inspectors (1978) *Primary education in England and Wales*. HMSO: London.

Her Majesty's Inspectors (1986) *Geography from 5 to 16*. HMSO: London.

Her Majesty's Inspectors (1989) *Environmental education from 5 to 16*. HMSO: London.

Herman, J.F. (1980) 'Children's cognitive maps of large-scale spaces: effects of exploration, direction and repeated experience'. *Journal of Experimental Child Psychology*, **29**, 126–43.

Herman, J.F. and Siegel, A.W. (1978) 'The development of cognitive mapping of the large-scale environment'. *Journal of Experimental Child Psychology*, **26**, 389–406.

Herman, J.F., Heins, J.A. and Cohen, D.S. (1987) 'Children's spatial knowledge of their neighbourhood environment.' *Journal of Applied Developmental Psychology*, **8**, 1–15.

Herman, J.F., Kail, J.V. and Siegel, A.W. (1979) 'Cognitive maps of a college campus: a new look at freshman orientation'. *Bulletin of the Psychonomic Society*, **13**, 183–6.

Herman, J.F., Kolker, R.G. and Shaw, M.L. (1982) 'Effects of motor activity on children's intentional and incidental memory for spatial locations'. *Child Development*, **53**, 239–44.

Herman, J.F., Norton, L.M. and Klein, C.A. (1986) 'Children's distance estimates in a large-scale environment'. *Environment and Behavior*, **18**, 533-58.

Herman, J.F., Norton, L.M. and Roth, S.F. (1983) 'Children and adults' distance estimations in a large-scale environment'. *Journal of Experimental Child Psychology*, **36**, 453–70.

Herman, J.F., Roth, S.F. and Norton, L.M. (1984) 'Time and distance in spatial cognition development'. *International Journal of Behavioral Development*, **7**, 35–51.

Herman, J.F., Shiraki, J.H. and Miller, B.S. (1985) 'Young children's ability to infer spatial relationships: evidence from a large, familiar environment'. *Child Development*, **56**, 1195–203.

Hess, R. and Torney, J.V. (1967) *The development of political attitudes in children*. Aldine : Chicago.

Heth, C.D. and Cornell, E.H. (1980) 'Three experiences affecting spatial discrimination learning by ambulatory children'. *Journal of Experimental Child Psychology*, **30**, 246–64.

Hewes, G. (1971) 'Personal communication to Blaut, J.M.' cited in Stea, D. (1976) 'Program notes on a spatial fugue'. In Moore, G.T. and Golledge, R.G. (Eds) *Environmental knowing*. Dowden, Hutchinson and Ross: Stroudsburg, Pennsylvania.

Hibberd, D. (1983) 'Children's images of the Third World'. *Teaching Geography*, **8**, 68–71.

Hicks, E.P. and Beyer, B.R. (1968) 'Images of Africa'. *Social Education*, **32**, 779–84.

Hill, F. and Friendly, M. (1980) 'The "whole city catalogue" project'. *Ekistics*, **281**, 138–9.

Hill, F. and Michelson, W. (1981) 'Towards a geography of urban children and youth'. In Herbert, D.T. and Johnston, R.J. (Eds) *Geography and the urban environment*, **IV**.

Wiley: Chichester.

Hill, P. (1978) *Play spaces for preschoolers: design guidelines for the development of preschool play spaces in residential environments.* Central Mortgage and Housing Corporation: Ottawa, Canada.

Himmelweit, H.T., Oppenheim, A.N. and Vince, P. (1958) *Television and the child.* Nuffield Foundation: London.

Hole, V. (1966) *Children's play on housing estates.* HMSO: London.

Hole, V. and Miller, A. (1969) 'Children's play on housing estates'. *Architects' Journal,* **143,** 1529–36.

Homenuck, P.H. (1973) *A study of high rise: effects, preferences and perceptions.* Institute of Environmental Research: Toronto.

Houssiadas, L. and Brown, L.B. (1980) 'Egocentrism in language and space perception: an examination of the concept'. *Genetic Psychology Monographs,* **101,** 183–214.

Hughes, M. (1978) 'Sequential analysis of exploration and play'. *International Journal of Development,* **1,** 83–7.

Hutorowicz, H.D. (1911) 'Maps of primitive peoples'. *Bulletin, American Geographical Society,* **43,** 669–79.

Hutt, S.J. and Hutt, C. (1970) *Direct observation and measurement of behavior.* Charles Thomas: Springfield.

Huttenlocher, J. and Presson, C.C. (1973) 'Mental rotation and the perspective problem'. *Cognitive Psychology,* **4,** 277–99.

Huttenlocher, J. and Presson, C.C. (1979) 'The coding and transformation of spatial information'. *Cognitive Psychology,* **11,** 375–94.

Ittelson, W.H. (Ed.) (1973) *Environment and cognition.* Seminar Press: New York.

Ittelson, W.H., Proshansky, H., Rivlin, L. and Winkel, G. (1974) *An introduction to environmental psychology.* Holt, Rinehart and Winston: New York.

Jacobs, J. (1976) 'The uses of sidewalks: assimilating children'. In Proshansky, H.M., Ittelson, W.H. and Rivlin, L.G. (Eds) *Environmental psychology.* Holt, Rinehart and Winston: New York.

Jacobs, E. and Jacobs, P. (1980) 'Children as managers'. *Ekistics,* **281,** 135–7.

Jahoda, G. (1963) 'The development of children's ideas about country and nationality'. *British Journal of Educational Psychology,* **33,** 47–60 and 143–53.

Jakle, J.A., Brunn, S. and Roseman, C. (1976) *Human spatial behavior.* Duxbury Press: Massachusetts.

Jaspers, J., van der Geer, J., Tajfel, H. and Johnson, N.B. (1983) 'On the development of national attitudes in children'. *European Journal of Social Psychology,* **2,** 347–69.

Johnson, N.B., Middleton, M.R. and Tajfel, H. (1970) 'The relationship between children's preferences for and knowledge about other nations'. *British Journal of Social and Clinical Psychology,* **9,** 232–40.

Jones, P. (1979) 'Ethnic areas in British cities'. In Herbert, D.T. and Smith, D.M. (Eds) *Social problems and the city.* Oxford University Press: Oxford.

Jones, T.P. and McEvoy, D. (1978) 'Race and space in cloud-cuckoo land'. *Area,* **10,** 162–6.

Jung, C. (1969) *Memories, dreams, reflections.* Collins: London.

Kahl, H.B., Harman, J.F. and Klein, C.A. (1984) 'Distance distortions in cognitive maps: an examination of the information storage model'. *Journal of Experimental Child Psychology,* **38,** 134–46.

Kaluger, G. and Kaluger, M.F. (1974) *Human development: the span of life.*

Mosby: St Louis.

Kaminoff, R.D. and Proshansky, H.M. (1982) 'Stress as a consequence of the urban built environment'. In Goldberger, L. and Breznitz, S. (Eds.) *Handbook of stress*. Free Press: New York.

Kaplan, B. (1967) 'Meditations on genesis'. *Human Development*, 10, 65–87.

Kaplan, S. (1972) 'The challenge of environmental psychology: a proposal for a new functionalism'. *American Psychologist*, 27, 140–3.

Kaplan, S. (1973) 'Cognitive maps in perception and thought'. In Downs, R.M. and Stea, D. (Eds) *Image and environment*. Aldine: Chicago.

Kaplan, S. (1976) 'Adaptation, structure and knowledge'. In Moore, G.T. and Golledge, R.G. (Eds) *Environmental knowing*. Dowden, Hutchinson and Ross: Stroudsburg, Pennsylvania.

Kaplan, S., Kaplan, R. and Wendt, J.S. (1972) 'Rated preferences and complexity for natural and urban visual material'. *Perception and Psychophysics*, 12, 354–6.

Karan, P.P., Bladon, W.A. and Singh, G. (1980) 'Slum dwellers' and squatters' images of a city'. *Environment and Behavior*, 12, 81–100.

Keating, D.P. (Ed.) (1976) *Intellectual talent: research and development*. John Hopkins University Press: Baltimore.

Kellerman, A. (1981) 'Centrographic measures in geography'. *Catmog*, 32 Geo-Abstracts: Norwich.

Kellert, S.R. (1978) 'Perception of animals in American society'. Paper presented at the 41st North American Wildlife Conference, New York.

Keogh, B.K. (1971) 'Pattern copying under three conditions of an expanded spatial field'. *Developmental Psychology*, 4, 25–31.

Keogh, B.K. and Ryan, S.R. (1971) 'Use of three measures of field organisation with younger children'. *Perceptual and Motor Skills*, 33, 466.

Kessen, W., Haith, M. and Salapatek, P. (1970) 'Human infancy: a bibliography and guide'. In Mussen, P. (Ed.) *Carmichael's manual of child psychology*. Wiley: New York.

Kinsbourne, M. and Hiscock, M. (1978) 'Does cerebral dominance develop?' In Segalowitz, S.J. and Gruber, F.A. (Eds) *Language development and neurological theory*. Academic Press: New York.

Kirasic, K.C., Siegel, A.W., Allen, G.L., Curtis, L.E. and Furlong, N. (1979) 'A comparison of methods of externalizing college students' cognitive maps of their campus'. Unpublished theses, University of Pittsburg. Cited in Siegel, A.W. and Cousins, J.H. (1985), 'The symbolizing and symbolized child in the enterprise of cognitive mapping'. In Cohen, R. (Ed.) *The development of spatial cognition*. Lawrence Erlbaum: Hillsdale, New Jersey.

Kirasic, L.C., Allen, G. L. and Siegel, A.W. (1984) 'Expression of configurational knowledge of large-scale environments: students' performance of cognitive tasks'. *Environment and Behavior*, 16, 687-712.

Klapper, J.T. (1960) *The effects of mass communication*. Free Press: Illinois.

Klein, H.J. (1967) 'The delimitation of the town-centre in the image of its citizens'. In Brill, E.J. (Ed.) *Urban core and inner city*. University of Leiden: Netherlands.

Knight, J. (1980) 'Guidelines for planning playspaces'. *Ekistics*, 281, 145-8.

Knox, P. (1987) *Urban social geography*. Longman: London.

Konner, M.J. (1972) 'Aspects of the developmental ethology of a foraging people'. In Blurton Jones, N. (Ed.) *Ethological studies of child behaviour*. Cambridge University Press: Cambridge.

Kosslyn, S.M., Heldmeyer, K.H. and Locklear, E.P. (1977) 'Children's drawings as data about internal representations'. *Journal of Experimental Child Psychology*, **23**, 191–211.

Kosslyn, S.M., Pick, H.L. and Fariello, G.R. (1974) 'Cognitive maps in children and men'. *Child Development*, **45**, 707–16.

Kozlowski, L.T. and Bryant, K.J. (1977) 'Sense of direction, spatial orientation and cognitive maps'. *Journal of Experimental Psychology*, **3**, 590–8.

Kreutzer, M.A., Leonard, C. and Flavell, J.H. (1975) 'An interview study of children's knowledge about memory'. *Monographs of the Society for Research in Child Development*, **40**.

Kruidenier, W. (1978) 'The effects of encapsulation of preschool children's imaginative play'. Master's Dissertation, Unversity of Illinois.

Kuipers, B.J. (1975) 'A frame for frames: representing knowledge for recognition'. In Borrow, D.G. and Collins, A. (Eds) *Representing and understanding: studies in cognitive science*. Academic Press: New York.

Kuipers, B.J. (1982) 'The "map in the head" metaphor'. *Environment and Behavior*, **14**, 202–20.

Kurdek, L.A. (1978) 'Perspective taking as the cognitive basis of children's moral development: a review of literature'. *Merrill-Palmer Quarterly*, **24**, 3–28.

Ladd, F.C. (1967) 'A note on "the world across the street" '. *Harvard Graduate School of Education Association Bulletin*, **12**, 47–8.

Ladd, F.C. (1970) 'Black youths view their environment: neighbourhood maps'. *Environment and Behavior*, **2**, 74–9.

Lambert, W.E. and Klineberg, O. (1967) *Children's views of foreign peoples*. Appleton-Century-Crofts: New York.

Lamy, B. (1967) 'The use of the inner city of Paris and social stratification'. In Brill, E.J. (Ed.) *Urban core and inner city*. University of Leiden: Netherlands.

Landau, B. (1986) 'Early map use as an unlearned ability'. *Cognition*, **22**, 201–23.

Landau, B. and Spelke, E. (1985) 'Spatial knowledge and its manifestations'. In Wellman, H.M. (Ed.) *Children's searching: the development of search skill and spatial representation*. Lawrence Erlbaum: Hillsdale, New Jersey.

Landau, B., Gleitman, H. and Spelke, E. (1981) 'Spatial knowledge and geometric representation in a child blind from birth'. *Science*, **213**, 1275-8.

Landau, B., Spelke, E. and Gleitman, H. (1984) 'Spatial knowledge in a young blind child'. *Cognition*, **16**, 225–60.

Landy, D. (1965) *Tropical childhood*. Harper and Row: New York.

Langer, J. (1969) *Theories of development*. Holt, Rinehart and Winston: New York.

Laurendeau, M. and Pinard, A. (1970) *The development of the concept of space in the child*. International Universities Press: New York.

Lee, R. (1985) 'Where have all the geographers gone?'. *Geography*, **306**, 45–59.

Lee, T.R. (1962) ' "Brennan's Law" of shopping behaviour'. *Psychological Reports*, **11**, 662.

Lee, T.R. (1963) 'On the relation between the school journey and social and emotional adjustment in rural infant children'. *British Journal of Educational Psychology*, **27**, 100.

Lee, T.R. (1970) 'Perceived distance as a function of direction in the city'. *Environment and Behavior*, **2**, 40–51.

Lemen, J. (1966) *L'espace figuratif et les structures de la personalité*. Press Universitaires de France: Paris.

Levine, M., Marchon, I. and Hanley, G. (1984) 'The placement and misplacement of you-are-here-maps'. *Environment and Behavior*, 16, 139–57.

Liben, L.S. (1981) 'Spatial representation and behavior: multiple perspectives'. In Liben, L.S., Patterson, A,M. and Newcombe, N. (Eds) *Spatial representation and behavior across the life span*. Academic Press: New York.

Liben, L.S., Moore, M.L. and Golbeck, S.L. (1982) 'Preschoolers' knowledge of their classroom environment: evidence from small-scale and life-size spatial tasks'. *Child Development*, 53, 1275–84.

Lieberson, S. (1981) 'An asymmetrical approach to segregation'. In Peach, C., Robinson, V. and Smith, S. (Eds) *Ethnic segregation in cities*. Croom Helm: London.

Linn, M.C. and Petersen, A.C. (1985) 'Emergence and characterization of sex differences in spatial ability: a meta-analysis'. *Child Development*, 56, 1479–98.

Little, B.R. (1980) 'The social ecology of children's nothings'. *Ekistics*, 281, 93–5.

Lombardo, T.J. (1987) *The reciprocity of perceiver and environment: the evolution of James J. Gibson's ecological psychology*. Lawrence Erlbaum: Hillsdale, New Jersey.

Long, M. (1974) *Handbook for geography teachers*. Methuen: London.

Loo, C. (1972) 'The effects of spatial density on the social behavior of children'. *Journal of Applied Social Psychology*, 2, 372–81.

Loo, C. and Smetland, J. (1977) 'The effect of crowding on the behaviors and perceptions of 10-year old boys'. *Environmental Psychology and Nonverbal Behavior*, 2, 226–49.

Lowrey, R.A. (1970) 'Distance concepts of urban residents'. *Environment and Behavior*, 2, 52–73.

Lukashok, A. and Lynch, K. (1956) 'Some childhood memories of the city'. *Journal of the American Institute of Planners*, 22, 142–52.

Lynch, K. (1960) *Image of the city*. MIT Press: Cambridge, Massachusetts.

Lynch, K. (1979) *Growing up in cities: studies of the spatial environment of adolescence in Cracow, Melbourne, Mexico City, Salta, Toluca and Warsaw*. MIT Press: Cambridge, Massachusetts.

Lynch, K. and Bannerjee, T. (1976) 'Growing up in cities'. *New Society*, 37, 281–4.

Lynch, M. (1975) 'Girls will be girls'. *Sunday Times*, 27th July.

Lyons, E. (1983) 'Demographic correlates of landscape preference'. *Environment and Behavior*, 75, 487–511.

Maccoby, E.E. and Jacklin, C.N. (1974) *The psychology of sex differences*. Stanford University Press: California.

Maccoby, E.E. and Jacklin, C.N. (1979) 'Sex hormones in umbilical cord blood: their relationship to sex, birth order and behavioral development'. Paper presented at the Biennial Meeting of the Society for Research in Child Development, San Francisco.

Mackay, D.B. (1976) 'The effect of spatial stimuli on the estimation of cognitive maps'. *Geographical Analysis*, 8, 439–51.

Mackay, D.B. and Olshavsky, R.W. (1975) 'Cognitive maps of retail locations: an investigation of some basic issues'. *Journal of Consumer Research*, 2, 197–205.

Maddux, J. (1982) 'Geography: the science most affected by existing sex-dimorphic cognitive abilities'. Paper presented at the 78th Annual Meeting of the Association of American Geographers.

Magana, J.R., Evans, G.W. and Romney, A.K. (1981) 'Scaling techniques in the analysis of environmental cognition data'. *Professional Geographer*, 33, 294-301.

Mark, L.S (1972) 'Modelling through toy-play: methodology for eliciting topographical representations in children'. In Mitchell, W.J. (Ed.) *Environmental design: research and practice*. University of California Press: Los Angeles.

Mason, G., Forrester, A. and Hermann, R. (1975) *Berkeley park use study*. Department of Parks and Recreation: Berkeley, California.

Matthews, M.H. (1980a) 'The mental maps of children: images of Coventry's city centre'. *Geography*, 65, 169–79.

Matthews, M.H. (1980b) 'Children represent their environment: mental maps of Coventry city centre'. *Geoforum*, 11, 385–97.

Matthews, M.H. (1981) 'Children's perception of urban distance'. *Area*, 4, 333–43.

Matthews, M.H. (1984a) 'Environmental cognition of young children: images of journey to school and home area'. *Transactions of the Institute of British Geographers, New Series*, 9, 89–106.

Matthews, M.H. (1984b) 'Cognitive maps of young children: a comparison of graphic and iconic techniques'. *Area*, 16, 31–41.

Matthews, M.H. (1984c) 'Cognitive mapping abilities of young girls and boys'. *Geography*, 69, 327–36.

Matthews, M.H. (1985a) 'Young children's representations of the environment: a comparison of techniques'. *Journal of Environmental Psychology*, 5, 261–78.

Matthews, M.H. (1985b) 'Environmental capability of the very young: some implications for environmental education in primary schools'. *Educational Review*, 37, 227–39.

Matthews, M.H. (1986a) 'Children as map makers'. *Geographical Magazine*, March, 124–9.

Matthews, M.H. (1986b) 'The influence of gender on the environmental cognition of young boys and girls'. *Journal of Genetic Psychology*, 147, 295–302.

Matthews, M.H. (1986c) 'Gender, graphicacy and geography'. *Educational Review*, 38, 259–71.

Matthews, M.H. (1987a) 'Gender, home range and environmental cognition'. *Transactions of the Institute of British Geographers, New Series*, 12, 43–56.

Matthews, M.H. (1987b) 'Children's urban space preferences'. *Research Memorandum*, 32, Coventry Polytechnic.

Matthews, M.H. (1987c) 'Sex differences in spatial competence: the ability of young children to map "primed" unfamiliar environments'. *Educational Psychology*, 7, 77–90.

Matthews, M.H. (1988) 'Geography and gender'. *Geographical Magazine*, August, 47–50.

Matthews, M.H. (1989a) 'Maps in mind: assessing spatial awareness in young children'. *The Times Educational Supplement*, April, 31–2.

Matthews, M.H. (1989b) 'Mapping matters: the development of spatial knowledge in young children'. *Links*, September, 4, 32–7.

Matthews, M.H. and Airey, A. (1990) 'Mapping behaviour and culture: a comparison of young children's mapping capabilities in Kenya and Britain'. *End-of-grant Report: Nuffield Foundation*.

Maurer, R. and Baxter, J.C. (1972) 'Images of neighborhood among Black, Anglo- and Mexican-American children'. *Environment and Behavior*, 4, 351–8.

Mays. P. (1985) *Teaching children through the environment*. Hodder and Stoughton: London.

McComas, J. and Field, J. (1984) 'Does early crawling experience affect infant's emerging spatial abilities?'. *New Zealand Journal of Psychology*, 13, 63–8.

McGee, C. (1982) 'Children's perceptions of symbols in maps and aerial photographs'.

Geographical Education, **4**, 51–9.

McGee, M. (1979) 'Human spatial abilities: psychometric studies and environmental, genetic, hormonal and neurological influences'. *Psychological Bulletin*, **86**, 889–918.

McGlone, J. (1980) 'Sex differences in human brain asymmetry: critical survey'. *The Behavioral and Brain Sciences*, **3**, 215–27.

McGuinness, D. (1974) 'Hearing: individual differences in perceiving'. *Perception*, **1**, 465–73.

McGuinness, D. (1976a) 'Sex differences in the organization of perception and cognition'. In Lloyd, B. and Archer, J. (Eds) *Exploring sex differences*. Academic Press: New York.

McGuinness, D. (1976b) 'Away from a unisex psychology: individual differences in visual sensory and perceptual processes'. *Perception*, **5**, 279–94.

McGuinness, D. and Pribram, K.H. (1979) 'The origins of sensory bias in the development of gender differences in perception and cognition'. In Bortner, M. (Ed.) *Cognitive growth and development*. Brunner, Mazel: New York.

McKechnie, G.E. (1977) 'The environmental response inventory in application'. *Environment and Behavior*, **9**, 225–76.

McKenzie, B.E. and Day, R.H. (1972) 'Object distance as a determinant of visual fixation in early infancy'. *Science*, **178**, 1108–10.

McKenzie, B.E., Day, R.H. and Ihsen, E. (1984) 'Localization of events in space: young infants are not always egocentric'. *British Journal of Developmental Psychology*, **2**, 1–9.

McNamara, T.P. (1986) 'Mental representations of spatial relations'. *Cognitive Psychology*, **18**, 723–32.

McNamara, T.P., Ratcliff, R. and McKoon. G. (1984) 'The mental representation of knowledge acquired from maps'. *Journal of Experimental Psychology: Learning, Memory and Cognition*, **10**, 723–2.

Mead, G.H. (1974) *Mind, self and society from the standpoint of a social behaviorist*. Chicago University Press: Chicago.

Mead, M. (1930) *Growing up in New Guinea*. Blue Ribbon Books: New York.

Mellaert, J. (1967) *Catal Huyuk: a neolithic town in Anatolia*. Thames and Hudson: New York.

Mercer, C. (1976) *Living in cities*. Penguin: Harmondsworth.

Michelson, W. and Roberts, E. (1979) 'Children and the urban physical environment'. In Michelson, W., Levine, S. and Spina, A. (Eds) *The child in the city*. University of Toronto Press: Toronto.

Michelson, W. and Michelson, E. (1980) 'Managing urban space in the interest of children: dimensions of the task'. *Ekistics*, **281**, 88–92.

Milgram, S., Greenwald, J., Kessler, S., McKenna, W. and Welters, J. (1972) 'A psychological map of New York City'. *American Scientist*, **60**, 194–200.

Miller, P. and Rutz, M. (1980) 'A comparison of scenic preference dimensions for children and adults'. Paper presented at the Annual Meetings of the Council of Educators in Landscape Architecture, Madison, West Indies.

Mills, D. (Ed.) (1981) (2nd ed. 1987) *Geographical work in primary and middle schools*. Geographical Association: Sheffield.

Minsky, M. (1975) 'A framework for representing knowledge'. In Winston, P.H. (Ed.) *The psychology of computer vision*. McGraw-Hill: New York.

Mitchelmore, M.C. (1974) 'The perceptual development of Jamaican students, with special reference to visualization and drawing of three-dimensional geometrical figures and the effects of spatial training'. Doctoral Dissertation, Ohio State University.

Mohr, D., Kucjaz, S. and Pick, H.L. (1975) 'Development of cognitive mapping capacities'. Paper presented at Society for Research in Child Development Conference, Denver, Colorado.

Moore, G.T. (1973) 'Developmental differences in environmental cognition'. In Pressner, W. (Ed.) *Environmental design and research*, 2. Dowden, Hutchinson and Ross: Stroudsburg, Pennsylvania.

Moore, G.T. (1974) 'The development of environmental knowing: an overview of an interactional-constructivist theory and some data on within-individual developmental variations'. In Canter, D. and Lee, T. (Eds) *Psychology and the built environment*. Architectural Press: London.

Moore, G.T. (1976) 'Theory and development of environmental knowing'. In Moore, G.T. and Golledge, R.G. (Eds) *Environmental knowing*. Dowden, Hutchinson and Ross: Stroudsburg, Pennsylvania.

Moore, G.T. and Cohen, U. (1978) 'Exceptional education and the physical environment: toward behaviorally-based design principles'. In Rogers, W. and Ittelson, W. (Eds) *New directions in environmental design*, 9. EDRA: Washington.

Moore, G.T. and Golledge, R.G. (1976) 'Environmental knowing: concepts and theories'. In Moore, G.T. and Golledge, R.G. (Eds) *Environmental knowing*. Dowden, Hutchinson and Ross: Stroudsburg, Pennsylvania.

Moore, R.C. (1978) 'Childhood use of the urban landscape' project. Cited in Moore, R.C. and Young, D. 'Childhood outdoors: toward a social ecology of the landscape'. In Altman, I. and Wohlwill, J.F. (Eds) *Children and the environment*. Plenum: New York.

Moore, R.C. (1986) *Childhood's domain: play and place in child development*. Croom Helm: London.

Moore, R.C. and Young, D. (1978) 'Childhood outdoors: toward a social ecology of the landscape'. In Altman, I. and Wohlwill, J.F. (Eds) *Children and the environment*. Plenum: New York.

Morrison, A. (1974) 'Testing the effectiveness of road speed maps and conventional maps'. *The Cartographic Journal*, 11, 102–16.

Morville, L. (1969) *Children's use of recreational areas*. Statens Byggeronskningstitat: Copenhagen.

Muchow, M. and Muchow, H. (1935) *Der Lebensraum des Grosstadtkindes*. Riegel: Hamburg.

Muir, M.E. and Blaut, J.M. (1969) 'The use of aerial photographs in teaching mapping to children in the first grade: an experimental study'. *The Minnesota Geographer*, 22, 4–19.

Muir, S. (1985) 'Understanding and improving students' map reading skills'. *Elementary School Journal*, 86, 207–16.

Munn, N, (1973) *Walbiri iconography: graphic representations and cultural symbolism in a central Australian society*. Ithaca: Cornell University.

Munroe, R.L. and Munroe, R.H. (1971) 'Effect of environmental experience on spatial ability in an East African society'. *Journal of Social Psychology*, 83, 15–22.

Murphy, D. (1968) 'The perception of Africa by seventh and eighth graders from the Grand Forks Air Base'. *University of North Dakota Department Paper*.

Murray, D. and Spencer, C. (1979) 'Individual differences in the drawing of cognitive maps: the effects of geographical mobility, strength of mental imagery and basic graphic ability'. *Transactions of the Institute of British Geographers, New Series*, **4**, 374–85.

Murray, R. (1974) 'The influence of crowding on children's behavior'. In Canter, D. and Lee, T. (Eds) *Psychology and the built environment*. Halstead Press: New York.

Nagy, J.N. and Baird, J.C. (1978) 'Children as environmental planners'. In Altman, I. and Wohlwill, J.F. (Eds) *Children and the environment*. Plenum: New York.

Nance, J. (1975) *The gentle Tasaday*. Harcourt Brace Jovanovich: New York.

Nash, S.C. (1979) 'Sex role as a mediator of intellectual functioning'. In Wittig, M.A. and Petersen, A.C. (Eds) *Sex-related differences in cognitive functioning*. Academic Press: New York.

Neisser, U. (1976) *Cognition and reality: principles and implications of cognitive psychology*. Freeman: San Francisco.

Nerlove, S.B., Munroe, R.H. and Munroe, R.L. (1971) 'Effect of environmental experience on spatial ability: a replication'. *Journal of Social Psychology*, **84**, 3–10.

Newcombe, N. (1982) 'Sex-related differences in spatial ability: problems and gaps in current approaches'. In Potegal, M. (Ed.) *Spatial abilities: development and physiological foundations*. Academic Press: New York.

Newcombe, N. (1985) 'Methods for the study of spatial cognition'. In Cohen, R. (Ed.) *The development of spatial cognition*. Lawrence Erlbaum: Hillsdale, New Jersey.

Newcombe, N. and Liben, S. (1982) 'Barrier effects in the cognitive maps of children and adults'. *Journal of Experimental Child Psychology*, **34**, 46–58.

Newson, J. and Newson, E. (1971) *Infant care in an urban community*. Penguin: Harmondsworth.

Newson, J. and Newson, E. (1976) *Seven years old in the home environment*. Allen and Unwin: London.

Newson, J. and Newson, E. (1977) *Perspectives on school at seven years old*. Allen and Unwin: London.

Newtson, D. (1980) 'An interactionist perspective on social knowing'. *Personality and Social Psychology Bulletin*, **6**, 520–31.

Nicholson, S. and Lorenzo, R. (1980) 'The political implications of child participation'. *Ekistics*, **281**, 160–3.

O'Keefe, J. and Nadel, L. (1978) *The hippocampus as a cognitive map*. Oxford University Press: London.

Orleans, P. (1973) 'Differential cognition of urban residents: effects of social scale on mapping'. In Downs, R.M. and Stea, D. (Eds) *Image and environment*. Aldine: Chicago.

Osgood, C.E. (1957) 'A behaviouralistic analysis of perception and language as cognitive phenomena'. In *Contemporary approaches to cognition: a symposium at the University of Colorado*. Harvard University Press: Cambridge, Massachusetts.

Pacione, M. (1982) 'Space preferences, locational decisions and the dispersal of civil servants from London'. *Environment and Planning, A*, **14**, 323–33.

Parke, R.D. (1978) 'Children's home environments: social and cognitive effects'. In Altman, I. and Wohlwill, J.F. (Eds) *Children and the environment*. Plenum: New York.

Parr, A.E. (1966) 'Psychological aspects of urbanology'. *Journal of Social Issues*, **22**, 39–45.

Parr, A.E. (1969) 'Problems of reason, feeling and habitat'. *Architectural Association Newsletter*, **1**, 5–10.

Passini, R. (1984) 'Spatial representations, a wayfinding perspective'. *Journal of Environmental Psychology*, **4**, 153–64.

Payne, R.J. and Jones, D.R.W. (1977) 'Children's urban landscapes in Huntington Hills, Calgary'. In Suedfeld, P. and Russel, J.A. (Eds) *The behavioral basis of design*. Dowden, Hutchinson and Ross: Stroudsburg, Pennsylvania.

Pearce, A. (1987) 'Teaching and learning through direct experience'. In Bailey, P.J. and Binns, J.A. (Eds) *A case for geography*. Geographical Association: Sheffield.

Pearce, J.C. (1977) *Magical child: rediscovering nature's plan for our children*. Dutton: New York.

Petchenik, B. (1987) 'Fundamental considerations about atlases for children'. *Cartographica*, **24**, 17–23.

Peters, A. (1983) *The new cartography*. Friendship Press: New York.

Phillips, R.J. and Noyes, A. (1982) 'An investigation of visual clutter in the topographic base of a geological map'. *The Cartographic Journal*, **29**, 397–400.

Piaget, J. (1937) *The construction of reality in the child*. Basic Books: New York.

Piaget, J. (1968) *On the development of memory and identity*. Clark University Press: Worcester, Massachusetts.

Piaget, J. (1969) *The mechanisms of perception*. Basic Books: New York.

Piaget, J. and Inhelder, B. (1956) *The child's conception of space*. Norton: New York.

Piaget, J. and Inhelder, B. (1967) *The child's conception of space*. Routledge and Kegan Paul: London.

Piaget, J. and Weil, A.M. (1951) 'Le développement, chez l'enfant, de l'idée de patrie et des relations avec l'étranger'. *Bulletin International des Sciences Sociales*, **13**, 605–21.

Piaget, J., Inhelder, B. and Szeminska, A. (1948) *The child's conception of geometry* (1st edition), Norton: New York.

Piaget, J., Inhelder, B. and Szeminska, A. (1960) *The child's conception of geometry* (2nd edition), Basic Books: New York.

Piché, D. (1977) 'The geographical understanding of children aged 5 to 8 years'. Doctoral Dissertation, University of London.

Piché, D. (1981) 'The spontaneous geography of the urban child'. In Herbert, D.T. and Johnston, R.J. (Eds) *Geography and the urban environment*. IV, Wiley: Chichester.

Pick, H.L. (1976) 'Transactional-constructivist approach to environmental learning: a commentary'. In Moore, G.T. and Golledge, R.G. (Eds) *Environmental knowing*. Dowden, Hutchinson and Ross: Stroudsburg, Pennsylvania.

Pick, H.L. and Acredolo, L.P. (Eds) (1983) *Spatial orientation: theory, research and application*. Plenum: New York.

Pick, H.L. and Lockman, J.J. (1981) 'From frames of reference to spatial representation'. In Liben, L.S., Patterson, A.H. and Liben, N. (Eds) *Spatial representation and behavior across the life span*. Academic Press: New York.

Pick, H.L., Yonas, A. and Rieser, J. (1976) 'Spatial reference systems in perceptual development'. In Bonstein, M.H. and Kesson, W. (Eds) *Psychological development from infancy: image to retention*. Lawrence Erlbaum: Hillsdale, New Jersey.

Poag, C.K., Cohen, R. and Weatherford, D.L. (1983) 'Spatial representations of young children: the role of self- versus adult-directed movement and viewing'. *Journal of Experimental Child Psychology*, **35**, 172–9.

Poag, C.K., Goodnight, J.A. and Cohen, R. (1985) 'The environments of children'. In Wellman, H.M. (Ed.) *Children's searching*. Lawrence Erlbaum: Hillsdale, New Jersey.

Pocock, D. (1976a) 'A comment on images derived from invitation-to-map exercises'.

Professional Geographer, **28**, 148–52.

Pocock, D. (1976b) 'Some characteristics of mental maps: an empirical study'. *Transactions of the Institute of British Geographers, New Series*, **1**, 493-512.

Pocock, D. and Hudson, R. (1978) *Images of the urban environment*. Macmillan: London.

Pollowy, A.M. (1977) *The urban nest*. Free Press: New York.

Porteous, J.D. (1977) *Environment and behavior*. Addison-Wesley: Minnesota.

Porteus, S.D. (1965) *Porteus Maze Test: fifty years application*. Pacific Books: California.

Pratt, D. (1972) *How to find and measure bias in textbooks*. Educational Technology Publications: Englewood Cliffs, New Jersey.

Presson, C.C. (1980) 'Spatial egocentrism and the effect of an alternate frame of reference'. *Journal of Experimental Child Psychology*, **29**, 391–402.

Presson, C.C. (1982) 'The development of map reading skills'. *Child Development*, **53**, 196–9.

Presson, C.C. and Ihrig, L.H. (1982) 'Using mother as a spatial landmark: evidence against egocentric coding in infancy'. *Developmental Psychology*, **18**, 699–703.

Presson, C.C. and Somerville, S.C. (1985) 'Beyond egocentrism: a new look at the beginnings of spatial representation'. In Wellman, H.M. (Ed.) *Children searching: the development of search skill and spatial representation*. Lawrence Erlbaum: Hillsdale, New Jersey.

Prior, F.M. (1959) 'The place of maps in the junior school'. Dissertation for the Diploma in Psychology of Childhood, University of Birmingham.

Rapoport, A. (1976) 'Environmental cognition in cross-cultural perspective'. In Moore, G.T. and Golledge, R.G. (Eds) *Environmental knowing*. Dowden, Hutchinson and Ross: Stroudsburg, Pennsylvania.

Rapoport, A. (1977) *Human aspects of urban form*. Pergamon: Oxford.

Rapoport, A. (1978) 'On the environment as an enculturating system'. In Weidmann, S. and Anderson, J.A. (Eds) *Priorities for environmental design research*. EDRA: Washington.

Rapoport, A. (1980) 'Cross-cultural aspects of environmental design'. In Altman, I. and Wohlwill, J.F. (Eds) *Environment and culture*. Plenum: New York.

Relph, E.C. (1976) *Place and placelessness*. Pion Press: London.

Rheingold, H.L. (1969) 'The effect of a strange environment on the behavior of infants'. In Foss, B.M. (Ed.) *Determinants of infant behavior*. Methuen; London.

Rheingold, H.L. and Cook, K.V. (1975) 'The content of boys' and girls' rooms as an index of parents' behavior'. *Child Development*, **46**, 459–63.

Rheingold, H.L. and Eckerman, C.O. (1973) 'Fear of the stranger: a critical examination'. In Reese, H.W. (Ed.) *Advances in child development and behavior*. Academic Press: New York.

Rieser, J.J. (1979) 'Spatial orientation of six-month-old infants'. *Child Development*, **59**, 1078–87.

Rieser, J.J. (1983) 'The generation and early development of spatial inferences'. In Pick, H.L. and Acredolo, L.P. (Eds) *Spatial orientation in natural and experimental settings*. Plenum: New York.

Robinson, V. (1980) 'Asians and council housing'. *Urban Studies*, **17**, 323–31.

Robinson, V. (1981) 'The development of South Asian settlement in Britain and the myth of return'. In Peach, C., Robinson, V. and Smith, S. (Eds) *Ethnic segregation in cities*. Croom Helm: London.

Robinson, V. (1984) 'Asians in Britain: a study of encapsulation and marginality'. In Clark, C., Ley, D. and Peach, C. (Eds) *Geography and ethnic pluralism*. Allen and

Unwin: London.

Roder, W. (1977) 'An alternative interpretation of men and women in geography'. *The Professional Geographer*, **29**, 397–400.

Rohane, K. (1981) 'Behavior-based design concepts for comprehensive school play-grounds: a review of playground design evolution'. *EDRA Yearbook*, **12**, 251–7.

Rose, H.M. (1969) 'Social processes in the city: race and urban residential choice'. *Resource Paper*, **6**. Association of American Geographers: Washington, D.C.

Rose, H.M. (1970) 'The development of an urban sub-system: the case of the negro ghetto'. *Annals of the Association of American Geographers*, **60**, 1–17.

Rose, H.M. (1972) 'The spatial development of black residential sub-systems'. *Economic Geographer*, **48**, 43–66.

Russell, J.A. and Ward, L.M. (1982) 'Environmental psychology'. *Annual Review of Psychology*, **33**, 651–88.

Saarinen, T.F. (1973) 'Student views of the world'. In Downs, R.M. and Stea, D. (Eds) *Image and environment*. Aldine: Chicago.

Saarinen, T.F. (1976) *Environmental planning: perception and behavior*. Houghton-Mifflin: Boston.

Saarinen, T.F. (1988) 'Centering of mental maps of the world'. *National Geographic Research*, **4**, 112–27.

Sadalla, E.K. and Magel, S.G. (1980) 'The perception of traversed distance'. *Environment and Behavior*, **12**, 65–79.

Sadalla, E.K. and Staplin, L.J. (1980a) 'An information storage model for distance cognition'. *Environment and Behavior*, **12**, 183–93.

Sadalla, E.K. and Staplin, L.J. (1980b) 'The perception of traversed distance'. *Environment and Behavior*, **12**, 167–82.

Saegart, S. and Hart, R. (1978) 'The development of environmental competence in boys and girls'. In Salter, M. (Ed.) *Play: anthropological perspectives*. Leisure Press: New York.

Sager, J. (1977) 'An investigation of unsupervised leisure time destinations among pre-adolescents in Toronto'. Master's Dissertation, University of Toronto.

Sanchez-Robles, J.C. (1980) 'The social conceptualization of home'. In Broadbent, G., Bunt, R. and Llorens, T. (Eds) *Meaning and behaviour in the built environment*. Wiley: Chichester.

Sandford, H.A. (1979) 'Things maps don't tell us'. *Geography*, **64**, 297–302.

Sanoff, H. and Dickerson, J. (1971) 'Mapping children's behavior in a residential setting'. *Journal of Architectural Education*, **25**, 98–103.

Satterly, D.J. (1964) 'Skills and concepts involved in map drawing and interpretation'. *New Era*, **1**, 263.

Scaife, M. and Bruner, J. (1975) 'The capacity for joint visual attention in the infant'. *Nature*, 24 January, 265–6.

Schaefer, K.H. and Sclar, E. (1975) *Access for all*. Penguin: Harmondsworth.

Schoggen, P. and Schoggen, M. (1985) 'Play, exploration and density'. In Wohlwill, J.F. and van Vliet, W. (Eds) *Habitats for children*. Lawrence Erlbaum: Hillsdale, New Jersey.

Schouela, D.A., Steinburg, L.M., Leveton, L.B. and Wapner, S. (1980) 'Development of the cognitive organization of an environment'. *Canadian Journal of Behavioral Science*, **12**, 1–16.

Scoffham, S. (1981) *Using the school's surroundings*. Ward Lock: London.

Scott, J.P. (1968) *Early experience and the organization of behavior*. Brooks, Cole: Belmont, California.

Sears, P.S. (1965) 'The effect of classroom conditions on the strength of achievement motive and work output of elementary schoolchildren'. Report on Co-operative Research Project OE873, Stanford University.

Searles, H. (1959) *The non-human environment in normal development and schizophrenia*. International Universities Press: New York.

Sharonov, Y.A. (1980) 'Designing children's spatial environment'. *Ekistics*, 281, 118–23.

Shemyakin, F.N. (1962) 'Orientation in space'. In Annayer, B.G. (Ed.) *Psychological sciences in the USSR. Office and Technical Services Report*, 62, Washington.

Sherrod, K., Vietze, P. and Friedman, S. (1978) *Infancy*. Brooks, Cole: Belmont, California.

Siegel, A.W. (1977) 'Finding one's way around the large-scale environment: the development of spatial representations'. In McGurk, H. (Ed.) *Ecological factors in human development*. North Holland: Amsterdam.

Siegel, A.W. (1981) 'The externalization of cognitive maps by children and adults: in search of ways to ask better questions'. In Liben, L.S., Patterson, A.H. and Newcombe, N. (Eds) *Spatial representation and behavior across the life span*. Academic Press: New York.

Siegel, A.W. and Cousins, J.H. (1985) 'The symbolizing and symbolized child in the enterprise of cognitive mapping'. In Cohen, R. (Ed.) *The development of spatial cognition*. Lawrence Erlbaum: Hillsdale, New Jersey.

Siegel, A.W. and Schadler, M. (1977) 'Young children's cognitive maps of their classroom'. *Child Development*, 48, 388–94.

Siegel, A.W. and White, S.H. (1975) 'The development of spatial representations of large-scale environments'. In Reese, H.W. (Ed.) *Advances in child development and behavior*. Academic Press: New York.

Siegel, A.W., Allen, G.L. and Kirasic, K.C. (1979) 'Children's ability to make bi-directional distance comparisons: the advantage of thinking ahead'. *Developmental Psychology*, 15, 656–7.

Siegel, A.W., Herman, J.F., Allen, G.L. and Kirasic, K.C. (1979) 'The development of cognitive maps of large-scale and small-scale spaces'. *Child Development*, 50, 582–5.

Siegel, A.W., Kirasic, K.C. and Kail, R.V. (1978) 'Stalking the elusive cognitive map'. In Altman, I. and Wohlwill, J.F. (Eds) *Children and the environment*. Plenum: New York.

Sieverts, T. (1967) 'Perceptual images of the city of Berlin'. In Brill, E.J. (Ed.) *Urban core and inner city*. University of Leiden: Netherlands.

Skinner, B.F. (1938) *The behaviour of organisms*. Appleton: New York.

Skinner, B.F. (1974) *About behaviourism*. Cape: London.

Skurnik, L.S. and George, F. (1967) *Psychology for everyman*. Penguin: Harmondsworth.

Smith, K.V. and Smith, W.M. (1962) *Perception and motion*. Saunders: Philadelphia.

Somerville, S.C. and Bryant, P.E. (1985) 'Young children's use of spatial co-ordinates'. *Child Development*, 56, 604–13.

Sommer, R. (1969) *Personal space: the behavioral basis of design*. Prentice-Hall: New Jersey.

Sophian, C. and Sage, S. (1985) 'Infants' search for hidden objects: developing skills for using information selectively'. *Infant Behavior and Development*, 8, 1–14.

Spencer, C. and Darvizeh, Z. (1981a) 'The case for developing a cognitive psychology that does not underestimate the abilities of young children'. *Journal of Environmental Psychology*, 1, 21–32.

Spencer, C. and Darvizeh, Z. (1981b) 'Young children's descriptions of their local environment: a comparison of information elicited by recall, recognition and performance techniques of investigation'. *Environmental Education and Information*, 1, 275–84.

Spencer, C. and Darvizeh, Z. (1983) 'Young children's place-descriptions, maps and route-finding: a comparison of nursery school children in Iran and Britain'. *International Journal of Early Childhood*, 15, 26–31.

Spencer, C. and Dixon, J. (1983) 'Mapping the development of feelings about the city: a longitudinal study of new residents' affective maps'. *Transactions of the Institute of British Geographers, New Series*, 8, 373-83.

Spencer, C. and Weetman, M. (1981) 'The microgenesis of cognitive maps: a longitudinal study of new residents of an urban area'. *Transactions of the Institute of British Geographers, New Series*, 6, 375–84.

Spencer, C., Blades, M. and Morsley, K. (1989) *The child in the physical environment*. Wiley: Chichester.

Spencer, C., Harrison, N. and Darvizeh, Z, (1980) 'The development of iconic mapping ability in young children'. *International Journal of Early Childhood*, 12, 57–64.

Spencer, C., Mitchell, S. and Wisdom, J. (1984) 'Evaluating environmental education in nursery and primary schools'. *Environmental Education and Information*, 3, 16–32.

Spencer, D. and Lloyd, J. (1974) 'A child's eye view of Small Heath, Birmingham'. *Research Memorandum*, 34, University of Birmingham.

Spink, J. and Moodie, D. (1972) 'Eskimo maps from the Canadian Eastern Arctic'. *Cartographica*, Monograph 5.

Spitz, R. (1945) 'Hospitalism: an inquiry into the genesis of psychiatric conditions in early childhood'. *Psychoanalytic Study of the Child*, 1, 53–74.

Spitz, R. (1965) *The first year of life*. International Universities Press: New York.

Stea, D. (1976) 'Program notes on a spatial fugue'. In Moore, G.T. and Golledge, R.G. (Eds) *Environmental knowing*. Dowden, Hutchinson and Ross: Stroudsburg, Pennsylvania.

Stea, D. and Blaut, J.M. (1973) 'Some preliminary observations on spatial learning in school children'. In Downs, R.M. and Stea, D. (Eds) *Image and environment*. Aldine: Chicago.

Stevens, A. and Coupe, P. (1978) 'Distortions in judged spatial relations'. *Cognitive Psychology*, 10, 422–37.

Stewart, W.F.R. (1970) *Children in flats*. National Society for the Prevention of Cruelty to Children: Melbourne.

Stiell, B. (1989) 'British and Indian children's views of their neighbourhood'. Batchelor of Science Dissertation, Coventry Polytechnic.

Stillwell, R. and Spencer, C. (1974) 'Children's early preferences for other nations and their subsequent acquisition of knowledge about those nations'. *European Journal of Social Psychology*, 3, 345–9.

Stradling, R. Noctor, M. and Baines, B. (1984) *Teaching controversial issues*. Edward Arnold: London.

Strelow, E. (1985) 'What is needed for a theory of mobility: direct perception and cognitive maps'. *Psychological Review*, 92, 226–48.

Strickland, E. (1979) 'Free play behaviors and equipment choices of third grade children in contrasting play environments'. Doctoral Dissertation, University of Texas, Austin.

Suttles, G.D. (1972) *The social construction of communities*. University of Chicago: Chicago.

Taeuber, K.E. and Taeuber, A.F. (1965) *Negroes in cities*. Aldine: Chicago.

Tajfel, H. (1981) *Human groups and social categories*. Cambridge University Press: Cambridge.

Tajfel, H. and Jahoda, G. (1966) 'Development in children of concepts and attitudes about their own countries'. Paper presented at the 18th International Congress of Psychology, Moscow.

Thomas, H., Jamison, W. and Hummel, D.D. (1973) 'Observation is insufficient for discovering that the surface of still water is invariantly horizontal'. *Science*, 81, 173–4.

Thompson, E.G., Harris, L.J. and Mann, I. (1980) 'Relationships among sex: measures of cognitive complexity and performance on spatial tasks in college students'. *British Journal of Psychology*, 73, 323–31.

Thornberg, J.M. (1973) 'Child's conception of places to live in'. In Preiser, W.F.E. (Ed.) *Environmental design research*. Dowden, Hutchinson and Ross: Stroudsburg, Pennsylvania.

Thorndyke, P.W. (1981) 'Distance estimation from cognitive maps'. *Cognitive Psychology*, 13, 526–50.

Tilly, C. (Ed.) (1974) *An urban child*. Little, Brown: Boston.

Tolman, E.C. (1973) 'Cognitive maps in rats and men'. First published in *Psychological Review*, (1948) 55, 189–208. Reprinted in Downs, R.M. and Stea, D. (Eds.) *Image and environment*. Aldine: Chicago.

Tolman, E.C. (1952) 'A cognition-motivation model'. *Psychological Review*, 59, 389–408.

Towler, J.O. (1970) 'The elementary school child: concept of reference systems'. *Journal of Geography*, 69, 89–93.

Towler, J.O. and Nelson, L.D. (1968) 'The elementary school child's concept of scale'. *Journal of Geography*, 67, 24–8.

Treib, M. (1980) 'Mapping experience'. *Design Quarterly*, 115, 1–54.

Tuan, Y.F. (1974) *Topophilia: a study of environmental perception, attitudes and values*. Prentice-Hall: Englewood Cliffs, New Jersey.

Tuan, Y.F (1978) 'Children and the natural environment'. In Altman, I. and Wohlwill, J.F. (Eds) *Children and the environment*. Plenum: New York.

Tuan, Y.F. (1979) *Space and place: the perspective of experience*. Edward Arnold: London.

Vandenberg, B. (1978) 'Play and development from an ethological perspective'. *American Psychologist*, 33, 724–38.

Vandenberg, S.G. and Kuse, A.R. (1979) 'Spatial ability: a critical review of the sex-linked major gene hypothesis'. In Wittig, M.A. and Petersen, A.C. (Eds) *Sex-related differences in cognitive functioning*. Academic Press: New York.

van den Berghe, P. (1974) 'Bringing beasts back in: toward a biosocial theory of aggression'. *American Sociological Review*, 39, 777–88.

van Staden, J.F. (1984) 'Urban early adolescents, crowding and the neighbourhood experience: a preliminary investigation'. *Journal of Environmental Psychology*, 4, 97–118.

van Valey, T.L., Roof, W.C. and Wilcox, J.E. (1977) 'Trends in residential segregation, 1960–1970'. *American Journal of Sociology*, 82, 826–44.

van Valkenberg, M. (1978) 'The design implications of grade school children's use of and attitudes about two way play areas in Carle Park, Urbana, Illinois'. In Rogers, W. and Ittelson, W. (Eds) *New dimensions in environmental design*, 9. EDRA: Washington.

van Vliet, W. (1983) 'Exploring the fourth environment: an examination of the home range of city and suburban teenagers'. *Environment and Behavior*, 15, 567–88.

Varanka, D. (1987) 'An analysis of contemporary map-like art'. Master's Dissertation, University of Illinois.

Verwer, D. (1980) 'Planning residential environments according to their real use by children and adults'. *Ekistics*, 281, 109–13.

Vogt, B., Raundalen, M. and Iversen, O. (1980) 'Selegrend: an experiment in environment design'. *Ekistics*, 281, 113–15.

Waber, D.P. (1976) 'Sex differences in cognition: a function of maturation rate'. *Science*, 192, 572–4.

Waber, D.P. (1977a) 'Biological substrates of field dependence: implications of the sex difference'. *Psychological Bulletin*, 84, 1076–87.

Waber, D.P. (1977b) 'Sex differences in mental abilities, hemispheric lateralization and rate of physical growth in adolescence'. *Developmental Psychology*, 13, 27–38.

Walker, R.J. (1978) 'An investigation into the development of map using abilities in primary school children'. Master's Dissertation, University of London.

Walker, R.J. (1980) 'Map using abilities of 5 to 9 year old children'. *Geographical Education*, 3, 545–54.

Wallace, A.F.C. (1972) *Housing and social structure*. Philadelphia Housing Authority: Philadelphia.

Walmsley, D.J. (1982) 'Personality and regional preference structures: a study of introversion–extraversion'. *Professional Geographer*, 34, 279–88.

Walmsley, D.J. (1988) *Urban living: the individual in the city*. Longman: London.

Walmsley, D.J. and Epps, W.R. (1988) 'Do humans have an innate sense of direction?'. *Geography*, 73, 31–40.

Walmsley, D.J. and Lewis, G.J. (1984) *Human geography: behavioural approaches*. Longman: London.

Walsh, D.A. Krauss, I.K. and Regner, V.A. (1981) 'Spatial ability, environmental knowledge, and environmental use: the elderly'. In Liben, L.S., Patterson, A.H. and Newcombe, N. (Eds) *Spatial representation and behavior across the life span*. Academic Press: New York.

Wapner, S. (1968) 'Age changes in perception of verticality and of the longitudinal body axis under body tilt'. *Journal of Experimental Child Psychology*, 6, 543–55.

Wapner, S. (1969) 'Organismic-developmental theory: some applications to cognition'. In Mussen, P.H. and Covington, M. (Eds) *Trends and issues in developmental psychology*. Holt, Rinehart and Winston: New York.

Ward, C. (1977) *The child in the city*. Architectural Press: London.

Warren, D. (1980) 'Support systems in different types of neighborhoods'. In Garbarino, J., Stocking, S. and Associates (Eds) *Protecting children from abuse and neglect*. Jossey-Bass: San Francisco.

Watson, J.B. (1913) 'Psychology as the behaviorist views it'. *Psychological Review*, 20, 158–77.

Webley, P. (1981) 'Sex differences in home range and cognitive maps in eight-year old children'. *Journal of Environmental Psychology*, 1, 293–302.

Webley, P. and Cutts, K. (1985) 'Children and nationhood'. *New Society*, 13, 451–3.

Wellman, H.M. (Ed.) (1985) *Children's searching: the development of search skill and spatial representation*. Lawrence Erlbaum: Hillsdale, New Jersey.

Wellman, H.M. and Somerville, S.C. (1982) 'The development of human search ability'. In Lamb, M.E. and Brown, A.L. (Eds) *Advances in developmental psychology*. 2, Lawrence Erlbaum: Hillsdale, New Jersey.

Wellman, H.M., Haake, R. and Somerville, S.C. (1981) 'An Easter egg hunt: young children's developing abilities in searching for missing objects'. Paper presented at the Biennial Meeting of the Society for Research in Child Development, Boston.

Wellman, H.M., Somerville, S.C. and Haake, R. (1979) 'Development of search procedures in real-life spatial environments'. *Developmental Psychology*, 15, 530–42.

Werner, H. (1948) *Comparative psychology of mental development*. International Universities Press: New York.

Werner, H. (1957) 'The concept of development from a comparative and organismic point of view'. In Harris, D.B. (Ed.) *The concept of development*. University of Minnesota Press: Minneapolis.

White, R.K. (1965) 'Images in the context of international conflict: Soviet perceptions of the US and USSR'. In Kelman, H. (Ed.) *International behavior*. Holt, Rinehart, Winston: New York.

White, S.H. (1980) 'Cognitive competence and performance in everyday environments'. *Bulletin of the Orton Society*, 30, 29–45.

White, S.H. and Siegel, A.W. (1976) 'Cognitive development: the new inquiry'. *Young children*, 31, 425–35.

Williams, E. (1977) 'Experimental comparisons of face-to-face and mediated communication'. *Psychological Bulletin*, 84, 963–76.

Williams, R. (1962) *Communication*. Penguin: Harmondsworth.

Willis, S.G., Wheatley, G.H. and Mitchell, O.R. (1979) 'Cerebral processing of spatial and verbal analytic tasks: an EEG study'. *Neuropsychologia*, 17, 473–84.

Wilson, J.R., DeFries, J.C., McClearn, C.E., Vandenberg, S.G., Johnson, R.C. and Rashad, M.N. (1975) 'Cognitive abilities: use of family data to assess sex and age differences in two ethnic groups'. *International Journal of Ageing and Human Development*, 6, 261–76.

Witkin, H.A., Dyk, R.B., Paterson, G.E., Goodenough, D.R. and Karp, S.A. (1962) *Psychological differentiation*. Wiley, New York.

Witkin, H.A., Goodenough, D.R. and Karp, S.A. (1967) 'Stability of cognitive style from childhood to young adulthood'. *Journal of Personality and Social Psychology*, 7, 291–300.

Witkin, H.A., Oltman, P.K., Raskin, E.R. and Karp, S.A. (1971) *Manual for the embedded figures test*. Consulting Psychologists Press: California.

Wohlwill, J.F. (1981) 'Experimental, developmental, differential: which way the royal road to knowledge about spatial cognition?'. In Liben, L.S., Patterson, A.H. and Newcombe, N. (Eds) *Spatial representation and behavior across the life span*. Academic Press: New York.

Wood, D. and Beck, R. (1976) 'Talking with Environmental A, an experimental mapping language'. In Moore, G.T. and Golledge, R.G. (Eds) *Environmental knowing*. Dowden, Hutchinson and Ross: Stroudsburg, Pennsylvania.

Woods, R.I. (1976) 'Aspects of the scale problem in the calculation of segregation indices: London and Birmingham, 1961 and 1971'. *Tijdschrift voor Economische en Sociale Geografie*, 69, 169–74.

Wright, D.R. (1979) 'Visual images in geography texts: the case of Africa'. *Geography*, 64, 205–10.

Wright, H.F. (1971) 'Urban space as seen by the child'. *Courrier: revue medico-sociale de l'enfance*, 21, 485–95.

Zube, E.H. (1984) *Environmental evaluation*. Cambridge University Press: Cambridge.

Zube, E.H., Pitt, D.G. and Anderson, T.W. (1974) *Perception and measurement of scenic resources in the Connecticut River valley*. University of Massachusetts Press: Amherst.

Index